THE LION

CHRISTIAN
POETRY
COLLECTION

compiled by

Mary Batchelor

A LION BOOK

Published by
Lion Publishing plc
Sandy Lane West, Oxford, England
www.lion-publishing.co.uk
ISBN 0 7459 5057 4

First hardback edition 1995
First paperback edition 2001
10 9 8 7 6 5 4 3 2 1 0

A catalogue record for this book is available
from the British Library

Printed and bound in Finland

CONTENTS

INTRODUCTION

The main purpose of this anthology is to give pleasure. I hope that it will appeal widely and be enjoyed by many readers who might find a more academic approach rather daunting. Some of the poems cut across accepted patterns of Christian thought and provide new insights into the nature of God and of our world in a way that stimulates thinking and strengthens faith. The seeing eye of the poet can often sharpen our less focused vision.

The poems in the book are mainly the work of Christian poets, though not necessarily in the mainstream of Christian tradition. Where a poet has sought to express the spiritual dimension within a framework of Christian thought, I have felt justified in including the poem. I have also included work by Christian poets which is not obviously 'religious', for, as one Christian poet put it: 'I think that if the mind is directed in faith, then all poetry, as all action, is religious.'

I have included within the anthology a number of verses which are usually thought of as hymns. I hope that in this context they will be read as poetry, freed from the association they will have for some readers with tune and congregation.

I have tried to provide a broad spectrum of poetic thought and feeling, drawing on many ages and various cultures. English-speaking countries well represented are Britain, the United States, Canada, Australia and the Caribbean.

My brief, which I was more than happy to follow, was for an anthology arranged by topic rather than by chronology. The mixing of styles, centuries and cultures, linked by a common topic, has yielded a rich pattern. And I have had great pleasure in the actual juxtaposition of material: sometimes putting two poems of very different style next to each other, for contrast; on other occasions retaining the mood or approach of one poem on through the next. Clear indexing enables those who wish to do so to read all the poems by a particular poet, or to take a section in historical order.

The poetry of one period contrasts in poetic style and form, and also in subject matter, with that of another. Every century seems to have its own special preoccupations.

Death and coming judgment were vivid realities in the past. In medieval times, when life was short and harsh, poets were strongly aware of death's imminence. In the seventeenth century poets were 'much possessed by death and saw the skull beneath the skin'. In the eighteenth century Cowper wrote verses on the county's mortality figures, bemoaning the fact that none took the inevitability of death seriously. For the Victorians death was still a part of most people's day-to-day experience. It is only in our own age that the consideration of death has become marginalized and ignored, even by most of our poets.

Doubt—including religious doubt—on the other hand, has become more widespread in the last century and a half. Early poets often embraced the Christian doctrines with very little questioning. In the Victorian age, when scientific study seemed to be overturning long-held beliefs, doubt flooded in. In 'Dover Beach', Matthew Arnold laments the turning of the tide against belief. Instead of faith, he sees faithful love between man and woman as providing the strong tie that can give life meaning and stability. Today doubt has been replaced by wholesale unbelief, and only avowedly Christian poets write with any certainty of spiritual realities.

But poets of our own day write with intensity about the moral dilemmas that face society, many brought about by new medical and scientific discovery.

I have avoided using translations, except a few from medieval Latin and those from Anglo-Saxon or Middle English. Sometimes the modern version approximates almost entirely to the original, merely substituting words in modern usage for archaisms. In other cases the present-day translator has created a new poem, preserving the spirit rather than the letter of the original. The finest examples of this kind of translation are Ronald Tamplin's renderings from Langland's 'Piers Plowman'. His translations are poems in their own right, yet also wonderfully preserve the style and flavour of Langland. I am particularly grateful to Mr Tamplin for providing a translation of one extract, 'Love In Action', specially for this anthology.

Some other small textual changes have been made. I have extracted verses from long poems, rather than weary the reader with overlong works. (This is indicated by the word 'From' before the title and ellipses within the poem.) I have consistently used lower case for 'he' and 'him' and other pronouns referring to God—a precedent set by all Bible translations. I have also updated some archaic spellings.

Poetry is currently staging a come-back. Perhaps in a largely materialistic age men and women are beginning to recognize the importance of the spiritual insight and prophetic voice of poetry. 'Where there is no vision the people perish.' Christian poets in particular provide that vision for us and we accept the gift with gratitude and joy.

Mary Batchelor

In Touch with God

Presence

Expecting him, my door was open wide:
    Then I looked round
    If any lack of service might be found,
And saw him at my side:
    How entered, by what secret stair,
    I know not, knowing only he was there.

T.E. Brown
1830–97

The Search

Apparition

How shall I find him, who can be my guide?
    Wears he a human form, a tear-marred face,
By blood-red raiment may he be descried,
    Or broods he far withdrawn through stellar space?
Perchance, informing all, his coils entwine
    And bind the monstrous fabric cell to cell,
Or, veiled in service, 'neath this Bread and Wine
    A homely God, he deigns with men to dwell.
Lo! just beyond the skyline he may stand,
    Speak just without the waftage of mine ear,
I all but touch him with my outstretched hand,
    Clear to my senses he may straight appear.

I hush my drumming heart, I stay my breath
To catch his step, to hearken what he saith.

Eugene Mason
1862–1935

Lost and Found

I missed him when the sun began to bend;
I found him not when I had lost his rim;
With many tears I went in search of him,
Climbing high mountains which did still ascend,
And gave me echoes when I called my friend;
Through cities vast and charnel-houses grim,
And high cathedrals where the light was dim,
Through books and arts and works without an end,
But found him not—the friend whom I had lost.
And yet I found him—as I found the lark,
A sound in fields I heard but could not mark;
I found him nearest when I missed him most;
I found him in my heart, a life in frost,
A light I knew not till my soul was dark.

George MacDonald
1824–1905

A New Hymn for Solitude

I found thee in my heart, O Lord,
　　As in some secret shrine;
I knelt, I waited for thy word,
　　I joyed to name thee mine.

I feared to give myself away
　　To that or this; beside
Thy altar on my face I lay,
　　And in strong need I cried.

Those hours are past. Thou art not mine,
　　And therefore I rejoice,
I wait within no holy shrine,
　　I faint not for the voice.

In thee we live; and every wind
　　Of heaven is thine; blown free
To west, to east, the God unshrined
　　Is still discovering me.

Edward Dowden
1843–1913

Wait a Little

Lord, thou clepedest* me,
And I nought ne answerèd thee
But wordès slow and sleepy:
'Thole* yet! Thole a little!'
But 'yet' and 'yet' was endèless,
And 'thole a little' a long way is.

Anonymous
Medieval

* *clepedest:* you called me ; *thole:* wait

Come in at My Door

Who is at my window? Who? Who?
Go from my window! Go! Go!
Who calls there, like a stranger,
Go from my window! Go!

—Lord, I am here, a wretched mortal,
That for thy mercy doth cry and call
Unto thee, my lord celestiàl,
See who is at thy window, who?—

Remember thy sin, remember thy smart,
And also for thee what was my part,
Remember the spear that pierced my heart,
And in at my door thou shalt go.

I ask no thing of thee therefore,
But love for love, to lay in store.
Give me thy heart; I ask no more,
And in at my door thou shalt go.

Who is at my window? Who?
Go from my window! Go!
Cry no more there like a stranger,
But in at my door thou go!

Anonymous
about 1500

No Coming to God without Christ

Good and great God! How should I fear
To come to thee, if Christ not there!
Could I but think, he would not be
Present, to plead my cause for me;
To Hell I'd rather run, than I
Would see thy face, and he not by.

Robert Herrick
1591–1674

To Find God

Weigh me the fire; or canst thou find
A way to measure out the wind;
Distinguish all those floods that are
Mixed in the watery theatre;
And taste thou them as saltless there,
As in their channel first they were.
Tell me the people that do keep
Within the kingdoms of the deep;
Or fetch me back that cloud again,
Beshivered into seeds of rain;
Tell me the motes, dust, sands, and spears
Of corn, when summer shakes his ears;
Show me the world of stars, and whence
They noiseless spill their influence:
This if thou canst; then show me him
That rides the glorious cherubim.

Robert Herrick
1591–1674

Divine Possession

He fumbles at your soul
As players at the keys
Before they drop full music on.
He stuns you by degrees,
Prepares your brittle nature
For the ethereal blow
By fainter hammers further heard,
Then nearer, then so slow
Your breath has time to straighten,
Your brain to bubble cool,
Deals one imperial thunderbolt
That scalps your naked soul.

When winds take forests in their paws
The universe is still.

Emily Dickinson
1830–86

Disclosure

Prayer is like watching for the
Kingfisher. All you can do is
Be where he is likely to appear, and
Wait.
Often, nothing much happens;
There is space, silence and
Expectancy.
No visible sign, only the
Knowledge that he's been there
And may come again.
Seeing or not seeing cease to matter,
You have been prepared.
But sometimes, when you've almost
Stopped expecting it,
A flash of brightness
Gives encouragement.

Ann Lewin
20th century

None Other Lamb

None other Lamb, none other Name,
　None other Hope in heaven or earth or sea,
None other Hiding-place from guilt and shame,
　None beside thee.

My faith burns low, my hope burns low
　Only my heart's desire cries out in me
By the deep thunder of its want and woe
　Cries out to thee.

Lord, thou art Life tho' I be dead,
　Love's Fire thou art, however cold I be:
Nor heaven have I, nor place to lay my head,
　Nor home, but thee.

Christina Rossetti
1830–94

The Search for God

To those I sought thee round about, O thou my God,
      To find thy abode:
I said unto the earth, 'Speak, art thou he?'
      She answered me,
'I am not.' I enquired of creatures all
      In general,
Contained therein: they with one voice proclaim
That none amongst them challenged such a name.

I asked the seas, and all the deeps below,
      My God to know:
I asked the reptiles, and whatever is
      In the abyss:
Even from the shrimp to the leviathan
      My enquiry ran:
But in those deserts, which no line can sound,
The God I sought for was not to be found.

I asked the air, if that were he, but know
      It told me, 'No':
I from the towering eagle to the wren
      Demanded then
If any feathered fowl 'mong them were such:
      But they, all much
Offended at my question, in full quire
Answered, to find my God I must look higher...

And now, my God, by thy illumining grace,
      Thy glorious face
(So far forth as thou wilt discovered be)
      Methinks I see:
And though invisible and infinite;
      To human sight
Thou in thy mercy, justice, truth, appearest,
In which to our frail senses thou com'st nearest.

O, make us apt to seek and quick to find,
      Thou God most kind:
Give us love, hope, and faith in thee to trust,
      Thou God most just:
Remit all our offences, we entreat,
      Most good, most great:
Grant that our willing though unworthy quest
May, through thy grace, admit us 'mongst the blest.

Thomas Heywood 1574–1641

Insatiableness

1

No walls confine! Can nothing hold my mind?
Can I no rest nor satisfaction find?
  Must I behold eternity
      And see
  What things above the heav'ns be?
     Will nothing serve the turn?
     Not earth, nor seas, nor skies?
      Till I what lies
    In time's beginning find;
Must I till then forever burn?

Not all the crowns; not all the heaps of gold
On earth; not all the tales that can be told,
  Will satisfaction yield to me:
      Nor tree,
  Nor shade, nor sun, nor Eden, be
     A joy: nor gems in gold,
     (Be't pearl or precious stone,)
      Nor spring, nor flowers,
    Answer my craving powers,
Nor anything that eyes behold.

Till I what was before all time descry,
The world's beginning seems but vanity.
  My soul doth there long thoughts extend;
      No end
  Doth find, or being comprehend:
     Yet somewhat sees that is
     The obscure shady face
      Of endless space,
    All rooms within; where I
Expect to meet eternal bliss.

2

This busy, vast, inquiring soul
    Brooks no control,
    No limits will endure,
Nor any rest: it will all see
Not time alone, but ev'n eternity.
  What is it? Endless sure.

'Tis mean ambition to desire
    A single world:

To many I aspire,
Though one upon another hurled:
Nor will they all, if they be all confined
Delight my mind...

'Tis nor delight nor perfect pleasure
To have a purse
That hath a bottom in its treasure,
Since I must thence endless expense disburse.
Sure there's a God (or else there's no delight)
One infinite.

Thomas Traherne
1636?–74

The Prayer

Wilt thou not visit me?
The plant beside me feels thy gentle dew,
    And every blade of grass I see
From thy deep earth its quickening moisture drew.

    Wilt thou not visit me?
Thy morning calls on me with cheering tone;
    And every hill and tree
Lend but one voice—the voice of thee alone.

    Come, for I need thy love,
More than the flower the dew or grass the rain;
    Come, gently as thy holy dove;
And let me in thy sight rejoice to live again.

    I will not hide from them
When thy storms come, though fierce may be their wrath,
    But bow with leafy stem,
And strengthened follow on thy chosen path.

    Yes, thou wilt visit me:
Nor plant nor tree thine eye delights so well,
    As, when from sin set free,
My spirit loves with thine in peace to dwell.

Jones Very
1813–80

The Divine Guest

My spirit longeth for thee
   Within my troubled breast;
Although I be unworthy
   Of so divine a Guest.

Of so divine a Guest,
   Unworthy though I be;
Yet has my heart no rest,
   Unless it comes from thee.

Unless it comes from thee,
   In vain I look around:
In all that I can see,
   No rest is to be found.

No rest is to be found,
   But in thy blessed love;
O, let my wish be crowned,
   And send it from above.

John Byrom
1692–1763

A Stranger in this Land

Lord, I am lonely
And the sun is shining,
Listless, while the wind
Shakes the ageing leaves.
The harvest has been gathered
All is bagged and barned,
Silos burst with grain.
   Why, Lord, must I still stand
Dropping blind seeds
On to a barren soil?

Come, sweet Jesus, cut me down
With the sickle of your mercy,
For I am lonely
And a stranger in this land.

Cliff Ashby
20th century

An Invocation

To God, the everlasting, who abides,
One Life within things infinite that die:
To him whose unity no thought divides
Whose breath is breathèd through immensity.

Him neither eye hath seen, nor ear hath heard;
Nor reason, seated in the souls of men,
Though pondering oft on the mysterious word,
Hath e'er revealed his being to mortal ken.

Earth changes, and the starry wheels roll round;
The seasons come and go, moons wax and wane;
The nations rise and fall, and fill the ground,
Storing the sure results of joy and pain:

Slow knowledge widens towards a perfect whole,
From that first man who named the name of heaven,
To him who weighs the planets as they roll,
And knows what laws to every life are given.

Yet he appears not. Round the extreme sphere
Of science still thin ether floats unseen:
Darkness still wraps him round; and ignorant fear
Remains of what we are, and what have been.

Only we feel him; and in aching dreams,
Swift intuitions, pangs of keen delight,
The sudden vision of his glory seems
To sear our souls, dividing the dull night . . .

O God, unknown, invisible, secure,
Whose being by dim resemblances we guess,
Who in man's fear and love abidest sure,
Whose power we feel in darkness and confess!

Without thee nothing is, and thou art nought
When on thy substance we gaze curiously:
By thee impalpable, named force and thought,
The solid world still ceases not to be.

Lead thou me, God, law, reason, duty, life!
All names for thee alike are vain and hollow—
Lead me, for I will follow without strife;
Or, if I strive, still must I blindly follow.

John Addington Symonds 1840–93

Lord of the Winds

Lord of the winds, I cry to thee,
  I that am dust,
And blown about by every gust
  I fly to thee.

Lord of the waters, unto thee I call.
  I that am weed upon the waters borne,
    And by the waters torn,
Tossed by the waters, at thy feet I fall.

Mary Coleridge
1861–1907

The Great Intruder

It is exasperating
to be called
so persistently
when the last thing
we want to do
is get up
and go
but God
elects
to keep on haunting
like some
holy ghost.

Thomas John Carlisle
20th century

From: Religio Laici

1

Thus man by his own strength to heaven would soar:
And would not be obliged to God for more.
Vain, wretched creature, how art thou misled
To think thy wit these God-like notions bred!
These truths are not the product of thy mind,
But dropped from heaven, and of a nobler kind.
Revealed religion first informed thy sight,
And *reason* saw not till *faith* sprung the light.
Hence all thy natural worship takes the source:
'Tis *revelation* what thou thinkst *discourse.*

2

But if there be a *Power* too just and strong
To wink at crimes and bear unpunished wrong,
Look humbly upward, see his will disclose
The forfeit first, and then the fine impose,
A mulct* thy poverty could never pay
Had not eternal wisdom found the way
And with celestial wealth supplied thy store;
His justice makes the fine, his mercy quits the score.
See God descending in thy human frame;
The offended, suffering in the offender's name.
All thy misdeeds to him imputed see,
And all his righteousness devolved on thee.

John Dryden
1631–1700

* *mulct:* fine

Beyond the Headlines

Then I saw the wild geese flying
In fair formation to their bases in Inchicore
And I knew that these wings would outwear the wings of war
And a man's simple thoughts outlive the day's loud lying.
Don't fear, don't fear, I said to my soul.
The Bedlam of Time is an empty bucket rattled,
'Tis you who will say in the end who best battles.
Only they who fly home to God have flown at all.

Patrick Kavanagh
20th century

Song

I scan you on the figured page
in tales of every distant age
and chant you in a holy song
but yet I hear, I see you wrong

I am so small
you are so all

and I would scent you in a flower
that flares and fails from hour to hour
and count your liberality
in berries bright upon the tree

but they are small
and you are all

or might I feel you in the sky
your cloudwind lifts my soul so high
or might I taste you in the spring
new-risen, cleanly carolling

I am so small
you are so all

but narrow is my inward sight
I do not spell your meanings right
and guttering my outward gaze
I do not steady trace your ways

my steps are small
to map your all

then break me wide your raging word
in flintstruck light from darkness stirred
and break me wide your dancing love
that soars the hawk, that swoops the dove

I am so small
you are so all in all.

Veronica Zundel
20th century

From: Wrestling Jacob

(GENESIS 32)

Come, O thou Traveller unknown,
I need not tell thee who I am,
   My misery, or sin declare,
Thyself has called me by my name,
   Look on thy hands, and read it there,
But who, I ask thee, who art thou?
Tell me thy name, and tell me now.

In vain thou strugglest to get free,
   I never will unloose my hold:
Art thou the Man who died for me?
   The secret of thy love unfold.
Wrestling I will not let thee go,
Till I thy name, thy nature know...

What though my shrinking flesh complain,
   And murmur to contend so long,
I rise superior to my pain,
   When I am weak then I am strong,
And when my all of strength shall fail,
I shall with the God-Man prevail...

I know thee, Saviour, who thou art,
   Jesus, the feeble sinner's friend;
Nor wilt thou with the night depart,
   But stay, and love me to the end;
Thy mercies never shall remove,
Thy nature and thy name is Love.

Charles Wesley
1707–88

Resurrection

Each time you go, I'm buried and I hear
seething with honest worms, the truthful loam.
But coming again, you riddle at my ear
with promises of being in air, at home.
I'm comfortable enough, cupboarded in earth—
Oh, I would take the idiom of air:
sirens and chimes and mother's shrieks in birth
and silence in perpetual repair.
But repeated resurrection I can't hear.
Let me grow into death the way of a stone
or let me wear the wind against my ear
eternally I'm worried like a bone.
Above, I hear your footsteps: in your mouth
promises raucous as the sky when geese fly south.

Jeanne Murray Walker
20th century

Surrender

Batter my heart, three-personed God, for you
As yet but knock, breathe, shine, and seek to mend;
That I may rise and stand, o'erthrow me and bend
Your force to break, blow, burn, and make me new.
I, like an usurped town, to another due,
Labour to admit you, but O, to no end.
Reason, your viceroy in me, me should defend,
But is captived and proves weak or untrue.
Yet dearly I love you and would be loved fain,
But am betrothed unto your enemy.
Divorce me, untie, or break that knot again,
Take me to you, imprison me, for I,
Except you enthrall me, never shall be free,
Nor ever chaste, except you ravish me.

John Donne
1572–1631

Hymn

Thou hidden love of God, whose height,
  Whose depth unfathomed no man knows,
I see from far thy beauteous light,
  Inly I sigh for thy repose;
My heart is pained, nor can it be
At rest, till it finds rest in thee.

Thy secret voice invites me still,
  The sweetness of thy yoke to prove:
And fain I would: but though my will
  Seems fixed, yet wide my passions rove;
Yet hindrances strew all the way;
I aim at thee, yet from thee stray.

'Tis mercy all, that thou hast brought
  My mind to seek her peace in thee;
Yet while I seek, but find thee not,
  No peace my wandering soul shall see;
O when shall all my wanderings end,
And all my steps to thee-ward tend! . . .

O Love, thy sovereign aid impart,
  To save me from low-thoughted care:
Chase this self-will through all my heart,
  Through all its latent mazes there:
Make me thy duteous child, that I
Ceaseless may Abba, Father, cry! . . .

Each moment draw from earth away
  My heart that lowly waits thy call:
Speak to my inmost soul, and say,
  I am thy love, thy God, thy all!
To feel thy power, to hear thy voice,
To taste thy love, be all my choice.

John Wesley
1703–91

The Invitation

Lord, what unvalued pleasures crowned
  The days of old;
When thou wert so familiar found,
  Those days were gold;—

When Abram wished thou couldst afford
  With him to feast;
When Lot but said, 'Turn in, my Lord,'
  Thou wert his guest.

But, ah! this heart of mine doth pant,
  And beat for thee;
Yet thou art strange, and wilt not grant
  Thyself to me.

What, shall thy people be so dear
  To thee no more?
Or is not heaven to earth as near
  As heretofore?

The famished raven's hoarser cry
  Finds out thine ear;
My soul is famished, and I die
  Unless thou hear.

O thou great ALPHA! King of kings
  Or bow to me,
Or lend my soul seraphic wings,
  To get to thee.

Anonymous
17th century

Walking With God

Alas, my God, that we should be
   Such strangers to each other!
O that as friends we might agree,
   And walk and talk together!

May I taste that communion, Lord,
   Thy people have with thee?
Thy Spirit daily talks with them,
   O let it talk with me!

Like Enoch, let me walk with God,
   And thus walk out my day,
Attended with the heavenly guards,
   Upon the King's highway.

When wilt thou come unto me, Lord?
   O come, my Lord most dear!
Come near, come nearer, nearer still:
   I'm well when thou art near.

There's no such thing as pleasure here;
   My JESUS is my all:
As thou dost shine or disappear,
   My pleasures rise and fall.

When wilt thou come unto me, Lord?
   For, till thou dost appear,
I count each moment for a day,
   Each minute for a year.

Thomas Shepherd
1665–1739

From: Uriel

Reach forth thy hand!
Sunder the clouds, for we have lost our way;
Reach forth thy hand and guide us thro' this darkness.
Thou in thy wisdom having dwelt in us,
Thou wilt not with thy kindred heart condemn us
To know thee once, once only, and only a little,
Nor wilt thou in thy justice, when our hearts
Respond, and long to know thee more and more
Wither us into dust and nothingness.
A homeless dog looked up to me, as I
Look up to thee, he came and trusted me,
Tho' strange my ways to him past finding out;
Strange are thy ways to me, but I am glad
We three are kinsmen, and thou art to me
As I am to the friendship-craving beast.
We trust, but then the freezing shadow falls,
Our vision fails, we cannot understand;
Even the Heart of the World, nailed to the Cross,
Cried out, 'Forsaken!'—but never was forsaken;
He died, he lives, with nothing lost, all gained.

I see thee putting forth thy hand to write
A crimson line above the western hills,
And here, in night's cottage, we detained can tell
Where thy great sun, in strength undimmed, rides on
Beyond the cloud-thatched eaves of dying day.

William Force Stead
1889–?

From: The Task

I was a stricken deer, that left the herd
Long since; with many an arrow deep infixt
My panting side was charged, when I withdrew
To seek a tranquil death in distant shades.
There was I found by one who had himself
Been hurt by th'archers. In his side he bore,
And in his hands and feet, the cruel scars.
With gentle force soliciting the darts,
He drew them forth, and healed, and bade me live.
Since then, with few associates, in remote
And silent woods I wander, far from those
My former partners of the peopled scene;
With few associates, and not wishing more.

William Cowper
1731–1800

God our Refuge

If there had anywhere appeared in space
    Another place of refuge where to flee,
Our hearts had taken refuge in that place,
    And not with thee.

For we against creation's bars had beat
    Like prisoned eagles, through great worlds had sought
Though but a foot of ground to plant our feet,
    Where thou wert not.

And only when we found in earth and air,
    In heaven or hell, that such might nowhere be—
That we could not flee from thee anywhere,
    We fled to thee.

Richard Chenevix Trench
1807–86

From: The Hound of Heaven

I fled him, down the nights and down the days;
  I fled him, down the arches of the years;
I fled him, down the labyrinthine ways
  Of my own mind; and in the mist of tears
I hid from him, and under running laughter.
      Up vistaed hopes I sped;
      And shot, precipitated,
Adown Titanic glooms of chasmed fears,
    From those strong Feet that followed, followed after.
      But with unhurrying chase,
      And unperturbèd pace,
    Deliberate speed, majestic instancy,
      They beat—and a Voice beat
      More instant than the Feet—
    'All things betray thee, who betrayest me.' . . .

    Halts by me that footfall:
    Is my gloom, after all,
Shade of his hand, outstretched caressingly?
    'Ah, fondest, blindest, weakest,
    I am he whom thou seekest!
Thou dravest love from thee, who dravest me.'

              Francis Thompson
              1859–1907

A Dig through Dust

I dream a dig through dust:
a pit I cannot tell how deep,
Sheol, the grave perhaps,
timber long since riddled to ash.
I scratch and sieve for goods;
ornaments, spindle-whorls and bones.

Find none. A post-hole then
whose tree and cross-tree raised a roof;
I comb the flinty ground
for sherds, grain, signs of the sacred
or profane, black layers
of occupation; and find none.

But for three Roman nails,
rust-cankered. Post-hole then, and grave.
Out of the dig's raised dust
a man—a gardener—appears
to set a seed in it.
Water, he says. I wake in tears.

Paul Hyland
20th century

That Holy Thing

They were all looking for a king
    To slay their foes and lift them high:
Thou cam'st, a little baby thing
    That made a woman cry.

O Son of Man, to right my lot
    Naught but thy presence can avail;
Yet on the road thy wheels are not,
    Nor on the sea thy sail!

My how or when thou wilt not heed,
    But come down thine own secret stair,
That thou mayst answer all my need—
    Yea, every bygone prayer.

George MacDonald
1824–1905

Prayer

I asked for Peace—
  My sins arose,
  And bound me close,
I could not find release.

I asked for Truth—
  My doubts came in,
  And with their din
They wearied all my youth.

I asked for Love—
  My lovers failed,
  and griefs assailed
Around, beneath, above.

I asked for thee—
  And thou didst come
  To take me home
Within thy heart to be.

Digby Mackworth Dolben
1848–67

Felicity

No, 'tis in vain to seek for bliss;
  For bliss can ne'er be found
Till we arrive where Jesus is,
  And tread on heavenly ground.

There's nothing round these painted skies,
  Or round this dusty clod;
Nothing, my soul, that's worth thy joys,
  Or lovely as thy God.

'Tis heaven on earth to taste his love,
  To feel his quickening grace;
And all the Heaven I hope above
  Is but to see his face.

Isaac Watts
1674–1748

Christ my All-in-all

I've found the pearl of greatest price,
  My heart doth sing for joy;
And sing I must, for Christ is mine,
  Christ shall my song employ.

Christ is my Prophet, Priest, and King:
  My Prophet full of light,
My great High Priest before the throne,
  My King of heavenly might.

For he indeed is Lord of lords,
  And he the King of kings;
He is the Sun of Righteousness,
  With healing in his wings.

Christ is my peace; he died for me,
  For me he gave his blood;
And as my wondrous sacrifice
  Offered himself to God.

Christ Jesus is my All-in-all,
  My comfort and my love;
My life below; and he shall be
  My glory-crown above.

John Mason
about 1645–94

The Search

Pilgrim remember
For all your pain
The Master you seek abroad
You will find at home—
Or walk in vain.

Anonymous
7th century

God's Mercy and Forgiveness

God's mercy

God's boundless mercy is (to sinful man)
Like to the ever-wealthy ocean:
Which though it sends forth thousand streams, 'tis ne'er
Known, or else seen, to be the emptier;
And though it takes all in, 'tis yet no more
Full, and filled full, than when full filled before.

Robert Herrick
1591–1674

'Neither Shadow of Turning'

I could not name a single blessing
   That came to me in disguise;
The gifts I asked arrived unmasked
   Under broad day's honest skies.

God does not play a senile game
   That wraps his mercies round
With a leprous sheet, a scabbed deceit:
   His good, from the start, is sound.

There is no heaven disguised as hell,
   No jail by which we're freed;
A twist that mocks is no paradox—
   It's the devil's twist indeed.

'Deliver us from evil'—why,
   If the evil has good inside?
God's war is grim—we are bruised with him:
   HIS gifts never mystified.

Jack Clemo
20th century

Saul Kane's Conversion

FROM: THE EVERLASTING MERCY

All earthly things that blessed morning
Were everlasting joy and warning.
The gate was Jesus' way made plain,
The mole was Satan foiled again,
Black blinded Satan snouting way
Along the red of Adam's clay;
The mist was error and damnation,
The lane the road unto salvation,
Out of the mist into the light;
O blessed gift of inner sight.
The past was fading like a dream;
There come the jingling of a team,
A ploughman's voice, a clink of chain,
Slow hoofs, and harness under strain.
Up the slow slope a team came bowing,
Old Callow at his autumn ploughing,
Old Callow, stooped above the hales,
Ploughing the stubble into wales;
His grave eyes looking straight ahead,
Shearing a long straight furrow red;
His plough-foot high to give it earth
To bring new food for men to birth.

O wet red swathe of earth laid bare,
O truth, O strength, O gleaming share,
O patient eyes that watch the goal,
O ploughman of the sinner's soul.
O Jesus, drive the coulter deep
To plough my living man from sleep ...

O Christ who holds the open gate,
O Christ who drives the furrow straight,
O Christ, the plough, O Christ, the laughter
Of holy white birds flying after,
Lo, all my heart's field red and torn,
And thou wilt bring the young green corn,
The young green corn divinely springing,
The young green corn for ever singing;
And when the field is fresh and fair
Thy blessèd feet shall glitter there.
And we will walk the weeded field,
And tell the golden harvest's yield,

The corn that makes the holy bread
By which the soul of man is fed,
The holy bread, the food unpriced,
Thy everlasting mercy, Christ

John Masefield
1878–1967

Christian Arrives at the Cross and Sepulchre

(FROM: THE PILGRIM'S PROGRESS)

Thus far did I come loaden with my sin,
Nor could aught ease the grief that I was in
Till I came hither. What a place is this!
Must here be the beginning of my bliss?
Must here the burden fall from off my back?
Blessed Cross! Blessed Sepulchre! Blessed rather be
The man that there was put to shame for me.

John Bunyan
1622–88

Conversion

He was a born loser,
accident-prone too;
never won a lottery,
married a girl who
couldn't cook, broke
his leg the day before
the wedding
and forgot the ring.
He was the kind
who ended up behind a post
in almost any
auditorium. Planes
he was booked to fly on
were delayed
by engine trouble
with sickening regularity.
His holidays at the beach
were almost always
ruined by rain. All
his apples turned out
wormy. His letters
came back marked
'Moved, left no
address.' And it was
his car that was cited
for speeding
from among a flock of others
going 60 in a
55 mile zone.

So it was a real shocker
when he found himself
elected, chosen by Grace
for Salvation, felt
the exhilaration of
an undeserved and wholly
unexpected Joy
and tasted, for the
first time, the Glory
of being on
the winning side.

Luci Shaw
20th century

CONFESSION AND FORGIVENESS

A Hymn

Drop, drop, slow tears
 and bathe those beauteous feet,
Which brought from heaven
 the news and Prince of peace:
Cease not, wet eyes,
 his mercy to entreat;
To cry for vengeance
 sin doth never cease:
In your deep floods
 drown all my faults and fears;
Nor let his eye
 see sin, but through my tears.

Phineas Fletcher
1582–1650

Holy Sonnets

2

At the round earth's imagined corners blow
Your trumpets, angels, and arise, arise
From death, you numberless infinities
Of souls, and to your scattered bodies go:
All whom the flood did, and fire shall o'erthrow,
All whom war, dearth, age, agues, tyrannies,
Despair, law, chance hath slain, and you whose eyes
Shall behold God and never taste death's woe.
But let them sleep, Lord, and me mourn a space,
For if above all these my sins abound,
'Tis late to ask abundance of thy grace
When we are there. Here on this holy ground
Teach me how to repent; for that's as good
As if thou hadst sealed my pardon with thy blood.

John Donne
1572–1631

Forgive the Prodigal Heart

Behold the prodigal! To thee I come,
To hail my Father and to seek my home.
Nor refuge could I find, nor friend abroad,
Straying in vice and destitute of God.

O let thy terrors and my anguish end!
Be thou my refuge and be thou my friend:
Receive the son thou didst so long reprove,
Thou that art the God of love!

Matthew Prior
1664–1721

From: Murder in the Cathedral

Forgive us, O Lord, we acknowledge ourselves as type of the common man,
Of the men and women who shut the door and sit by the fire;
Who fear the blessing of God, the loneliness of the night
of God, the surrender required, the deprivation inflicted;
Who fear the injustice of men less than the justice of God;
Who fear the hand at the window, the fire in the thatch
the fist in the tavern, the push into the canal,
Less than we fear the love of God.
We acknowledge our trespass, our weakness, our fault; we acknowledge
That the sin of the world is upon our heads; that the
blood of the martyrs and the agony of the saints
Is upon our heads.
Lord, have mercy upon us.
Christ, have mercy upon us.
Lord, have mercy upon us.
Blessed Thomas, pray for us.

T.S. Eliot
1888–1965

Judgment and Mercy

O whither shall I fly? what path untrod
Shall I seek out to 'scape the flaming rod
Of my offended, of my angry God?

Where shall I sojourn? what kind sea will hide
My head from thunder? where shall I abide,
Until his flames be quenched or laid aside?

What if my soul should take the wings of day,
And find some desert? If she springs away,
The wings of vengeance clip as fast* as they...

'Tis vain to flee; 'tis neither here nor there
Can 'scape that hand, until that hand forbear;
Ah me! where is he not, that's everywhere?...

Great God! there is no safety here below;
Thou art my fortress, thou that seem'st my foe.
'Tis thou, that strik'st the stroke, must guard the blow.

Thou art my God, by thee I fall or stand;
Thy grace hath given me courage to withstand
All tortures, but my conscience and thy hand.

I know thy justice is thyself; I know,
Just God, thy very self is mercy too;
If not to thee, where, whither shall I go?

Then work thy will; if passion bid me flee,
My reason shall obey; my wings shall be
Stretch'd out no further than from thee to thee.

Francis Quarles
1592–1644

* *clip as fast:* grip as firmly

Mercy

Mercy is hendest* where sin is most,
Mercy is slower where sin is least;
Mercy abideth and looketh all day
When man from sin will turn away;
Mercy saveth that law would spill:*
Mercy asketh but God's will.

Anonymous
Medieval

* *hendest:* readiest; *spill:* destroy

Conscience

If I could shut the gate against my thoughts
    And keep out sorrow from this room within,
Or memory could cancel all the notes
    Of my misdeeds, and I unthink my sin:
How free, how clear, how clean my soul should lie
Discharged of such a loathsome company!

Or were there other rooms within my heart
    That did not to my conscience join so near,
Where I might lodge the thoughts of sin apart
    That I might not their clamorous crying hear;
What peace, what joy, what ease should I possess,
Freed from their horrors that my soul oppress!

But, O my Saviour, who my refuge art,
    Let thy dear mercies stand 'twixt them and me
And be the wall to separate my heart
    So that I may at length repose me free;
That peace, and joy, and rest may be within,
And I remain divided from my sin.

Anonymous
17th century

Second Lazarus

O come, dear Lord, unbind: like Lazarus, I
lie wrapped in stifling grave clothes of self-will.
Come give me life that I to death may die.
I stink: the grave of sin is worm-filled still
despite our turning from its rottenness,
unwilling to admit that we are bound,
too proud to mention our begottenness.
Come, open sin's sarcophagus. I'm wound
in selfishness, self-satisfaction, pride,
fear of change, demands of love, greed,
self-hate, sweet sins that come in fair disguise.
Help me accept this death and open wide
the tight-closed tomb. If pain comes as we're freed,
Your daylight must have hurt first Lazarus's eyes.

Madeleine L'Engle
20th century

The Penitent

Lord, I have sinned, and the black number swells
To such a dismal sum,
That should my stony heart and eyes,
And this whole sinful trunk a flood become,
And melt to tears, their drops could not suffice
        To count my score,
        Much less to pay:
But thou, my God, hast blood in store,
Yet, since the balsam of thy blood,
Although it can, will do not good,
Unless the wound be cleansed in tears before;
Thou in whose sweet, but pensive face,
Laughter could never steal a place,
        Teach but my heart and eyes
        To melt away,
And then one drop of balsam will suffice.

Jeremy Taylor
1613–67

A Prayer in Old Age

Bring no expectance of a heaven unearned
No hunger for beatitude to be
Until the lesson of my life is learned
Through what thou didst for me.

Bring no assurance of redeemèd rest
No intimation of awarded grace
Only contrition, cleavingly confessed
To thy forgiving face.

I ask one world of everlasting loss
In all I am, that other world to win.
My nothingness must kneel below thy Cross.
There let new life begin.

Siegfried Sassoon
1886–1967

A Hymn to God the Father

Wilt thou forgive that sin where I begun,
　　Which is my sin, though it were done before?
Wilt thou forgive those sins through which I run,
　　And do them still, though still I do deplore?
　　　　When thou hast done, thou hast not done,
　　　　　For I have more.

Wilt thou forgive that sin by which I won
　　Others to sin, and made my sin their door?
Wilt thou forgive that sin which I did shun
　　A year or two, but wallowed in a score?
　　　　When thou hast done, thou hast not done,
　　　　　For I have more.

I have a sin of fear, that when I've spun
　　My last thread, I shall perish on the shore;
Swear by thyself that at my death thy sun
　　Shall shine as it shines now, and heretofore;
　　　　And having done that, thou hast done,
　　　　　I have no more.

John Donne
1572–1631

Frailty

Fain would I say, 'Forgive my foul offence!'
    Fain promise never more to disobey;
But, should my Author health again dispense,
    Again I might desert fair virtue's way;
Again in folly's path might go astray;
    Again exalt the brute and sink the man;
Then how should I for heavenly mercy pray,
    Who act so counter heavenly mercy's plan?
Who sin so oft have mourned, yet to temptation ran?

Robert Burns 1759–96

Little Prayer for Samson and Delilah

When all virtue
like Samson's Rastafarian locks
lies strewn about us,
have mercy, Lord,
on those who sleep in weakness
and those who have shorn us of strength.

Like the growing stubble on Samson's head,
let us be renewed to undertake
the phenomenal as matter of course
when we awaken
from the lap of philistine ease.

Diane Karay Tripp 20th century

Times without Number

Times without number have I prayed
    'This only once forgive';
Relapsing, when thy hand was stayed,
    And suffered me to live:—

Yet now the kingdom of thy peace,
    Lord, to my heart restore;
Forgive my vain repentances,
    And bid me sin no more.

Charles Wesley 1707–88

A Hymn to God the Father

Hear me, O God!
　A broken heart
　Is my best part:
Use still thy rod
　That I may prove
　Therein thy love.

If thou hadst not
　Been stern to me,
　But left me free,
I had forgot
　Myself and thee.

For sin's so sweet,
　As minds ill bent
　Rarely repent
Until they meet
　Their punishment.

Who more can crave
　Than thou hast done,
　That gav'st a son
To free a slave,
　First made of nought,
　With all since bought?

Sin, Death, and Hell
　His glorious Name
　Quite overcame,
Yet I rebel,
　And slight the same.

But I'll come in,
　Before my loss
　Me farther toss,
As sure to win
　Under his cross.

Ben Jonson
1572–1637

Heaven's Sun Shining on my Soul

But, ah, our sins, our clouds benight the air;
Lord, drain the fens of this my boggy soul,
Whose grosser vapours make my day so foul;
The Son hath strength to chase away
These rising fogs, and make a glorious day:
Rise, and shine always clear; but, most of all
Let me behold thy glory, in thy fall;
That being set, poor I (my flesh being hurled
From this) may meet thee, in another world.

Francis Quarles
1592–1644

A Prayer for Grace

View me, Lord, a work of thine:
Shall I then lie drowned in night?
Might thy grace in me but shine,
I should seem made all of light.

But my soul still surfeits so
On the poisoned baits of sin,
That I strange and ugly grow,
All is dark and foul within.

Cleanse me, Lord, that I may kneel
At thine altar, pure and white:
They that once thy mercies feel,
Gaze no more on earth's delight.

Worldly joys like shadows fade,
When the heavenly light appears;
But the cov'nants thou hast made,
Endless, know nor days, nor years.

In thy word, Lord, is my trust,
To thy mercies fast I fly;
Though I am but clay and dust,
Yet thy grace can lift me high.

Thomas Campion
1567–1620

Comfort in Extremity

Alas! my Lord is going,
> Oh my woe!
It will be mine undoing:
> If he go,
I'll run and overtake him;
> If he stay,
I'll cry aloud, and make him
> Look this way.
> O stay, my Lord, my Love, 'tis I;
> Comfort me quickly, or I die.

'Cheer up thy drooping spirits;
> I am here.
Mine all-sufficient merits
> Shall appear
Before the throne of glory
> In thy stead:
I'll put into thy story
> What I did.
> Lift up thine eyes, sad soul, and see
> Thy Saviour here. Lo, I am he.'

Alas, shall I present
> My sinfulness
To thee? Thou wilt resent
> The loathsomeness.
'Be not afraid, I'll take
> Thy sins on me,
And all my favour make
> To shine on thee.'
> Lord, what thou'lt have me, thou must make me.
> 'As I have made thee now, I take thee.'

Christopher Harvey
1597–1663

Thankfulness and Praise

From: Providence

Of all the creatures both in sea and land,
Only to man thou hast made known thy ways,
And put the pen alone into his hand,
And made him secretary of thy praise.

George Herbert
1593–1633

Non Nobis Domine

Non nobis Domine!—
    Not unto us, O Lord!
The praise or glory be
    Of any deed or word;
For in thy judgement lies
    To crown or bring to nought
All knowledge or device
    That man has reached or wrought.

And we confess our blame—
    How all too high we hold
That noise which men call fame,
    That dross which men call gold.
For these we undergo
    Our hot and godless days,
But in our hearts we know
    Not unto us the praise.

O Power by whom we live—
    Creator, Judge, and Friend,
Upholdingly forgive
    Nor fail us at the end:
But grant us well to see
    In all our piteous ways—
Non nobis Domine!—
    Not unto us the praise!

Rudyard Kipling
1865–1936

Fill the World with Praise

From all that dwell below the skies
Let the Creator's praise arise;
Let the Redeemer's name be sung
Through every land by every tongue.

Eternal are thy mercies, Lord;
Eternal truth attends thy word;
Thy praise shall sound from shore to shore,
Till suns shall rise and set no more.

In every land begin the song;
To every land the strains belong:
In cheerful sounds all voices raise
And fill the world with loudest praise.

Isaac Watts
1674–1748

Antiphon

Let all the world in ev'ry corner sing,
    My God and King!
  The heavens are not too high,
  His praise may thither fly;
  The earth is not too low,
  His praises there may grow.

Let all the world in ev'ry corner sing,
    My God and King!
  The church with psalms must shout,
  No door can keep them out;
  But above all, the heart
  Must bear the longest part.

Let all the world in ev'ry corner sing,
    My God and King!

George Herbert
1593–1633

May 20:
Very Early Morning

all the field praises him/all
dandelions are his glory/gold
and silver all trilliums unfold
white flames above their trinities
of leaves all wild strawberries
and massed wood violets reflect his skies'
clean blue and white
all brambles/all oxeyes
all stalks and stems lift to his light
all young windflower bells
tremble on hair
springs for his air's
carillon touch/last year's yarrow (raising
brittle star skeletons) tells
age is not past praising
all small low unknown
unnamed weeds show his impossible greens
all grasses sing
tone on clear tone
all mosses spread a spring-
soft velvet for his feet
and by all means
all leaves/buds/all flowers cup
jewels of fire and ice
holding up
to his kind morning heat
a silver sacrifice

now
make of our hearts a field
to raise your praise

Luci Shaw
20th century

A Psalm for Sunday Night

O sing the glories of our Lord;
    His grace and truth resound,
And his stupendous acts record,
    Whose mercies have no bound!

He made the all-informing light
    And hosts of angels fair;
'Tis he with shadows clothes the night,
    He clouds or clears the air.

Those restless skies with stars enchased
    He on firm hinges set;
The wave-embracèd earth he placed
    His hanging cabinet.

We in his summer-sunshine stand,
    And in his favour grow;
We gather what his bounteous hand
    Is pleasèd to bestow.

When he contracts his brow, we mourn,
    And all our strength is vain;
To former dust in death we turn,
    Till he inspire again.

Thomas Pestel 1584?–1659?

Anthem

Let us praise our Maker, with true passion extol him.
Let the whole creation give out another sweetness,
Nicer in our nostrils, a novel fragrance
From cleansed occasions in accord together
As one feeling fabric, all flushed and intact,
Phenomena and numbers announcing in one
Multitudinous ecumenical song
Their grand givenness of gratitude and joy,
Peacable and plural, their positive truth
An authoritative This, an unthreatened Now
When, in love and in laughter, each lives itself,
For, united by his Word, cognition and power,
System and Order, are a single glory,
And the pattern is complex, their places safe.

W.H. Auden 20th century

From: A Song to David

Praise above all—for praise prevails;
Heap up the measure, load the scales,
   And good to goodness add:
The generous soul her Saviour aids,
But peevish obloquy degrades;
   The Lord is great and glad...

Glorious the sun in mid career;
Glorious the assembled fires appear;
   Glorious the comet's train:
Glorious the trumpet and alarm;
Glorious the Almighty's stretched-out arm;
   Glorious the enraptured main:

Glorious the northern lights a-stream;
Glorious the song, when God's the theme;
   Glorious the thunder's roar:
Glorious Hosanna from the den;
Glorious the catholic Amen;
   Glorious the martyr's gore:

Glorious—more glorious is the crown
Of him that brought salvation down
   By meekness, called the Son;
Thou that stupendous truth believed,
And now the matchless deed's achieved
   Determined, dared and done.

Christopher Smart
1722–71

All Praise

To God, ye choir above, begin
　A hymn so loud and strong
That all the universe may hear
　And join the grateful song.

Praise him, thou sun, who dwells unseen
　Amidst transcendent light,
Where thy refulgent beam would seem
　A spot, as dark as night.

Thou silver moon, ye host of stars,
　The universal song
Through the serene and silent night
　To listening worlds prolong.

Sing him, ye distant worlds and suns,
　From whence no travelling ray
Hath yet to us, through ages past,
　Had time to make its way.

Assist, ye raging storms, and bear
　On rapid wings his praise,
From north to south, from east to west,
　Through heaven, and earth, and seas.

Exert your voice, ye furious fires
　That rend the watery cloud,
And thunder to this nether world
　Your Maker's words aloud.

Ye works of God, that dwell unknown
　Beneath the rolling main;
Ye birds, that sing among the groves,
　And sweep the azure plain;

Ye stately hills, that rear your heads,
　And towering pierce the sky;
Ye clouds, that with an awful pace
　Majestic roll on high;

Ye insects small, to which one leaf
　Within its narrow sides
A vast extended world displays,
　And spacious realms provides;

Ye race, still less than these, with which
   The stagnant water teems,
To which one drop, however small,
   A boundless ocean seems;

—Whate'er ye are, where'er ye dwell,
   Ye creatures great or small,
Adore the wisdom, praise the power,
   That made and governs all.

Philip Skelton
1707–87

O Rex Gentium

O King! thou art the wall-stone
which of old the workmen
from their work rejected!
Well it thee beseemeth
that thou hold the headship
of this Hall of glory,
and should'st join together
with a fastening firm
the broad-spaced walls
of the flint unbreakable
all fitly framed together;
that among the earth's dwellers
all with sight of eyes
may for ever wonder.
O Prince of glory!
now through skill and wisdom
manifest thy handiwork,
true-fast and firm-set
in sovereign splendour.

From Cynewulf,
based upon the antiphon 'O Rex Gentium' about 820

Jesus Christ the Apple Tree

The tree of life my soul hath seen,
Laden with fruit, and always green:
The trees of nature fruitless be
Compared with Christ the apple tree.

His beauty doth all things excel:
By faith I know, but ne'er can tell
The glory which I now can see
In Jesus Christ the apple tree.

For happiness I long have sought,
And pleasure dearly I have bought:
I missed of all; but now I see
'Tis found in Christ the apple tree.

I'm weary with my former toil,
Here I will sit and rest awhile:
Under the shadow I will be,
Of Jesus Christ the apple tree.

This fruit doth make my soul to thrive,
It keeps my dying faith alive;
Which makes my soul in haste to be
With Jesus Christ the apple tree.

From Divine Hymns or Spiritual Songs,
compiled by Joshua Smith, New Hampshire 1784

Song of Creation

Now we must praise the Guardian of Heaven,
the might of the Lord and his purpose of mind,
the work of the Glorious Father; for he,
God eternal, established each wonder,
he, Holy Creator, first fashioned
heaven as a roof for the sons of men.
Then the Guardian of Mankind adorned
this middle-earth below, the world for men,
Everlasting Lord, Almighty King.

Caedmon's Song
late 7th century?

A Prayer

O mighty God, which for us men
   Didst suffer on the cross
The painful pangs of bitter death,
   To save our souls from loss,
I yield thee here most hearty thanks,
   In that thou dost vouchsafe,
Of me most vile and sinful wretch,
   So great regard to have.
Alas, none ever had more cause
   To magnify thy name,
Than I, to whom thy mercies showed
   Do witness well the same.
So many brunts of fretting foes
   Whoever could withstand,
If thou had'st not protected me,
   With thy most holy hand?
A thousand times in shameful sort
   My sinful life had ended,
If by thy gracious goodness, Lord,
   I had not been defended.
In stinking pools of filthy vice
   So deeply was I drowned,
That none there was but thee alone,
   To set my foot on ground.
When as the fiend had led my soul
   E'en to the gates of hell,
Thou call'dst me back, and dost me choose
   In heaven with thee to dwell:—
Let furies now fret on their fill,
   Let Satan rage, and roar,
As long as thou art on my side,
   What need I care for more?

Humfrey Gifford
about 1580

Praise

The glorious armies of the sky
　　To thee, Almighty King,
Triumphant anthems consecrate,
　　And hallellujahs sing.

But still their most exalted flights
　　Fall vastly short of thee:
How distant then must human praise
　　From thy perfections be!

Yet how, my God, shall I refrain
　　When to my ravished sense
Each creature everywhere around
　　Displays thy excellence!

The active lights that shine above,
　　In their eternal dance,
Reveal their skilful Maker's praise
　　With silent elegance.

The blushes of the morn confess
　　That thou art still more fair,
When in the east its beams revive,
　　To gild the fields of air.

The fragrant, the refreshing breeze
　　Of ev'ry flowery bloom
In balmy whispers own, from thee
　　Their pleasing odours come.

The singing birds, the warbling winds,
　　And waters murmuring fall
To praise the first Almighty Cause
　　With different voices call.

Thy numerous works exalt thee thus,
　　And shall I silent be?
No, rather let me cease to breathe,
　　Than cease from praising thee!

Elizabeth Rowe
1674–1737

Bermudas—Song of the Emigrants

Where the remote Bermudas ride
In the ocean's bosom unespied,
From a small boat that rowed along,
The listening winds received this song.
   'What should we do but sing his praise
That led us through the watery maze,
Unto an isle so long unknown
And yet far kinder than our own?
Where he the huge sea-monsters wracks,
That lift the deep upon their backs.
He lands us on a grassy stage,
Safe from the storm's and prelates' rage.
He gave us this eternal spring,
Which here enamels everything;
And sends the fowls to us in care,
On daily visits through the air.
He hangs in shades the orange bright,
Like golden lamps in a green night,
And does in the pom'granates close
Jewels more rich than Ormus shows.
He makes the figs our mouths to meet,
And throws the melons at our feet;
But apples* plants of such a price
No tree could ever bear them twice.
With cedars, chosen by his hand,
From Lebanon, he stores the land;
And makes the hollow seas that roar
Proclaim the ambergris on shore.
He cast (of which we rather boast)
The Gospel's pearl upon our coast,
And in these rocks for us did frame
A temple, where to sound his name.
Oh let our voice his praise exalt,
Till it arrive at heaven's vault,
Which thence, perhaps, rebounding may
Echo beyond the Mexique Bay.'
   Thus sung they in the English boat,
An holy and a cheerful note,
And all the way, to guide their chime,
With falling oars they kept the time.

Andrew Marvell
1621–78

* *apples:* pineapples

From: The Dream of Gerontius

Praise to the Holiest in the height,
    And in the depth be praise,
In all his words most wonderful,
    Most sure in all his ways.

Oh loving wisdom of our God!
    When all was sin and shame,
A second Adam to the fight
    And to the rescue came.

Oh wisest love! that flesh and blood,
    Which did in Adam fail,
Should strive afresh against the foe,
    Should strive and should prevail.

And that a higher gift than grace
    Should flesh and blood refine,
God's presence and his very self,
    And essence all-divine.

Oh generous love! that he who smote
    In man for man the foe,
The double agony in man
    For man should undergo;

And in the garden secretly,
    And on the cross on high,
Should teach his brethren, and inspire
    To suffer and to die.

Praise to the Holiest in the height,
    And in the depth be praise,
In all his words most wonderful,
    Most sure in all his ways.

John Henry Newman
1801–90

How Shall I Praise?

How shall I sing that majesty
    Which angels do admire?
Let dust in dust and silence lie;
    Sing, sing, ye heavenly choir.
Thousands of thousands stand around
    Thy throne, O God most high;
Ten thousand times ten thousand sound
    Thy praise; but who am I?

Thy brightness unto them appears;
    While I thy footsteps trace
A sound of God comes to my ears,
    But they behold thy face.
They sing because thou art their Sun;
    Lord, send a beam on me;
For where heaven is but once begun
    There Hallelujahs be.

Enlighten with faith's light my heart
    Inflame it with love's fire;
Then shall I sing and bear a part
    With that celestial choir.
I shall, I fear, be dark and cold,
    With all my fire and light;
Yet when thou dost accept their gold,
    Lord, treasure up my mite.

How great a being, Lord, is thine,
    Which doth all beings keep!
Thy knowledge is the only line
    To sound so vast a deep.
Thou art a sea without a shore,
    A sun without a sphere;
Thy time is now and evermore,
    Thy place is everywhere.

John Mason
about 1645–94

King of Glory

King of glory, King of peace,
　　I will love thee;
And that love may never cease,
　　I will move thee.

Thou hast granted my request,
　　Thou hast heard me:
Thou didst note my working breast,
　　Thou hast spared me.

Wherefore with my utmost art
　　I will sing thee,
And the cream of all my heart
　　I will bring thee.

Though my sins against me cried
　　Thou didst clear me;
And alone, when they replied,
　　Thou didst hear me.

Seven whole days, not one in seven,
　　I will praise thee.
In my heart, though not in heaven,
　　I can raise thee.

Thou grew'st soft and moist with tears,
　　Thou relentedst;
And when Justice called for fears,
　　Thou dissentedst.

Small it is in this poor sort
　　To enrol thee:
Ev'n eternity is too short
　　To extol thee.

George Herbert
1593–1633

In Thankful Remembrance

FOR MY DEAR HUSBAND'S SAFE ARRIVAL

What shall I render to thy name
  Or how thy praises speak?
My thanks how shall I testify?
  O Lord, thou knowest I'm weak.

I owe so much, so little can
  Return unto thy name,
Confusion seizes on my soul,
  And I am filled with shame.

O thou that hearest prayers, Lord,
  To thee shall come all flesh,
Thou hast me heard and answerèd,
  My plaints have had access.

What did I ask for but thou gav'st?
  What more could I desire?
But thankfulness even all my days -
  I humbly this require.

Thy mercies, Lord, have been so great
  In number numberless,
Impossible for to recount
  Or any way express.

O help thy saints that sought thy face
  To return unto thee praise
And walk before thee as they ought,
  In strict and upright ways.

Anne Bradstreet
1612–72

True Delight

To music bent is my retired mind.
    And fain would I some song of pleasure sing,
But in vain joys no comfort now I find;
    From heavenly thoughts all true delight doth spring.
Thy power, O God, thy mercies to record,
Will sweeten every note and every word.

All earthly pomp or beauty to express
    Is but to carve in snow, on waves to write.
Celestial things, though men conceive them less,
    Yet fullest are they in themselves of light;
Such beams they yield as know no means to die,
Such heat they cast as lifts the spirit high.

Thomas Campion
1567–1620

From: The Christian Year

IN CHOIRS AND PLACES WHERE THEY SING, HERE FOLLOWETH THE ANTHEM.

Lord, make my heart a place where angels sing!
    For surely thoughts low-breathed by thee
Are angels gliding near on noiseless wing;
    And where a home they see

Swept clean, and garnished with adoring joy,
    They enter in and dwell,
    And teach that heart to swell
With heavenly melody, their own untired employ.

John Keble
1792–1866

God's Unending Mercies

When all thy mercies, O my God,
　My rising soul surveys;
Transported with the view, I'm lost
　In wonder, love and praise.

O how shall words with equal warmth
　Thy gratitude declare,
That glows within my ravished heart!
　But thou canst read it there.

Thy providence my life sustained
　And all my wants redressed,
When in the silent womb I lay,
　And hung upon the breast.

To all my weak complaints and cries,
　Thy mercy lent an ear,
Ere yet my feeble thoughts had learnt
　To form themselves in prayer.

Unnumbered comforts to my soul
　Thy tender care bestowed,
Before my infant heart conceived
　From whom these comforts flowed.

When in the slippery path of youth
　With heedless steps I ran.
Thine arm unseen conveyed me safe
　And led me up to man ...

Through every period of my life
　Thy goodness I'll pursue,
And after death, in distant worlds,
　The glorious theme renew ...

Through all eternity to thee
　A joyful song I'll raise;
But oh! eternity's too short
　To utter all thy praise.

Joseph Addison
1672–1719

In Praise of God

Ay me, dear Lord, that ever I might hope,
For all the pains and woes that I endure,
To come at length unto the wishèd scope
Of my desire; or might my self assure,
That happy port for ever to recure*.
Then would I think these pains no pains at all,
And all my woes to be but penance small.

Then would I sing of thine immortal praise
An heavenly hymn, such as the angels sing,
And thy triumphant name then would I raise
'Bove all the gods, thee only honouring,
My guide, my God, my victor, and my king;
Till then, dread Lord, vouchsafe to take of me
This simple song, thus framed in praise of thee.

Edmund Spenser
1552–99

* *recure:* recover

Two Graces for Children

What God gives, and what we take,
'Tis a gift for Christ his sake:
Be the meal of beans and peas,
God be thanked for those, and these.
Have we flesh, or have we fish,
All are fragments from his dish.
He his church save, and the king,
And our peace here, like a spring,
Make it ever flourishing.

Here a little child I stand,
Heaving up my either hand;
Cold as paddocks* though they be
Here I lift them up to thee,
For a benison* to fall
On our meat, and on us all.

Robert Herrick
1591–1674

* *paddocks:* toads; *benison:* blessing

Dust

Sweet sovereign Lord of this so pined-for Spring,
How breathe the homage of but one poor heart
With such small compass of thy everything?

Ev'n though I knew this were my life's last hour,
It yet would lie, past hope, beyond my power
One instant of my gratitude to prove,
My praise, my love.

That 'Everything'!—when this, my human dust,
Whereto return I must,
Were scant to bring to bloom a single flower!

Walter de la Mare
1873–1956

Praise and Prayer

Praise is devotion fit for mighty minds,
    The differing world's agreeing sacrifice;
Where heaven divided faiths united finds:
    But Prayer in various discord upward flies.

For Prayer the ocean is where diversely
    Men steer their course, each to a several coast;
Where all our interests so discordant be
    That half beg winds by which the rest are lost.

By Penitence when we ourselves forsake,
    'Tis but in wise design on piteous Heaven;
In praise we nobly give what God may take,
    And are, without a beggar's blush, forgiven.

Sir William Davenant
1606–68

God Is Near

God Made Known

Lord, grant us calm, if calm can set forth thee;
  Or tempest, if a tempest set thee forth;
Wind from the east or west or south or north,
  Or congelation of a silent sea,
With stillness of each tremulous aspen tree.

Still let fruit fall, or hang upon the tree;
  Still let the east and west, the south and north,
Curb in their winds, or plough a thundering sea;
  Still let the earth abide to set thee forth,
Or vanish like a smoke to set forth thee.

Christina Rossetti
1830–94

The Uninvited Guest

He seems to come in like the leaves—
Blown in at the open window,
And always on a light and airy day.
Never in stormy weather.
And always, I've noticed,
At an inconvenient time—
Right in the middle of the washing.
He looks at me and shows me these holes in his hands.
And, well, I can see them in his feet.
'Not again,' I say.
'Please don't stand there bleeding
All over the kitchen floor.'

Sometimes he comes softly, sadly,
At night—close, by the side of my bed—
Sometimes I latch the door—

But he never goes away.

Thelma Laycock
20th century

Approaches

When thou turn'st away from ill,
Christ is this side of thy hill.

When thou turnest towards good,
Christ is walking in thy wood.

When thy heart says, 'Father, pardon!'
Then the Lord is in thy garden.

When stern Duty wakes to watch,
Then his hand is on the latch.

But when Hope thy song doth rouse,
Then the Lord is in the house.

When to love is all thy wit,
Christ doth at thy table sit.

When God's will is thy heart's pole,
Then is Christ thy very soul

George MacDonald
1824–1905

God in Everything

I am the wind which breathes upon the sea,
I am the wave of the ocean,
I am the murmur of the billows,
I am the ox of the seven combats,
I am the vulture upon the rocks,
I am a beam of the sun,
I am the fairest of plants,
I am a wild boar in valour,
I am a salmon in the water,
I am a lake in the plain,
I am a word of knowledge,
I am the point of the lance in battle,
I am the God who creates in the head the fire.
Who is it that throws light into the meeting on the mountain?
Who announces the ages of the moon?
Who teaches the place where couches the sun?

Anonymous.
Said to be by the legendary poet Amergin, when he first set foot in Ireland.

Wholeness

What if the foot, ordained the dust to tread,
Or hand, to toil, aspired to be the head?
What if the head, the eye, or ear repined
To serve mere engines to the ruling mind?
Just as absurd for any part to claim
To be another, in this general frame;
Just as absurd, to mourn the tasks or pains
The great Directing Mind of all ordains.
All are but parts of one stupendous whole,
Whose body Nature is, and God the soul;
That, changed through all, and yet in all the same;
Great is the earth, as in the ethereal frame;
Warms in the sun, refreshes in the breeze,
Glows in the stars, and blossoms in the trees;
Lives through all life, extends through all extent;
Spreads undivided, operates unspent!
Breathes in our soul, informs our mortal part,
As full, as perfect, in a hair as heart;
As full, as perfect in vile man that mourns,
As the rapt seraph that adores and burns;
To him no high, no low, no great, no small;
He fills, he bounds, connects, and equals all.

Alexander Pope
1688–1744

After St Augustine

Sunshine let it be or frost,
Storm or calm, as thou shalt choose;
Though thine every gift were lost,
Thee thyself we could not lose.

Mary Coleridge
1861–1907

God's Aid

God to enfold me,
    God to surround me,
God in my speaking,
    God in my thinking.

God in my sleeping,
    God in my waking,
God in my watching,
    God in my hoping.

God in my life,
    God in my lips,
God in my soul,
    God in my heart.

God in my sufficing,
    God in my slumber,
God in mine ever-living soul,
    God in mine eternity.

Traditional Celtic
Collected by Alexander Carmichael
19th century

News

The only news I know
Is bulletins all day
From immortality.

The only shows I see
Tomorrow and today,
Perchance eternity.

The only one I meet
Is God, the only street
Existence; this traversed,

If other news there be
Or admirabler show,
I'll tell it you.

Emily Dickinson
1830–84

The Divine Image

To Mercy, Pity, Peace, and Love
All pray in their distress;
And to these virtues of delight
Return their thankfulness.

For Mercy, Pity, Peace, and Love
Is God, our father dear,
And Mercy, Pity, Peace, and Love
Is Man, his child and care.

For Mercy has a human heart,
Pity a human face,
And Love, the human form divine,
And Peace, the human dress.

Then every man, of every clime,
That prays in his distress,
Prays to the human form divine,
Love, Mercy, Pity, Peace.

And all must love the human form,
In Heathen, Turk, or Jew;
Where Mercy, Love, and Pity dwell
There God is dwelling too.

William Blake 1757–1827

'Lo, I am with you always'

Wide fields of corn along the valleys spread;
The rain and dew mature the swelling vine;
I see the Lord in multiplying bread;
    I see him turning water into wine;
    I see him working all the works divine
He wrought when Salemward his steps were led;
    The selfsame miracles around him shine;
He feeds the famished; he revives the dead;
    He pours the flood of light on darkened eyes;
He chases tears, diseases, fiends away;
    His throne is raised upon these orient skies;
His footstool is the pave whereon we pray.
    Ah, tell me not of Christ in Paradise,
For he is all around us here today.

John Charles Earle late 19th—20th century?

The Guest

Yet if his Majesty, our sovereign lord,
Should of his own accord
Friendly himself invite,
And say 'I'll be your guest tomorrow night,'
How should we stir ourselves, call and command
All hands to work! 'Let no man idle stånd!

'Set me fine Spanish tables in the hall;
See they be fitted all;
Let there be room to eat
And order taken that there want no meat.
See every sconce and candlestick made bright,
That without tapers they may give a light.

'Look to the presence: are the carpets spread,
The dazie* o'er the head,
The cushions in the chairs,
And all the candles lighted on the stairs?
Perfume the chambers, and in any case
Let each man give attendance in his place!'

Thus, if a king were coming, would we do;
And 'twere good reason too;
For 'tis a duteous thing
To show all honour to an earthly king,
And after all our travail and our cost,
So he be pleased, to think no labour lost.

But at the coming of the King of Heaven
All's set at six and seven;
We wallow in our sin,
Christ cannot find a chamber in the inn.
We entertain him always like a stranger,
And, as at first, still lodge him in the manger.

Anonymous 17th century
* *dazie:* dais, canopy

'I am not worthy'

Thy God was making haste into thy roof,
Thy humble faith, and fear, keeps him aloof:
He'll be thy guest, because he may not be,
He'll come—into thy house? no, into thee.

Richard Crashaw 1613–49

Immortal Love

Immortal love for ever full,
  For ever flowing free,
For ever shared, for ever whole,
  A never-ebbing sea!

Our outward lips confess the name,
  All other names above;
Love only knoweth whence it came
  And comprehendeth love.

We may not climb the heavenly steeps
  To bring the Lord Christ down;
In vain we search the lowest deeps,
  For him no depths can drown;

But warm, sweet, tender, even yet
  A present help is he;
And faith still has its Olivet,
  And love its Galilee.

The healing of his seamless dress
  Is by our beds of pain;
We touch him in life's throng and press,
  And we are whole again.

Through him the first fond prayers are said,
  Our lips of childhood frame;
The last low whispers of our dead
  Are burdened with his name.

Alone, O love ineffable,
  Thy saving name is given;
To turn aside from thee is hell,
  To walk with thee is heaven.

John Greenleaf Whittier
1807–92

God's Dwelling

What happy, secret fountain,
Fair shade or mountain,
Whose undiscovered virgin glory
Boasts it this day, though not in story
Was then thy dwelling? did some cloud
Fixed to a tent, descend and shroud
My distrest Lord? or did a star
Beckoned by thee, though high and far,
In sparkling smiles haste gladly down
To lodge light and increase her own?
My dear, dear God! I do not know
What lodged thee then, nor where, nor how;
But I am sure, thou dost now come
Oft to a narrow, homely room,
Where thou too hast but the least part
My God, I mean *my sinful heart.*

Henry Vaughan
1621–95

Pax

All that matters is to be at one with the living God
to be a creature in the house of the God of Life.

Like a cat asleep on a chair
at peace, in peace
and at one with the master of the house, with the mistress,
at home, at home in the house of the living,
sleeping on the hearth, and yawning before the fire.

Sleeping on the hearth of the living world,
yawning at home before the fire of life
feeling the presence of the living God
like a great reassurance
a deep calm in the heart
a presence
as of a master sitting at the board
in his own and greater being,
in the house of life.

D.H. Lawrence
1885–1930

God with Us

Fountain of sweets! eternal Dove!
Which leav'st thy glorious perch above,
And hovering down, vouchsafest thus
To make thy nest below with us.

Soft as thy softest feathers, may
We find thy love to us today;
And in the shelter of thy wing
Obtain thy leave and grace to sing.

Joseph Beaumont
1615–99

In Portugal, 1912

And will they cast the altars down,
Scatter the chalice, crush the bread?
In field, in village, and in town
 He hides an unregarded head.

Waits in the corn-lands far and near,
Bright in his sun, dark in his frost,
Sweet in the vine, ripe in the ear—
 Lonely unconsecrated Host.

In ambush at the merry board
The Victim lurks unsacrificed;
The mill conceals the harvest's Lord,
 The wine-press holds the unbidden Christ.

Alice Meynell
1847–1922

Heed not the Withered Gods

The mummied gods are set in stone
deep in the deserts terrible.
But one was wrapped in faith alone
and lay beneath a lighter spell.

The kingly gods in golden ways
lay down with sceptre and with sword,
prepared to sleep a million days.
But one awoke upon the third.

So I, his roused and fortunate,
heed not the withered gods who bless
with silence where their temples wait
long in the moonlight motionless.

But journeying in joy instead
from cross to cross, from pain to pain,
I clutch him in the broken bread,
I taste his wine within the rain.

James E. Warren Jr.
20th century

Most Blessed Vine

Most blessed Vine!
Whose juice so good
I feel as wine,
But thy fair branches felt as blood;
How wert thou pressed
To be my feast!
In what deep anguish
Didst thou languish,
What springs of sweat and blood did drown thee!
How in one path
Did the full wrath
Of thy great Father
Crowd and gather,
Doubling thy griefs, when none would own thee!

Henry Vaughan
1622–95

At Communion

Whether I kneel or stand or sit in prayer,
I am not caught in time nor held in space,
but thrust beyond this posture I am where
time and eternity come face to face;
infinity and space meet in this place
where crossbar and high upright hold the one
in agony and in all Love's embrace.
The power in helplessness that was begun
when all the brilliance of the flaming sun
contained itself in the small confines of a child
now comes to me in this strange action done
in mystery. Break me, break space, O wild
and lovely power. Break me: thus am I dead,
am resurrected now in wine and bread.

Madeleine L'Engle
20th century

Thou art God

Thou art the peace of all things calm
Thou art the place to hide from harm
Thou art the light that shines in dark
Thou art the heart's eternal spark
Thou art the door that's open wide
Thou art the guest who waits inside
Thou art the stranger at the door
Thou art the calling of the poor
Thou art my Lord and with me still
Thou art my love, keep me from ill
Thou art the light, the truth, the way
Thou art my Saviour this very day.

David Adam
20th century

From: Christ's Victory in Heaven

What hath man done that man shall not undo,
Since God to him is grown so near akin?
Did his foe slay him? He shall slay his foe.
Hath he lost all? He all again shall win.
Is sin his master? He shall master sin.
   Too hardy soul, with sin the field to try;
   The only way to conquer was to fly.
But thus long death hath lived, and now death's self shall die.

He is a path, if any be misled;
He is a robe, if any naked be;
If any chance to hunger, he is bread;
If any be a bondman, he is free;
If any be but weak, how strong is he!
   To dead men life he is, to sick men health;
   To blind men sight, and to the needy wealth,
A pleasure without loss, a treasure without stealth.

Giles Fletcher
1586–1623

God in me

God be in my head,
And in my understanding;
God be in mine eyes,
And in my looking;
God be in my mouth
And in my speaking;
God be in my heart,
And in my thinking;
God be at my end and at my departing.

Anonymous
16th century

Love and Trust

Jesus my Knight

Jesu, I now begin
To love thee day and night.
My soul from earth to wean
I shall do all my might.
'Twas all my love to win
Jesu became my knight.

Anonymous
Medieval

A Prayer to Jesus

Jesu, since thou me made and bought,
Thou be my love and all my thought,
And help that I may to thee be brought;
Withouten thee I may do nought.

Jesu, since thou must do thy will,
And nothing is that thee may let*;
With thy grace my heart fulfil,
My love and my liking in thee set.

Jesu, at thy will
I pray that I might be;
All my heart fulfil
With perfect love to thee.

That I have done ill,
Jesu, forgive thou me;
And suffer me never to spill*,
Jesu, for pity. Amen.

Richard Rolle
1290–1349

* *let:* forbid, stop; *spill:* perish

Name

A name written in sand
by a child's hand;
on a San Quentin wall
by an inmate's fingernail;
in blood stains
on doorposts;
in small-print footnotes
of dissertations

a name sprinkled
on little heads;
sung over bodies
in immersion tanks

A name breathed
in wind-touched silence
of lost paradise;
carried on wings
of one-day butterflies

A name on quivering lips
of combat soldier
alone in a foxhole;
clattering between teeth
of an ageing woman;
tremored by a
protestant voice

A name remains
when writing is no more
and voices die

A name given to
what has no name

Between desire
and silence
falls a name:

Jesus, the Christ.
Paradise regained.

Cor W. Barendrecht
20th century

A Song

Lord, when the sense of thy sweet grace
Sends up my soul to seek thy face,
Thy blessed eyes breed such desire,
I die in love's delicious fire.
   O love, I am thy sacrifice.
Be still triumphant, blessed eyes.
Still shine on me, fair suns! that I
Still may behold, though still I die.

Though still I die, I live again;
Still longing so to be still slain,
So gainful is such loss of breath.
I die even in desire of death.
   Still live in me this loving strife
Of living death and dying life.
For while thou sweetly slayest me
Dead to my self, I live in thee.

Richard Crashaw 1613–49

True Love

All other love is like the moon
That waxeth or waneth as flower in plain
As flower that blooms and fadeth soon,
As day that showereth and ends in rain.

All other love begins with bliss,
In weeping and woe makes its ending;
No love there is that's our whole bliss
But that which rests on heaven's king.

His love is fresh and ever green
And ever full without waning;
His love makes sweet and gives no pain,
His love is endless, enduring.

All other love I flee for thee;
Tell me, tell me where thou liest.
'In Marìe, mild and free
I shall be found, but more in Christ'.

Anonymous about 1350

At Home

Long did I toil and knew no earthly rest,
Far did I rove and found no certain home;
At last I sought them in his sheltering breast,
Who opes his arms and bids the weary come:
With him I found a home, a rest divine,
And I since then am his, and he is mine.

The good I have is from his store supplied,
The ill is only what he deems the best;
He for my friend I'm rich with nought beside,
And poor without him, though of all possessed;
Changes may come, I take or I resign,
Content while I am his, while he is mine.

Whate'er may change, in him no change is seen,
A glorious Sun that wanes not nor declines,
Above the storms and clouds he walks serene,
And on his people's inward darkness shines;
All may depart, I fret not, nor repine,
While I my Saviour's am, while he is mine.

While here, alas! I know but half his love,
But half discern him and but half adore;
But when I meet him in the realms above
I hope to love him better, praise him more,
And feel, and tell, amid the choir divine,
How fully I am his and he is mine.

J. Quarles 1624–65
H.F. Lyte 1793–1847

Love in Action

Truth proclaims it: love the wonder healer—
No blemish left, if that herb is used.
As God wished, the world was shaped in love.
Revealed to Moses, it was the best of things,
Heaven's image, priceless, the plant of peace.
But heaven could not contain the weight of love,
Till, here on earth, it fed to the full, took
Flesh and blood. After that, no leaf there was
On tree so light as love, mobile in air, plunging
As a needle point, no steel could stop it,
Nor castle wall. So, on earth as in heaven,
Love leads God's people, like a mayor,
Agent between the commons and the king. Love
Directs all, frames law, fixes fines
For the people's crimes. Know it for sure,
Love comes surging from the power of God,
Its source, its mountain spring, the human heart.

From Piers Plowman *by William Langland*
1330?–1400?
translated by Ronald Tamplin

A Child my Choice

Let folly praise that fancy love, I praise and love that Child
Whose heart no thought, whose tongue no word,
    whose hand no deed defiled.
I praise him most, I love him best, all praise and love is his;
While him I love, in him I live, and cannot live amiss.
Love's sweetest mark, laud's highest theme, man's most desirèd light,
To love him life, to leave him death, to live in him delight.
He mine by gift, I his by debt, thus each to other due,
First friend he was, best friend he is, all times will try him true.

Robert Southwell
1561–95

Hard God

Candles and rose light
through cathedral glass
poorly define him.
No gentle picker of pale
violets in grass.
No wandering shepherd
breathing wisdom and hymns
in shaded vale.
Let it pass.

I serve a hard God.

Liken him to a raging fire.

Remember him
forcing Pharaoh higher
to cliff's edge,
then to churning sea;
see him swallowing Korah
in an extemporaneous tomb;
recall his intended pyre
to be built
from his erring
but chosen sons,
quenched only by Moses' plea.

I serve a hard God.

He walks a stern path
through the earth.
His voice roars
in thunder,
giving birth
to terror;
oceans leap
in his wake
waves are hurled
mountains quake—
desolations are his footprints
in the world.

He is hard
and his way was stone,
tough and free
from gentility

like nails
driven through bone
and splintered to a tree.

He thunders and kills
from below, in, above;
he consumes all dross.

He is stern
like love
and hard
like a cross.

Nancy Thomas
20th century

Christ's Love

Love me brought,
And love me wrought
Man to be thy fere*
Love me fed,
And love me led
And love me lettet* here.

Love me slew
And love me drew,
And love me laid on bier.
Love is my peace;
For love I chese*
Man to buyen dear.

Ne dread thee nought,
I have thee sought,
Bothen day and night,
To haven thee
Well is me,
I have thee won in fight.

Anonymous
From The Commonplace Book of Friar John Grimeston, *copied 1372*

* *fere:* mate; *lettet:* allows; *chese:* chose

Discipline

Throw away thy rod,
Throw away thy wrath:
   O my God,
Take the gentle path.

For my heart's desire
Unto thine is bent:
   I aspire
To a full consent.

Not a word or look
I affect to own,
   But by book,
And thy book alone.

Though I fail, I weep;
Though I halt in pace,
   Yet I creep
To the throne of grace.

Then let wrath remove;
Love will do the deed;
   For with love
Stony hearts will bleed.

Love is swift of foot,
Love's a man of war,
   And can shoot,
And can hit from far.

Who can 'scape his bow?
That which wrought on thee,
   Brought thee low,
Needs must work on me.

Throw away thy rod:
Though man frailties hath,
   Thou art God:
Throw away thy wrath.

George Herbert
1593–1633

'O Lord, Seek Us'

O Lord, seek us, O Lord, find us
   In thy patient care;
By thy love before, behind us,
   Round us everywhere:
Lest the god of this world blind us,
   Lest he speak us fair,
Lest he forge a chain to bind us,
   Lest he bait a snare.
Turn not from us, call to mind us,
   Find. embrace us, bear;
Be thy love before, behind us,
   Round us, everywhere.

Christina Rossetti
1830–94

Christ, my Beloved

Christ, my Beloved, which still doth feed
   Among the flowers, having delight
   Among his faithful lilies,
Doth take great care for me indeed,
   And I again with all my might
   Will do what so his will is.

My Love in me and I in him,
   Conjoined by love, who still abide
   Among the faithful lilies
Till day do break, and truth do dim
   All shadows dark and cause them slide,
   According as his will is.

William Baldwin
about 1547

Love's Sacrifice

O thou who camest from above,
    The pure, celestial fire to impart,
Kindle a flame of sacred love
        On the mean altar of my heart,
There let it for thy glory burn
    With inextinguishable blaze.
And trembling to its Source return,
        In humble prayer and fervent praise.

Jesus, confirm my heart's desire
    To work, and speak, and think for thee,
Still let me guard the holy fire,
        And still stir up thy gift in me,
Ready for all thy perfect will
    My acts of faith and love repeat,
'Till death thy endless mercies seal,
        And make my sacrifice complete.

Charles Wesley
1707–88

From: Little Gidding

IV

The dove descending breaks the air
With flame of incandescent terror
Of which the tongues declare
The one discharge from sin and error.
The only hope, or else despair
    Lies in the choice of pyre or pyre—
    To be redeemed from fire by fire.

Who then devised the torment? Love.
Love is the unfamiliar Name
Behind the hands that wove
The intolerable shirt of flame
Which human power cannot remove.
    We only live, only suspire
    consumed by either fire or fire.

T.S. Eliot
1888–1965

•

Lovest Thou Me?

Hark, my soul! It is the Lord;
'Tis thy Saviour, hear his word;
Jesus speaks, and speaks to thee:
'Say, poor sinner, lov'st thou me?

'I delivered thee when bound,
And, when wounded, healed thy wound;
Sought thee wandering, set thee right,
Turned thy darkness into light.

'Can a woman's tender care
Cease towards the child she bare?
Yes, she may forgetful be,
Yet will I remember thee.

'Mine is an unchanging love,
Higher than the heights above;
Deeper than the depths beneath,
Free and faithful, strong as death.

'Thou shalt see my glory soon,
When the work of grace is done;
Partner of my throne shalt be:
Say, poor sinner, lov'st thou me?'

Lord, it is my chief complaint
That my love is weak and faint;
Yet I love thee and adore,
O for grace to love thee more!

William Cowper
1731–1800

The Divine Lover

Me, Lord? Canst thou mispend
One word, misplace one look on me?
　Call'st me thy Love, thy Friend?
Can this poor soul the object be
Of these love-glances, those life-kindling eyes?
What? I the centre of thy arms' embraces?
　Of all thy labour I the prize?
　Love never mocks, truth never lies.
Oh how I quake: hope fear, fear hope displaces:
I would, but cannot hope: such wondrous love amazes.

　See, I am black as night,
See, I am darkness: dark as hell.
　Lord, thou more fair than light;
Heaven's sun thy shadow: suns can dwell
With shades? 'twixt light and darkness what commerce?
True: thou art darkness, I thy Light: my ray
　Thy mists and hellish fogs shall pierce.
　With me, black soul, with me converse;
I make the foul December flowery May.
Turn thou thy night to me; I'll turn thy night to day.

　See, Lord, see I am dead:
Tombed in myself: myself my grave.
　A drudge: so born, so bred:
Myself even to myself a slave.
Thou freedom, life: can life and liberty
Love bondage, death? *Thy freedom I: I tied*
　To loose thy bonds: be bound to me:
　My yoke shall ease, my bonds shall free.
Dead soul, thy spring of life, my dying side:
There die with me to live: to live in thee I died.

Phineas Fletcher
1582–1650

A Hymn to Christ

AT THE AUTHOR'S LAST GOING INTO GERMANY, 1619

In what torn ship soever I embark,
That ship shall be my emblem of thy ark;
What sea soever swallow me, that flood
Shall be to me an emblem of thy blood.
Though thou with clouds of anger do disguise
Thy face: yet through that mask I know those eyes,
   Which, though they turn away sometimes,
   They never will despise.

I sacrifice this island unto thee,
And all whom I loved there, and who loved me;
When I have put our seas 'twixt them and me,
Put thou thy sea betwixt my sins and thee.
As the tree's sap doth seek the root below
In winter, in my winter now I go
   Where none but thee, the eternal root
   Of true love, I may know.

Nor thou nor thy religion dost control*
The amorousness of an harmonious soul,
But thou wouldst have that love thyself. As thou
Art jealous, Lord, so I am jealous now.
Thou lov'st not, till from loving more thou free
My soul. Whoever gives, takes liberty.
   O, if thou car'st not whom I love,
   Alas, thou lov'st not me.

Seal then this bill of my divorce to all
On whom those fainter beams of love did fall;
Marry those loves which in youth scattered be
On fame, wit, hopes (false mistresses), to thee.
Churches are best for prayer that have least light;
To see God only, I go out of sight,
   And to 'scape stormy days I choose
   An everlasting night.

John Donne
1572–1631

* *control*: censure, or check.

Splendidis Longum Valedico Nugis

Leave me, O love, which reachest but to dust;
   And thou, my mind, aspire to higher things;
Grow rich in that which never taketh rust;
   Whatever fades but fading pleasure brings.
Draw in thy beams, and humble all thy might
   To that sweet yoke where lasting freedoms be;
Which breaks the clouds and opens forth the light,
   That doth both shine and give us sight to see.
O take fast hold; let that light be thy guide
In this small course which birth draws out to death,
   And think how evil becometh him to slide,
Who seeketh heaven, and comes of heavenly breath.
   Then farewell, world; thy uttermost I see;
   Eternal Love, maintain thy life in me.

Sir Philip Sidney
1554–86

'And she washed his feet with her tears, and wiped them with the hair of her head.'

The proud Egyptian Queen, her Roman guest,
(To express her love in height of state, and pleasure)
With pearl dissolved in gold, did feast,
   Both food and treasure.

And now (dear Lord!) thy lover, on the fair
And silver tables of thy feet, behold!
Pearl in her tears, and in her hair,
   Offers thee gold.

Sir Edward Sherburne
1618–1702

During his Courtship

Christ, my Life, my Only Treasure,
    Thou alone
    Mould thine own,
After thy good pleasure.

Thou, who paidst my price, direct me!
    Thine I am
    Holy Lamb,
Save, and always save me.

Order thou my whole condition,
    Choose my state
    Fix my fate
By thy wise decision.

From all earthly expectation
    Set me free,
    Seize for thee
All my strength of passion.

Into absolute subjection
    Be it brought,
    Every thought,
Every fond affection.

That which most my soul requires
    For thy sake
    Hold it back
Purge my best desires.

Keep from me thy loveliest creature,
    Till I prove
    JESUS' love
Infinitely sweeter;

Till with purest passion panting
    Cries my heart
    'Where thou art
Nothing more is wanting.'

Blest with thine abiding Spirit,
    Fully blest
    Now I rest,
All in thee inherit.

Heaven is now with Jesus given;
Christ in me,
Thou shalt be
Mine eternal heaven.

Charles Wesley
1707–88

The Measure of Love

If love be strong, hot, mighty and fervènt,
There may be trouble, grief or sorrow fall,
But that the lover would be well content
All to endure and think it eke too small,
Though it were death, so he might therewithal
The joyful presence of that person get
On whom he hath his heart and love y-set.

Thus should of God the lover be content
Any distress or sorrow to endure,
Rather than to be from God absènt,
And glad to die, so that he may be sure
By his departing hence for to procure,
After this valley dark, the heavenly light,
And of his love the glorious blessed sight.

Not only a lover content is in his heart
But coveteth eke and longeth to sustain
Some labour, incommodity, or smart,
Loss, adversity, trouble, grief or pain:
And of his sorrow, joyful is and fain,
And happy thinketh himself that he may take
Some misadventure for his lover's sake.

Thus shouldest thou, that lovest God also.
In thine heart wish, covet, and be glad
For him to suffer trouble, pain and woe:
For whom if thou be never so woe bestead,
Yet thou ne shalt sustain (be not adread)
Half the dolour, grief and adversity
That he already suffered hath for thee.

Sir Thomas More
1478–1535

Love

Love bade me welcome; yet my soul drew back,
  Guilty of dust and sin.
But quick-eyed Love, observing me grow slack
  From my first entrance in,
Drew nearer to me, sweetly questioning
  If I lacked anything.

'A guest', I answered, 'worthy to be here.'
  Love said, 'You shall be he.'
'I, the unkind, ungrateful? Ah, my dear,
  I cannot look on thee.'
Love took my hand, and smiling did reply,
  'Who made the eyes but I?'

'Truth, Lord, but I have marred them; let my shame
  Go where it doth deserve.'
'And know you not', says Love, 'who bore the blame?'
  'My dear, then I will serve.'
'You must sit down', says Love, 'and taste my meat.'
  So I did sit and eat.

George Herbert 1593–1633

Lachrimae Amantis

What is there in my heart that you should sue
so fiercely for its love? What kind of care
brings you as though a stranger to my door
through the long night and in the icy dew

seeking the heart that will not harbour you,
that keeps itself religiously secure?
At this dark solstice filled with frost and fire
your passions's ancient wounds must bleed anew.

So many nights the angel of my house
has fed such urgent comfort through a dream,
whispered 'your lord is coming, he is close'

that I have drowsed half-faithful for a time
bathed in pure tones of promise and remorse:
'tomorrow I shall wake to welcome him.'

Geoffrey Hill 20th century

From: Preparatory Meditations Before my Approach to the Lord's Supper

What love is this of thine, that cannot be
  In thine infinity, O Lord, confined,
Unless it in thy very person see
  Infinity, and finity, conjoined?
  What! Hath thy Godhead, as not satisfied,
  Married our manhood, making it its bride?

Oh, matchless love! Filling Heaven to the brim!
  O'er-running it; all running o'er beside
This world! Nay, overflowing hell, wherein
  For thine elect there rose a mighty tide,
  That there our veins might through thy person bleed
  To quench those flames that else would on us feed!

Oh, that thy love might overflow my heart
  To fire the same with love! For love I would.
But oh, my straitened breast! My lifeless spark!
  My fireless flame! What, chilly, love, and cold?
  In measure small? In manner chilly? See!
  Lord, blow the coal. Thy love inflame in me.

Edward Taylor
1645?–1729

From: In Memoriam

Love is and was my Lord and King,
  And in his presence I attend
  To hear the tidings of my friend,
Which every hour his couriers bring.

Love is and was my King and Lord,
  And will be, though as yet I keep
  Within his court on earth, and sleep
Encompassed by his faithful guard,

And hear at times a sentinel
  Who moves about from place to place,
  And whispers to the world of space,
In the deep night, that all is well.

Alfred, Lord Tennyson
1809–92

Heart's Music

(FROM: CAMPION'S FIRST BOOK OF AIRS)

Tune thy music to thy heart
   Sing thy joy with thanks, and so thy sorrow.
   Though devotion needs not art
Sometimes of the poor the rich may borrow.

   Strive not yet for curious ways;
Concord pleaseth more the less 'tis strained.
   Zeal affects not outward praise,
Only strives to show a love unfeigned.

   Love can wondrous things effect,
Sweetest sacrifice all wrath appeasing.
   Love the Highest doth respect;
Love alone to him is ever pleasing.

Anonymous
about 1600?

A Prayer

Grant, I thee pray, such heat into mine heart
That to this love of thine may be equàl;
Grant me from Satan's service to astart,
With whom me rueth so long to have been thrall;
Grant me, good Lord and creator of all,
The flame to quench of all sinful desire
And in thy love set all mine heart afire.

That when the journey of this deadly life
My silly* ghost hath finishèd, and thence
Departen must without his fleshly wife,
Alone into his Lordès high presènce,
He may thee find, O well of indulgènce,
In thy lordship not as a lord, but rather
As a very tender, loving father.

Sir Thomas More
1478–1535

* silly: defenceless

THE WORLD WE LIVE IN

God's Grandeur

The world is charged with the grandeur of God.
　It will flame out, like shining from shook foil;
　It gathers to a greatness, like the ooze of oil
Crushed. Why do men then now not reck his rod?
Generations have trod, have trod, have trod;
　And all is seared with trade; bleared, smeared with toil;
　And wears man's smudge and shares man's smell: the soil
Is bare now, nor can foot feel, being shod.

And for all this, nature is never spent;
　There lives the dearest freshness deep down things;
And though the last lights off the black West went
　Oh, morning, at the brown brink eastward, springs—
Because the Holy Ghost over the bent
　World broods with warm breast and with ah! bright wings.

Gerard Manley Hopkins
1844–89

Nature and Landscape

Flower in the Crannied Wall

Flower in the crannied wall,
I pluck you out of the crannies;—
Hold you here, root and all, in my hand,
Little flower—but if I could understand
What you are, root and all, and all in all,
I should know what God and man is.

Alfred, Lord Tennyson
1809–92

Six O'Clock Feeling

You ever feel
dat 6 o'clock feeling
6 o'clock shadow falling
wrappin you up
meking you stop
and tink
bout all dese tings
God doin
6 o'clock bee calling
all dem tree
tekking strange, strange shape
and stan up
sharp! sharp! gainst dat sky
you know dem 6 o'clock colour
pink an orange an blue an purple an black
dat 6 o'clock feeling
mekkin you feel like touchin
mekkin you feel so small
you could cry
or fall down pun you knee
and thank God
you could still
see he 6 o'clock sky

Kamal Singh
20th century

Oil of Spikenard

What a spendthrift you are, sir,
a squanderseed wastrel!
Did they never teach you
the Puritan virtues?
Look at those puffball heads.
You toss your hair like a petulant schoolgirl, and there—
how untidy you are!—it's like dandruff.
Then there's sperm,
not to mention the sand and the stars and the orange pips.
It's embarrassing, all this extravagance.

And not five minutes ago you painted a skyscape
in a whole fruit salad of pastels,
a study in citrous shades.
So now what are you up to?
You've rubbed it out and started again with blue.
Stop a minute and give us viewing time,
you throwaway artist.
Even when invention funds
are unlimited, surely the waste...

Couldn't this oil of spikenard
have been sold and given to the poor?

Anne Ashworth
20th century

Ode

The spacious firmament on high
With all the blue ethereal sky,
And spangled heavens, a shining frame,
Their great Original proclaim:
The unwearied sun, from day to day,
Does his Creator's power display,
And publishes to every land
The work of an almighty hand.

Soon as the evening shades prevail,
The moon takes up the wondrous tale,
And nightly to the listening earth
Repeats the story of her birth:
Whilst all the stars that round her burn,
And all the planets in their turn,
Confirm the tidings as they roll,
And spread the truth from pole to pole.

What though, in solemn silence, all
Move round the dark, terrestrial ball?
What though nor real voice nor sound
Amid their radiant orbs be found?
In reason's ear they all rejoice,
And utter forth a glorious voice,
For ever singing, as they shine,
'The hand that made us is divine'.

Joseph Addison
1672–1719

Nature's Hymn to the Deity

All nature owns with one accord
The great and universal Lord;
The sun proclaims him through the day,
The moon when daylight drops away,
The very darkness smiles to wear
The stars that show us God is there,
On moonlight seas soft gleams the sky,
And, 'God is with us,' waves reply.

Winds breathe from God's abode, 'We come,'
Storms louder own God is their home,
And thunder yet with louder call,
Sounds, 'God is mightiest over all';
Till earth, right loath the proof to miss,
Echoes triumphantly, 'He is,'
And air and ocean makes reply,
'God reigns on earth, in air and sky.'

All nature owns with one accord
The great and universal Lord:
Insect and bird and tree and flower—
The witnesses of every hour—
Are pregnant with his prophecy
And 'God is with us', all reply.
The first link in the mighty plan
Is still—and all upbraideth man.

John Clare
1793–1864

The Very Thought

I love the very thought of Heaven:
Where angels sing
In perfect, perpetual Choir Practice.
Where Father, Son, and Spirit
Rule, unchallenged,
And are honoured in full measure.
I love the very thought of Heaven:
But I was not made
To live there.

I was not made
To walk on clouds,
And bask eternally
In immaterial splendour.
I was made for this green planet:
This tight ball
Of infinite beauty,
Alive with unending possibilities
Of his creative power.
I was made for the sunshine
That blazes through the veins of leaves,
And glints in the tiny, perfect back
Of a ladybird, crossing my arm.
I was made to be human
In this, most human place.
I was made for Earth:
The Earth is my home.
That's why I'm glad
that God, more than anyone,
Is a Friend of the Earth.
That he was prepared
To die for its restoration,
And that's why I'm glad
That the magnificent, jewelled foundations
Of the mighty Pearly Gates,
Will be anchored
Deeply and for ever
In the soil of Earth.

Gerard Kelly
20th century

West Head Secrets

(WEST HEAD, NORTH OF SYDNEY, IS THE SITE OF MANY HUNDREDS OF ABORIGINAL CARVINGS)

Men with brown skins found this place
 of rest, of promontory peacefulness;
 and here took time to sit and think,
 to formulate the insights of the years,
 the essence of the Dream Time, of the stories told around
 a million twinkling camp-fires, twinkling like the ice-fire stars
 that in these South-Land myths form both a mystery and a key,
 a guide for those who've come to know their signs.
These things the brown philosophers recalled
 and, as appropriate to a timeless theme,
 they carved their knowings in this rocky shrine
 of this the oldest continent, still yet unknown.

Today this ancient shrine again has seen
 solemn engravings, never to be smoothed;
 for from today, both of our hearts shall show
 the impressions deeply grooved of our bared souls.

The cultured superficiality
 of white man, sees the brown man's finest art
 as riddles, or an aimless hunter's play:
though no one else can share or understand
 in full these things we know, their truth
 is etched in pain upon our throbbing hearts.

Humphrey Babbage
20th century

Nature

The sky is low, the clouds are mean,
A travelling flake of snow
Across a barn or through a rut
Debates if it will go.

A narrow wind complains all day
How someone treated him;
Nature, like us, is sometimes caught
Without her diadem.

Emily Dickinson
1830–86

A Chant out of Doors

God of grave nights,
God of brave mornings,
God of silent noon,
Hear my salutation!
   For where the rapids rage white and scornful
   I have passed safely, filled with wonder;
   Where the sweet pools dream under willows
   I have been swimming, filled with joy.

God of round hills,
God of green valleys,
God of clear springs,
Hear my salutation!
   For where the moose feeds I have eaten berries,
   Where the moose drinks I have drunk deep;
   And under clear skies I have known love.

God of great trees,
God of wild grasses,
God of little flowers,
Hear my salutation!
   For where the deer crops and the beaver plunges
   Near the river I have pitched my tent;
   Where the pines cast aromatic needles
   On the still flowers I have known peace.

God of grave nights,
God of brave mornings,
God of silent noon,
Hear my salutation.

Marguerite Wilkinson
1883–1928

A Pastoral Hymn

Happy choristers of air
Who by your nimble flight draw near
   His throne, whose wondrous story
   And unconfinèd glory
Your notes still carol, whom your sound
And whom your plumy pipes rebound.

Yet do the lazy snails no less
The greatness of our Lord confess,
   And those whom weight hath chained
   And to the earth restrained,
Their ruder voices do as well,
Yea and the speechless fishes tell.

Great Lord, from whom each tree receives
Then pays again as rent, his leaves;
   Thou dost in purple set
   The rose and violet,
And giv'st the sickly lily white,
Yet in them all, thy name doth write.

John Hall
1627–56

Vegetation

O never harm the dreaming world,
the world of green, the world of leaves,
but let its million palms unfold
the adoration of the trees.

It is a love in darkness wrought
obedient to the unseen sun,
longer than memory, a thought
deeper than the graves of time.

The turning spindles of the cells
weave a slow forest over space,
the dance of love, creation,
out of time moves not a leaf,
and out of summer, not a shade.

Kathleen Raine
20th century

Nature's Melody

Hark, my soul, how everything
Strives to serve our bounteous King;
Each a double tribute pays;
Sings its part, and then obeys.

Nature's sweet and chiefest quire
Him with cheerful notes admire;
Chanting every day their lauds,
While the grove their song applauds.

Though their voices lower be,
Streams have too their melody;
Night and day they warbling run,
Never pause, but still sing on.

All the flowers that gild the spring
Hither their still music bring;
If Heaven bless them, thankful they
Smell more sweet, and look more gay.

Only we can scarce afford
This short office to our Lord;
We,—on whom his bounty flows,
All things gives, and nothing owes.

Wake, for shame, my sluggish heart,
Wake, and gladly sing thy part:
Learn of birds, and springs, and flowers,
How to use thy noble powers.

Call whole nature to thy aid,
Since 'twas he whole nature made;
Join in one eternal song,
Who to one God all belong.

Live for ever, glorious Lord,
Live, by all thy works adored;
One in three, and three in one,
Thrice we bow to thee alone.

John Austin
1613–69

The Storm

Rods of rain piledrive mercilessly into the tarmac
and bounce back
to the billowing, black clouds above;
the drains spew back the gurgling torrent's flow,
sweeping away bedraggled, drowning rats below.

Rrrrrumble … CRACK! The heavens tear themselves asunder;
buffeted pilots helplessly curse the thunder.
Lightning sizzles, the air's alight.
The moped driver anxiously looks for cover;
frightened children run to their frightened mother.

In agony radios hiss and spit;
a splintering tree screams as it is hit;
rain trickles from my squelching boots;
pea-pullers scatter to escape the carnage,
as God puts proud Man back into the Dark Age.

The digger's arm stretches imploringly towards the sky
but the arm of the cloud passes remorselessly by,
gradually disappearing over the hill;
the abandoned digger ruefully dips, weak and forlorn,
and thankful birds emerge to greet the second dawn.

Trevor Hoggard
20th century

Worry Wind

I hate gales. They remind me of everything
I haven't done: roof tiles not fixed; painting
Left; fence posts unsecured. I am found out.
I turn in the dark and think of all
Responsibilities. Have I taught
My sons enough, as they grow tall?
Have they the breath of faith? I cannot know.
A squall of sycamore keys rakes the window.
My own life rattles past.

Peter Walton
20th century

Bring me the Sunset

Bring me the sunset in a cup,
Reckon the morning's flagons up
And say how many dew,
Tell me how far the morning leaps,
Tell me what time the weaver sleeps
Who spun the breadths of blue.

Write how many notes there be
In the new robin's ecstasy
Among astonished boughs,
How many trips the tortoise makes,
How many cups the bee partakes,
The debauchee of dews.

Also, who laid the rainbow's piers,
Also, who leads the docile spheres
By withes of supple blue?
Whose fingers string the stalactite
Who counts the wampum* of the night
To see that none is due?
Who built this little alban house
And shut the windows down so close
My spirit cannot see?
Who'll let me out some gala day
With implements to fly away,
Passing pomposity?

Emily Dickinson
1830-1886

* wampum: string of beads used as memory aid,
and shell beads used as currency by native Americans.

Immanence

I come in the little things
Saith the Lord:
Not borne on morning wings
Of majesty, but I have set my feet
Amidst the delicate and bladed wheat
That springs triumphant in the furrowed sod.
There so I dwell, in weakness and in power;
Not broken or divided, saith our God!
In your strait garden plot I come to flower:
About your porch my vine
Meek, fruitful, doth entwine;
Waits, at the threshold, Love's appointed hour...

Evelyn Underhill   1875–1941

From: The Task

One spirit—his
Who wore the plaited thorns with bleeding brows—
Rules universal nature. Not a flower
But shows some touch, in freckle, streak or stain
Of his unrivalled pencil. He inspires
Their balmy odours, and imparts their hues,
And bathes their eyes with nectar, and includes,
In grains as countless as the sea-side sands,
The forms with which he sprinkles all the earth.
Happy who walks with him! whom what he finds
Of flavour or of scent in fruit or flower,
Or what he views of beautiful or grand
In nature, from the broad majestic oak
To the green blade that twinkles in the sun,
Prompts with remembrance of a present God!
His presence, who made all so fair, perceived,
Makes all still fairer. As with him no scene
Is dreary, so with him all seasons please.
Though winter had been none, had man been true,
And earth be punished for its tenant's sake,
Yet not in vengeance; as this smiling sky,
So soon succeeding such an angry night,
And these dissolving snows, and this clear stream
Recovering fast its liquid music, prove.

William Cowper   1731–1800

Christ in Creation

I see his blood upon the rose
And in the stars the glory of his eyes,
His body gleams amid eternal snows,
His tears fall from the skies.

I see his face in every flower;
The thunder and the singing of the birds
Are but his voice—and carven by his power
Rocks are his written words.

All pathways by his feet are worn,
His strong heart stirs the ever-beating sea,
His crown of thorns is twined with every thorn,
His cross is every tree.

Joseph Mary Plunkett
1887–1916

The Community

First chestnut tree, the candle master
Lights the dawn's church, birch serves the altar,
Oak in old age guides novice summer,
Elm bows to still the rooks' dark clamour,
Sycamore spreads the lessons' leaves,
Pines' song shapes the praying eaves
In needles sharp as finger tips;
Beech scurries, rustling, through the copse
And by the stream the willows tell
Litany of each circling shallow.

Gifts take a summer's life to form,
Brought to the apse with autumn's hymn,
Angel from sycamore and blood
Where holly stoops, the cornfield's bread
Where copse gives way to the wide acre,
Pasture to furrow and stooped shadow;
Pale song as spruce the crucifer
Snuffs sun and leaves the evening door
For mustard seed, the cellarer
To all the wild birds of the air.

Martyn Halsall
20th century

A Garden

(WRITTEN AFTER THE CIVIL WARS)

See how the flowers, as at parade,
Under their colours stand displayed:
Each regiment in order grows,
That of the tulip, pink, and rose.
But when the vigilant patrol
Of stars walks round about the pole,
Their leaves, that to the stalks are curled,
Seem to their staves the ensigns furled.
Then in some flower's beloved hut
Each bee, as sentinel, is shut,
And sleeps so too; but if once stirred,
She runs you through, nor asks the word.
    O thou, that dear and happy isle,
The garden of the world erewhile,
Thou paradise of the four seas
Which heaven planted us to please,
But, to exclude the world, did guard
With watery,if not flaming, sword;
What luckless apple did we taste
To make us mortal and thee waste!
Unhappy! shall we never more
That sweet militia restore,
When gardens only had their towers,
And all the garrisons were flowers;
When roses only arms might bear,
And men did rosy garlands wear?

Andrew Marvell
1621–78

Home Pictures in May

The sunshine bathes in clouds of many hues
And morning's feet are gemmed with early dews;
Warm daffodils about the garden beds
Peep through their pale slim leaves their golden heads,
Sweet earthly suns of spring; the gosling broods,
In coats of sunny green, about the road
Waddle in ecstasy; and in rich moods
The old hen leads her flickering chicks abroad,
Oft scuttling 'neath her wings to see the kite
Hang wavering o'er them in the spring's blue light.
The sparrows round their new nests chirp with glee
And sweet the robin spring's young luxury shares,
Tootling its song in feathery gooseberry tree
While watching worms the gardener's spade unbares.

John Clare *1793–1864*

Of an Orchard

Good is an orchard, the saint saith
To meditate on life and death,
With a cool well, a hive of bees,
A hermit's grot below the trees.

Good is an orchard: very good,
Though one should wear no monkish hood;
Right good when spring awakes her flute,
And good in yellowing time of fruit:

Very good in the grass to lie
And see the network 'gainst the sky,
A living lace of blue and green
And boughs that let the gold between.

The bees are types of souls that dwell
With honey in a quiet cell;
The ripe fruit figures goldenly
The soul's perfection in God's eye.

Prayer and praise in a country home
Honey and fruit: a man might come
Fed on such meats to walk abroad
And in his orchard talk with God.

Katharine Tynan Hinkson *1861–1931*

Under a Wiltshire Apple Tree

Some folks can afford,
So I've heard say,
Set up a sort of cross
Right in the garden way
To mind 'em of the Lord.

But I, when I do see
Thik apple tree
An' stoopin' limb
All spread wi' moss,
I think of him
And how he talks wi' me.

I think of God
And how he trod
That garden long ago;
He walked, I reckon, to and fro
And then sat down
Upon the groun'
Or some low limb
What suited him
Such as you see
On many a tree,
And on thik very one
Where I at set o' sun
Do sit and talk wi' he.

And, mornings too, I rise and come
An' sit down where the branch be low;
A bird do sing, a bee do hum,
The flowers in the border blow,
And all my heart's so glad and clear
As pools when mists do disappear:
As pools a-laughing in the light
When mornin' air is swep' and bright,
As pools what got all Heaven in sight
So's my heart cheer
When he be near.

He never pushed the garden door,
He left no footmark on the floor;
I never heard 'un stir nor tread
And yet his hand do bless my head,
And when 'tis time for work to start
I takes him with me in my heart.

And when I die, pray God I see
At very last thik apple tree
An' stoopin' limb,
And think of him
And all he been to me.

Anna Bunstan
late 19th—20th century?

Pied Beauty

Glory be to God for dappled things—
For skies of couple-colour as a brinded cow;
For rose-moles all in stipple upon trout that swim;
Fresh firecoal chestnut-falls; finches' wings;
Landscapes plotted and pieced—fold, fallow and plough;
And all trades, their gear and tackle and trim.

All things counter, original, spare, strange;
Whatever is fickle, freckled (who knows how?)
With swift, slow; sweet, sour; adazzle, dim;
He fathers-forth whose beauty is past change:
        Praise him.

Gerard Manley Hopkins
1844–89

Water and Seascape

The Life-tide

Each wave that breaks upon the strand,
How swift soe'er to spurn the sand
   And seek again the sea,
Christ-like, within its lifted hand
Must bear the stigma of the land
   For all eternity.

John Bannister Tabb
1845–1909

From: The Seafarer

On earth there is no man so self-assured,
so generous with his gifts or so bold in his youth,
so daring in his deeds or with such a gracious lord,
that he harbours no fears about his seafaring
as to what the Lord will ordain for him.

Wherefore my heart leaps within me,
my mind roams with the waves
over the whale's domain, it wanders far and wide
across the face of the earth, returns again to me
eager and unsatisfied; the solitary bird screams,
irresistible, urges the heart to the whale's way
over the stretch of the seas.

    So it is that the joys
of the Lord inspire me more than this dead life,
ephemeral on earth. I have no faith
that the splendours of this earth will survive for ever...

Great is the fear of God; through him the world turns.
He established the mighty plains, the face
of the earth and the sky above. Foolish is he
who fears not his Lord: death catches him unprepared.
Blessed is the humble man: mercy comes to him from heaven.
God gave man a soul because he trusts in his strength.

Anonymous
about 850

Belize Suite

1 SEA WALL

Only a gentle swish
Where waves would touch the land
no wind no turbulence
along this wall arranged by man
dividing land from sea

No cruise-ships light this harbour end to end
only that cluster
where the army lights
ride there at anchor...
cool darkness and deluding calm

houses sit silent near the water's edge
their calm precariousness like our peace
hoisted on stilts
like mokojumbies in the carnival
listening the ocean's gentle murmur
hearing its angry wail
what seems like decades now
when death rode loud and furious
on the hissing waves

From storm and earthquake Lord
deliver us
and us
and us

Velma Pollard
20th century

The Waterfall

With what deep murmurs through time's silent stealth
Doth thy transparent, cool, and watery wealth
    Here flowing fall,
    And chide and call,
As if his liquid loose retinue stayed
Lingering, and were of this steep place afraid,
    The common pass
    Where, clear as glass,
    All must descend
    Not to an end;
But quickened by this deep and rocky grave,
Rise to a longer course more bright and brave.

    Dear Stream, dear bank, where often I
    Have sat, and pleased my pensive eye,
    Why, since each drop of thy quick store
    Runs thither, whence it flowed before,
    Should poor souls fear a shade or night,
    Who came, sure, from a sea of light?
    Or since those drops are all sent back
    So sure to thee, that none doth lack,
    Why should frail flesh doubt any more
    That what God takes, he'll not restore?
    O useful element and clear!
    My sacred wash and cleanser here,
    My first consigner unto those
    Fountains of life, where the Lamb goes,
    What sublime truths, and wholesome themes
    Lodge in thy mystical, deep streams!
    Such as dull man can never find,
    Unless that Spirit lead his mind,
    Which first upon thy face did move,
    And hatched all with his quickening love.
    As this loud brook's incessant fall
    In streaming rings restagnates all,
    Which reach by course the bank, and then
    Are no more seen, just so pass men.
    O my invisible estate,
    My glorious liberty, still late!
    Thou art the channel my soul seeks,
    Not this with cataracts and creeks.

Henry Vaughan
1622–95

Kwikila, Waterless Place

(KWIKILA IS IN PAPUA NEW GUINEA)

Two still-green trees rub together
   as if for reassurance
   that the wind that grates
   will carry too;
   carry clouds, heavy clouds,
   full clouds and black;
   to fall and to dampen,
   to drench and to soak—
   deep into the pores of the earth.

The stream-beds are paths
   for the lizard and snake;
   the reed-beds are brown
   and blackened—(Last week
   another fire went along there)
   and the boulders which rolled along
   in the floods are quite still;
   still with the stillness of tragedy brooding,
   still with the stillness of death.

Men curse the wind
   for its transitory promises—
   dark clouds build up
   (and our hopes with them too)
   and are then blown away;
   or, worse still, come over,
   intact and enticing,
   to cynically spatter
   verandahs and faces
   before passing on ...

A desk—and textbooks strewn;
   lately my eyes have been wandering
   more and more. But my window
   still frames the same picture
   of a bright, empty sky
   (called *gorgeous* in Sydney
   where water comes piped),
   and grass, grey with despair—
Dust hangs in a curl
   (thrown up by a wheel);
   it seems, almost, to have been hanging there
   for months now.

O Lord, I murmur, and murmur again,
   Please send us rain.

   Humphrey Babbage 20th century

Eternity Seen from North Avenue
November 3

from the top of the
wet road
narrowed by
half a mile
& a steep slope
I see the grey
splay up & over
so that
for an afternoon
all space
is paved with
the same pale rain

there is
no difference
the road has
no end
the horizon
has been abolished
& what
is to stop me
from driving
up the sky?

Luci Shaw   *20th century*

The Shell

Upon the sandy shore an empty shell,
  Beyond the shell infinity of sea;
O Saviour, I am like that empty shell,
  Thou art the Sea to me.

A sweeping wave rides up the shore, and lo,
  Each dim recess the coiled shell within
Is searched, is filled, is filled to overflow
  By water crystalline.

Not to the shell is any glory then:
  All glory give we to the glorious sea.
And not to me is any glory when
  Thou overflowest me.

Sweep over me thy shell, as low I lie,
  I yield me to the purpose of thy will,
Sweep up, O conquering waves, and purify
  And with thy fulness fill.

Amy Carmichael
1867–1951

The Singularity of Shells

A shell—how small an empty space,
a folding out of pink and white,
a letting in of spiral light.
How random? and how commonplace?
(A million shells along the beach
are just as fine and full of grace
as this one here within your reach.)

But lift it, hold it to your ear
and listen. Surely you can hear
the swish and sigh of all the grey
and gleaming waters, and the play
of wind with rain and sun, encased
in one small jewel box and placed,
by God and oceans, in your way.

Luci Shaw
20th century

Town and City

Over the Great City

Over the great city,
Where the wind rustles through the parks and gardens,
In the air, the high clouds brooding,
In the lines of street perspective, the lamps, the traffic,
The pavements and the innumerable feet upon them,
I Am: make no mistake—do not be deluded.

Think not because I do not appear at the first glance
    —because the centuries have gone by and
    there is no assured tidings of me—that therefore I am not
    there.
Think not because all goes its own way that
    therefore I do not go my own way through all.
The fixed bent of hurrying faces in the street—each
    turned towards its own light, seeing no other
    —yet I am the Light towards which they
    all look.
The toil of so many hands to such multifarious ends,
    yet my hand knows the touch and twining of them
    all.

All come to me at last.
There is no love like mine;
For all other love takes one and not another;
And other love is pain, but this is joy eternal.

                    Edward Carpenter
                    1844–1929

Indifference

When Jesus came to Golgotha they hanged him on a tree,
They drave great nails through hands and feet, and made a Calvary;
They crowned him with a crown of thorns, red were his wounds and deep,
For those were crude and cruel days, the human flesh was cheap.

When Jesus came to Birmingham, they simply passed him by,
They never hurt a hair of him, they only let him die;
For men had grown more tender, and they would not give him pain,
They only passed down the street, and left him in the rain.

Still Jesus cried, 'Forgive them, for they know not what they do,'
And still it rained the winter rain that drenched him through and through;
The crowds went home and left the streets without a soul to see,
And Jesus crouched against a wall and cried for Calvary.

G.A. Studdert Kennedy 1883–1929

All Fools' Eve

From rooming-house to rooming-house
The toasted evening spells
City to hayrick, warming and bewildering
A million motes. From gilded tiers,
Balconies, and sombre rows,
Women see gopher-hawks, and rolling flaxen hills;
Smell a lost childhood's homely supper.
Men lean with folded newspapers,
Touched by a mushroom and root-cellar
Coolness. The wind flows,
Ruffles, unquickens. Crumbling ash
Leaves the west chill. The Sticks-&-Stones, this City,
Lies funeral bare.
Over its gaping arches stares
That haunt, the mirror mineral.
In cribs, or propped at plastic tablecloths,
Children are roundeyed, caught by a cold magic,
Fading of glory. In their dim
Cement-floored garden the zoo monkeys shiver.
Doors slam. Lights snap, restore
The night's right prose.
Gradually
All but the lovers' ghostly windows close.

Margaret Avison 20th century

Uxbridge Road

The Western Road goes streaming out to seek the cleanly wild,
It pours the city's dim desires towards the undefiled,
It sweeps betwixt the huddled homes about its eddies grown
To smear the little space between the city and the sown:
The torments of that seething tide who is there that can see?
There's one who walked with starry feet the western road by me!

He is the Drover of the soul; he leads the flock of men
All wistful on that weary track, and brings them back again.
The dreaming few, the slaving crew, the motley caste of life—
The wastrel and artificer, the harlot and the wife—
They may not rest, for ever pressed by one they cannot see:
The one who walked with starry feet the western road by me.

He drives them east, he drives them west, between the dark and light;
He pastures them in city pens, he leads them home at night.
The towery trams, the threaded trains, like shuttles to and fro
To weave the web of working days in ceaseless travel go.
How harsh the woof, how long the weft! who shall the fabric see?
The one who walked with starry feet the western road by me!

Throughout the living joyful year at lifeless tasks to strive,
And scarcely at the end to save gentility alive;
The villa plot to sow and reap, to act the villa lie,
Beset by villa fears to live, midst villa dreams to die;
Ah, who can know the dreary woe? and who the splendour see?
The one who walked with starry feet the western road by me.

Behold! he lent me as we went the vision of the seer;
Behold! I saw the life of men, the life of God shine clear.
I saw the hidden Spirit's thrust; I saw the race fulfil
The spiral of its steep ascent, predestined of the Will.
Yet not unled, but shepherded by one they may not see—
The one who walked with starry feet the western road by me!

Evelyn Underhill
1875–1941

Tower Block

The Council's plywood barricades
block up the frames where wired glass
was systematically smashed out.

Wet stains that pattern the bare
concrete walls, are covered up
by over-lapping spray-gun scrawls,

proclaiming loyalties and hates,
initials, names, the brute
ideograms of failing speech.

Inside the battered lifts a stench
of disinfectant still insinuates
those smells its wash has drowned.

Press on the broken button,
or climb up the glass-strewn stairs,
along the cloned, deserted landings

bolted doors conceal the warmth of homes
the pride of fitted carpets,
comforts of a frayed armchair, and

families as alive to laughter and pain
as those behind herbaceous borders,
safe along the neat suburban lanes.

Tony Lucas
20th century

An Absolutely Ordinary Rainbow

The word goes round Repins.
the murmur goes round Lorenzinis.
at Tattersalls, men look up from sheets of numbers.
the Stock Exchange scribblers forget the chalk in their hands
and men with bread in their pockets leave the Greek Club:
There's a fellow crying in Martin Place. They can't stop him.

The traffic in George Street is banked up for half a mile
and drained of motion. The crowds are edgy with talk
and more crowds come hurrying. Many run in the back streets
which minutes ago were busy main streets, pointing:
There's a fellow weeping down there. No one can stop him.

The man we surround, the man no one approaches
simply weeps, and does not cover it, weeps
not like a child, not like the wind, like a man
and does not declaim it, nor beat his breast, nor
even sob very loudly—yet the dignity of his weeping
holds us back from his space, the hollow he makes about him
in the midday light, in his pentagram of sorrow,
and uniforms back in the crowd who tried to seize him
stare out at him, and feel, with amazement, their minds
longing for tears as children for a rainbow.

Some will say, in the years to come, a halo
or force stood around him. There is no such thing.
Some will say they were shocked and would have stopped him
but they will not have been there. The fiercest manhood,
the toughest reserve the slickest wit amongst us

trembles with silence, and burns with unexpected
judgements of peace. Some in the concourse scream
who thought themselves happy. Only the smallest children
and such as look out of Paradise come near him
and sit at his feet, with dogs and dusty pigeons.

Ridiculous, says a man near me, and stops
his mouth with his hands, as if it uttered vomit—
and I see a woman, shining, stretch her hand
and shake as she receives the gift of weeping,
as many as follow her also receive it

and many weep for sheer acceptance, and more
refuse to weep for fear of all acceptance,
but the weeping man, like the earth, requires nothing,
the man who weeps ignores us, and cries out
of his writhen face and ordinary body

not words, but grief, not messages, but sorrow
hard as the earth, sheer, present as the sea—
and when he stops, he simply walks between us
mopping his face with the dignity of one
man who has wept, and now has finished weeping.

Evading believers, he hurries off down Pitt Street.

Les A. Murray
20th century

Yours, Not Ours

You are as inevitable as morning
and you are there
long before the first Woodbine croak is heard
at the bleary eyed bus stops of the city.
You watch and wonder
as the sound of waking
mumbles its chorus across roof tops
You see and hear lovers readjust their dreams
in the not quite right of day
You listen to the out of tune clatter of newspapers
drowning out the concert pitch spot-on of the trees
This is a tired morning, as street sweepers clock on
We have stolen it from you
and fashioned it in our own image
You have not yet charged us with theft
and when you do
our defence will be inadequate
the dog ends in the gutter have no apologies written on them
there are no acknowledgements in the personal columns
the milk bottles hold no thank you notes
and the morning yawns steadily onwards
the morning that is not ours
but always yours.

Stewart Henderson
20th century

All God's Creatures

The Bells of Heaven

'Twould ring the bells of Heaven
The wildest peal for years,
If Parson lost his senses
And people came to theirs,
And he and they together
Knelt down with angry prayers
For tamed and shabby tigers,
And dancing dogs and bears,
And wretched, blind pit ponies,
And little hunted hares.

Ralph Hodgson
1872–1962

From: To a Fish of the Brook

Enjoy thy stream, O harmless fish;
And when an angler for his dish,
   Through gluttony's vile sin,
Attempts, a wretch, to pull thee *out*
God give thee strength, O gentle trout,
   To pull the rascal *in!*

John Wolcot (Peter Pindar)
1738–1839

A Dream of Nature

Birds I saw in bushes made nests.
Even a simple one no man
Could ever make. And when and where
I wondered did the magpie learn
To weave sticks one with another
To secure her nest? Carpenters
Couldn't do anything as good,
No designer make a blueprint
For it either. It astonished
Me even more that many birds
Hid their eggs, carefully concealed,
So that only the parent birds
Themselves could find them. Some I saw
Did their breeding high in the trees
And hatched their young way up above
The ground. Diving birds plumped deep down
In swamps, moorland ponds and reedbeds,
Wherever there was water. 'Dear
God,' I cried, 'What school do all these
Wild things go to, to get such sense?'
And then the peacock; I saw how
He mated, how roughly the bird
Went about it. I marvelled at
His splendour along with his crude
Screaming voice. I looked at the sea
And on further to the high stars.
The whole world was full of wonders
Too many to put down now, flowers
In the fields, their dazzling colours,
So many different shades, sprung
From the same earth and grassy fields,
Some bitter to the taste, some sweet.
It seemed all one great miracle
Ranged too wide for me to record.
But what struck me and set me back
Was that reason seemed to govern
All creatures and how they acted
Except for man, except mankind.

From Piers Plowman *by William Langland*
1330?–1400?
translated by Ronald Tamplin

Jubilate Agno

Rejoice in God, O ye tongues; give glory to the Lord, and the Lamb.
Nations and languages, and every creature, in which is the breath of life.
Let man and beast appear before him, and magnify his name together.

Let Noah and his company approach the throne of grace,
    and do homage to the ark of their salvation.
Let Abraham present a ram, and worship the God of his redemption.
Let Isaac, the bridegroom, kneel with his camels,
    and bless the hope of his pilgrimage.
Let Jacob, and his speckled drove adore the good Shepherd of Israel.
Let Esau offer a scape goat for his seed,
    and rejoice in the blessing of God his father.
Let Nimrod, the mighty hunter, bind a leopard to the altar,
    and consecrate his spear to the Lord.
Let Ishmael dedicate a tyger, and give praise for the liberty,
    in which the Lord has let him at large.
Let Balaam appear with an ass, and bless the Lord his people
    and his creatures for a reward eternal...
Let Daniel come forth with a lion,
    and praise God with all his might through faith in Christ Jesus...
Let David bless with the bear—The beginning of victory to the Lord—
    to the Lord the perfection of excellence—
    Hallelujah from the heart of God,
    and from the hand of the artist inimitable,
    and from the echo of the heavenly harp
    in sweetness magnifical and mighty.
Let Solomon praise with the ant,
    and give the glory to the Fountain of all wisdom...
Let Mephibosheth with the cricket
    praise the God of cheerfulness, hospitality, and gratitude...
Let Job bless with the worm—
    the life of the Lord is in humiliation,
    the spirit also and the truth...
Let Benjamin bless and rejoice with the redbird,
    who is soft and soothing.
Let Dan rejoice with the blackbird,
    who praises God with all his heart, and biddeth to be of good cheer.

Christopher Smart
1722–71

INSECTS, BIRDS AND CREEPING THINGS

The House Sparrow

Citizen Philip Sparrow, who likes
To build and breed about our habitations—
  The little birds that fly through the city smoke—

Prolific, adaptable, bold,
Untidy, cheerfully vocal—
  The little birds that quarrel in the eaves—

Grant him his right of freedom and, of your charity,
His dole of crumbs and kitchen scraps—
  The little birds that stand in the eye of God

John Heath-Stubbs
20th century

From: 'Ducks'

When God had finished the stars and whirl of coloured suns
He turned his mind from big things to fashion little ones,
Beautiful tiny things (like daisies) he made, and then
He made the comical ones in case the minds of men
  Should stiffen and become
  Dull, humourless and glum:
And so forgetful of their Maker be
As to take even themselves—*quite seriously*...
All God's jokes are good—even the practical ones!...
And as for the duck, I think God must have smiled a bit
Seeing those bright eyes blink on the day he fashioned it.
And he's probably laughing still at the sound that came out of its bill!

F.W. Harvey
1888–1957

The Visitor

Twice,
that sleety twilit afternoon
I glanced up sharply from the ironing
and saw, out in the dismal garden,
beyond the thickening window
our reluctant great-tit,
persuaded by winter's argument
towards the pendulous, swinging coconut;—

almost as if the Lord,
temporarily leaving aside weightier matters
had quietly entered the room
and tapped me on the shoulder,
saying

Do look, don't miss him,
isn't he wonderful?
Put down that shirt, just for a moment,
and join in my delight,
for I love you even as I love him,
and I want you to share my pleasure
in this tiny ruffled topknot
of my Creation,

pecking at life's cold shell
cupped in my wide hands;—

and tasting joy.

Jan Godfrey
20th century

The Unemployed

the cormorants
    a black dole queue
stand on Marsden rock
    totally unemployed

there are still the working ones
the kittiwakes mewing busily
around the rocks in the sea

but for the cormorants there is
nothing to do

    one flaps off slowly
and another returns
    with no news of work
the rest just stand around.

Rodney Ward
20th century

Noise

When I play
my records
(at full volume,
in stereo)
I have to
close all
the windows.

I can't stand
the noise
of the birds
outside
in the trees.

Steve Turner
20th century

The Sparrow's Skull

MEMENTO MORI: WRITTEN AT THE FALL OF FRANCE

The kingdoms fall in sequence, like the waves on the shore.
All save divine and desperate hopes go down, they are no more.
Solitary is our place, the castle in the sea,
And I muse on those I have loved, and on those who have loved me.

I gather up my loves, and keep them all warm,
While above our heads blows the bitter storm:
The blessed natural loves, of life-supporting flame,
And those whose name is Wonder, which have no other name.

The skull is in my hand, the minute cup of bone,
And I remember her, the tame, the loving one,
Who came in at the window, and seemed to have a mind
More towards sorrowful man than to those of her own kind.

She came for a long time, but at length she grew old;
And on her death-day she came, so feeble and so bold;
And all day, as if knowing what the day would bring,
She waited by the window, with her head beneath her wing.

And I will keep the skull, for in the hollow here
Lodged the minute brain that had outgrown a fear;
Transcended an old terror, and found a new love,
And entered a strange life, a world it was not of.

Even so, dread God! even so, my Lord!
The fire is at my feet, and at my breast the sword:
And I must gather up my soul, and clap my wings, and flee
Into the heart of terror, to find myself in thee.

Ruth Pitter
20th century

Saint Francis Preaches to the Computers

Saint Francis found his way (saints, in a dream,
An ecstasy, slip in and out of time)
Into the computer shop. The chipper little chaps
All chrome and plastic, stainless steel,
Gleaming and winking, chirped and buzzed and whirred
And pipped and peeped, much like the congregation
The saint had just been preaching to—of Ruddocks, Dunnocks
Citrils, Serins, Siskins, Spinks,
Orphean warblers, Ortolans, Golden Orioles.
So he began to do his stuff again—
You know the kind of thing that he would say:—he told them
To praise the Lord who had created them,
Had made them bright and new, had programmed them
Had plugged them in, and kept them serviceable.
But somehow they looked glum; hint of a minor key
Seemed to infect their electronic singing:
'Alas,' they said, 'for we were not created
By God, whoever he or she may be,
But by the shaved ape, the six-foot Siamang
The pregnant mandrake root, cumulus in pants,
Glassily-essenced Man. We are no more clever
Than he who made us, though we think faster. Nor
    were we programmed
With thoughts that take off into timelessness,
Nor trans-death longings. But we have one fear,
And it is rust, is rust, is rust,
The eternal rubbish tip and the compressor.'
'My little mechanical brothers,' rejoined the saint
'I'll tell you something that a Mullah said,
One that was in the Soldan's entourage,
That time I visited his camp. They postulate
A moderate-sized menagerie in heaven.
I'll only mention Balaam's percipient ass,
Tobias' toby dog, that other faithful fido
Who hunted in his dreams in that Ephesian den
The seven sleepers snorted in, and snarled
At Roman persecutors, and, golden-crested,
Cinnamon-breasted, with broad dappled wings
The hoopoe, which was wise King Solomon's
Special envoy to the queen of Sheba—
That sweet blue-stocking with the donkey's toes.'

'If these could pass into eternity,
It was for love and service. And Eternity,
Loving through mankind, loved them,

And lifted them into a resurrection, as shall be lifted
The whole creation, groan though it does and travail.
And if these brute beasts were loved, then so may you be,
Along with the Puffing Billies, Chitty Chitty Bang Bangs,
Barnacled Old Superbs, Ezekiel's Wheels,
Elijah's fiery space-ship. You shall be built as stones
That gleam in the High-priestly breastplate
Which is the wall of that bright golden city—
Itself the human body glorified.'

John Heath-Stubbs
20th century

St Francis and the Birds

When Francis preached love to the birds
They listened, fluttered, throttled up
Into the blue like a flock of words

Released for fun from his holy lips,
Then wheeled back, whirred about his head,
Pirouetted on brothers' capes.

Danced on the wing, for sheer joy played
And sang, like images took flight.
Which was the best poem Francis made,

His argument true, his tone light.

Seamus Heaney
20th century

Dear St Francis

Some creatures of our God and King
distract one at funeral moments
trundle across the floor on six legs
in their own gospel procession

Other creatures of our God and Queen
pop in and out feeding young
At the frantic nestbox when I try to join
in spirit in committal prayers.

Diana Downing
20th century

To a Waterfowl

Whither, midst falling dew,
While glow the heavens with the last steps of day,
Far, through their rosy depths, dost thou pursue
   Thy solitary way?

   Vainly the fowler's eye
Might mark thy distant flight to do thee wrong,
As, darkly seen against the crimson sky,
   Thy figure floats along.

   Seek'st thou the plashy brink
Of weedy lake, or marge of river wide,
Or where the rocking billows rise and sink
   On the chafed ocean-side?

   There is a Power whose care
Teaches thy way along that pathless coast—
The desert and illimitable air—
   Lone wandering, but not lost.

   All day thy wings have fanned,
At that far height, the cold, thin atmosphere,
Yet stoop not, weary, to the welcome land,
   Though the dark night is near.

   And soon that toil shall end;
Soon shalt thou find a summer home, and rest,
And scream among thy fellows; reeds shall bend,
   Soon, o'er thy sheltered nest.

   Thou'rt gone, the abyss of heaven
Hath swallowed up thy form; yet on my heart
Deeply has sunk the lesson thou hast given,
   And shall not soon depart.

   He who, from zone to zone,
Guides through the boundless sky thy certain flight,
In the long way that I must tread alone,
   Will lead my steps aright.

William Cullen Bryant
1794–1878

The Kingfisher

When Noah left the Ark, the animals
Capered and gambolled on the squadgy soil,
Enjoying their new-found freedom; and the birds
Soared upwards, twittering, to the open skies.
But one soared higher than the rest, in utter ecstasy,
Till all his back and wings were drenched

With the vivid blue of heaven itself, and his breast scorched
With the upward-slanting rays of the setting sun.
When he came back to earth, he had lost the Ark;
His friends were all dispersed. So now he soars no more;
A lonely bird, he darts and dives for fish,
By streams and pools—places where water is—
Still searching, but in vain, for the vanished Ark
And rain-washed terraces of Ararat.

John Heath-Stubbs
20th century

The Prayer of the Cock

Do not forget, Lord,
it is I who make the sun rise.
I am your servant
but, with the dignity of my calling,
I need some glitter and ostentation.
Noblesse oblige ...
all the same,
I am your servant,
only... do not forget, Lord,
I make the sun rise.

Carmen de Gasztold   *20th century*
translated by Rumer Godden

The Fly

The Lord in his wisdom made the fly,
And then forgot to tell us why.

Ogden Nash
20th century

The Butterfly

My hands are warm to the butterfly
I am trying to set free.
Delicate, frail creature of beauty,
what can it know of me?
I am outside its comprehension.
It knows sunshine and showers,
darkness and the feel of flowers.
We do not ask it to do the impossible
and know Man.

So we, with God,
who looks with tenderness upon our frailty,
trying to guide us.
Trust him!
He knows the way, and, if we let him,
will open windows,
and, cradling us gently in hands we cannot comprehend.
will lift us up and set us free.

Margaret Orford
20th century

Be a Butterfly

Don't be a kyatta-pilla
Be a butterfly
old preacher screamed
to illustrate his sermon
of Jesus and the higher life

rivulets of well-earned
sweat sliding down
his muscly mahogany face
in the half-empty school church
we sat shaking with muffling
laughter
watching our mother trying to save
herself from joining the wave

only our father remaining poker face
and afterwards we always went home to
split peas Sunday soup
with dumplings, fufu and pigtail

Don't be a kyatta-pilla
Be a butterfly
Be a butterfly

That was de life preacher
and you was right

Grace Nichols
20th century

Student Taper

When
—At end of moon,
At end of day—
My lamp is lit,
Grant me a boon,
I pray,
And do
So order it

—That the small creatures,
Terrified and blind;
The gold and silvern moths
Of lovely kind,
Do not whirl to my taper,
Nor, therein,
Die, painfully,
And bring my light
To sin.

My light
Is innocent!
Grant
—That it may be
Harmless,
And helpful,
And remarked
Of thee.

James Stephens
1882–1950

Bestialities

When I get mad I stamp
sd the ant.

*

Sd the mother ladybug if you
know who you are it's
all in that and you may
leave it to the others with their
pads and blast off.

*

What are you doing sd the dolphin up a
gumtree eating peanuts:
(swimming?)

*

Because it was going to be
autumn the centipede was
sitting at a roadside table snapping
   the 3 buckles on the (each)
     foot's
       galoshes.

*

Better not call wings beautiful unless
you're flying with them sd
the dragonfly and then it's better than
wanting toes.

*

Sd the mite on the
single page of a sad letter
Eureka.

Margaret Avison
20th century

Upon a Spider Catching a Fly

Thou sorrow, venom elf:
Is this thy play,
To spin a web out of thyself
   To catch a fly?
     For why?

I saw a pettish wasp
   Fall foul therein:
Whom yet thy whorl pins did not hasp
   Lest he should fling
     His sting.

But as afraid, remote
   Didst stand hereat,
And with thy little fingers stroke
   And gently tap
     His back.

Then gently him didst treat
   Lest he should pet,
And in a froppish, aspish heat
   Should greatly fret
     Thy net.

Whereas the silly fly
   Caught by its leg,
Thou by the throat took'st hastily,
   And 'hinde the head
     Bite dead.

This goes to pot, that not
   Nature doth call.
Strive not above what strength hath got,
   Lest in the brawl
     Thou fall.

This fray seems thus to us:
   Hell's spider gets
His entrails spun to whip cords thus,
   And wove to nets,
     And sets.

To tangle Adam's race
   In's strategems
To their destructions, spoiled, made base

By venom things,
    Damned sins.

But mighty, gracious Lord,
    Communicate
Thy grace to break the cord; afford
    Us glory's gate
        And state.

We'll nightingale sing like,
    When perched on high
In glory's cage, thy glory bright:
    Yea, thankfully,
        For joy.

Edward Taylor
1645?–1729

The Prayer of the Ant

Lord,
I am always made out to be wrong;
a fable to the whole world.
Certainly I hoard
and make provision!
I have my rights!
And surely I can take a little joy
in the fruits of all my work
without some sob singer
coming to rob my store?
There is something in your justice
that I scarcely understand,
and, if you would allow me to advise,
it might be thought over again.
I have never been a burden to anybody,
and, if I may say so,
I manage my own business very well.
Then,
to the incorrigible improvidence
of some people,
must I, for all eternity, say
Amen.

Carmen de Gasztold
20th century
translated by Rumer Godden

Go To The Ant

I have always considered
the grasshopper
to be the finer fellow
He did not scrape and hoard
worldly possessions
He would not have turned away
a friend hungry
He had more fun
in one fiddle foot
than the ant in his
whole diligent body
Gladly the grasshopper
glorified God by the
sensuous enjoyment
of each irretrievable moment
while the ant
grieved his yesterdays
and grumbled each tomorrow

IS THERE A LIFE BEFORE DEATH?

wrote the grasshopper
on the lavatory wall
and added

NOT FOR ANTS

Barbara Dickinson
20th century

Song of the Death-Watch Beetle

Here come I, the death-watch beetle
Chewing away at the great cathedral;

Gnawing the mediaeval beams
And the magnificent carved rood screen

Gorging on gospels and epistles
From the illuminated missals;

As once I ate the odes of Sappho
And the histories of Manetho,

The lost plays of Euripides
And all the thought of Parmenides.

The Sibyl's leaves which the wind scattered,
And great Aunt Delia's love letters.

Turn down the lamp in the cooling room:
There stand I with my little drum.

Death. Watch, You are watching death.
Blow out the lamp with your last breath.

John Heath-Stubbs
20th century

The Serpent

The serpent is more subtle.
He is more subtle
than a rhineroceros
who cannot slither up unsuspectingly.
He is more subtle
than a lion
who cannot sing from branches.
He is more subtle
than a terrapin,

   a goat,
more subtle than truth.
You think he is a stick
until you collect him
for firewood.
You think he is a leaf
until he bends down
to kiss.
You think he is a stone,
    a tree,
    a good idea,
    your true self.
The serpent has more beauty.
He amazes you with his colour
which speaks with the sun.
He amazes you with his grace.
If you had not been told
you will want to take him in your hand,
you will want to take him home.

Steve Turner
20th century

CATS AND OTHER ANIMALS

From: Jubilate Agno

For I will consider my cat Jeoffrey.

For he is the servant of the living God duly and daily serving him.

For at the first glance of the glory of God in the East he worships in his way.

For this is done by wreathing his body seven times round with elegant quickness.

For then he leaps up to catch the musk, which is the blessing of God upon his prayer.

For he rolls upon prank to work it in.

For having done duty and received blessing he begins to consider himself.

For this he performs in ten degrees.

For first he looks upon his fore-paws to see if they are clean.

For secondly he kicks up behind to clear away there.

For thirdly he works upon stretch with the fore-paws extended.

For fourthly he sharpens his paws by wood.

For fifthly he washes himself.

For sixthly he rolls upon wash.

For seventhly he fleas himself, that he may not be interrupted upon the beat.

For eighthly he rubs himself against a post.

For ninthly he looks up for his instruction.

For tenthly he goes in quest of food.

For when his day's work is done his business more properly begins.

For he keeps the Lord's watch in the night against the adversary.

For he counteracts the powers of darkness by his electrical skin and glaring eyes.

For he counteracts the Devil, who is death, by brisking about the life.

For in his morning orisons he loves the sun and the sun loves him.

For he is of the tribe of tiger.

For the cherub cat is a term of the angel tiger.

For he has the subtlety and hissing of a serpent, which in goodness he suppresses.

For he will not do destruction, if he is well-fed, neither will he spit without
    provocation.

For he purrs in thankfulness, when God tells him he's a good cat.

For he is an instrument for the children to learn benevolence upon.

For every house is incomplete without him and a blessing is lacking in the spirit...

For he knows that God is his Saviour.

For there is nothing sweeter than his peace when at rest.

For there is nothing brisker than his life when in motion...

For the divine spirit comes about his body to sustain it in complete cat.

Christopher Smart
1722–71

The Game of Backsliding

The robins
rival
the starlings
for my seeds:
beans,
carrots,
peppers, melons,
radishes, pickles,
broccoli, and corn.

This morning
a quite contrary cat
fearlessly chooses
my garden—
how does it grow?—
to trampoline
in my tomatoes,
roll out the onions,
drag a dead rat
through the new strawberries.

I grin a wry
and guilty grimace
at the way
I too daily
sport with, spoil
the fragile shoots
of my May sowings,
his seeds of Christlike life.

Nevertheless,
I shoo the cat.

Merle Meeter
20th century

The Tyger

Tyger! Tyger! burning bright
In the forests of the night,
What immortal hand or eye
Could frame thy fearful symmetry?

In what distant deeps or skies
Burnt the fire of thine eyes?
On what wings dare he aspire?
What the hand dare seize the fire?

And what shoulder, and what art,
Could twist the sinews of thy heart?
And when thy heart began to beat,
What dread hand? and what dread feet?

What the hammer? What the chain?
In what furnace was thy brain?
What the anvil? what dread grasp
Dare its deadly terrors clasp?

When the stars threw down their spears,
And watered heaven with their tears,
Did he smile his work to see?
Did he who made the lamb make thee?

Tyger! Tyger! burning bright
In the forests of the night,
What immortal hand or eye,
Dare frame thy fearful symmetry?

William Blake
1757–1827

Reluctant Prophet

Both were dwellers
in deep places (one
in the dark bowels
of ships and great fish
and wounded pride.
The other
in the silvery belly
of the seas.) Both
heard God saying
'Go!'
but the whale
did as he was told.

Luci Shaw
20th century

The Lamb

Little lamb, who made thee?
Dost thou know who made thee?
Gave thee life, and bid thee feed,
By the stream and o'er the mead;
Gave thee clothing of delight,
Softest clothing, woolly, bright;
Gave thee such a tender voice,
making all the vale rejoice?
Little lamb, who made thee?
Dost thou know who made thee?

Little lamb, I'll tell thee,
Little lamb, I'll tell thee:
He is callèd by thy name,
For he calls himself a lamb.
He is meek and he is mild;
He became a little child.
I a child, and thou a lamb,
We are callèd by his name.
Little lamb, God bless thee!
Little lamb, God bless thee!

William Blake
1757–1827

The Late Passenger

The sky was low, the sounding rain was falling dense and dark,
And Noah's sons were standing at the window of the Ark.

The beasts were in, but Japhet said, 'I see one creature more
Belated and unmated there come knocking at the door.'

'Well let him knock,' said Ham, 'Or let him drown or learn to swim.
We're overcrowded as it is; we've got no room for him.'

'And yet it knocks, how terribly it knocks,' said Shem, 'Its feet
Are hard as horn—but oh the air that comes from it is sweet.'

'Now hush,' said Ham, 'You'll waken Dad, and once he comes to see
What's at the door, it's sure to mean more work for you and me.'

Noah's voice came roaring from the darkness down below,
'Some animal is knocking. Take it in before we go.'

Ham shouted back, and savagely he nudged the other two,
'That's only Japhet knocking down a brad-nail in his shoe.'

Said Noah, 'Boys, I hear a noise that's like a horse's hoof.'
Said Ham, 'Why, that's the dreadful rain that drums upon the roof.'

Noah tumbled up on deck and out he put his head;
His face went grey, his knees were loosed, he tore his beard and said,

'Look, look! It would not wait. It turns away. It takes its flight.
Fine work you've made of it, my sons, between you all tonight!

'Even if I could outrun it now, it would not turn again
—Not now. Our great discourtesy has earned its high disdain.

'Oh noble and unmated beast, my sons were all unkind;
In such a night what stable and what manger will you find?

Oh golden hoofs, oh cataracts of mane, oh nostrils wide
With indignation! Oh the neck wave-arched, the lovely pride!

'Oh long shall be the furrows ploughed across the hearts of men
Before it comes to stable and to manger once again,

And dark and crooked all the ways in which our race shall walk,
And shrivelled all their manhood like a flower with broken stalk,

'And all the world, oh Ham, may curse the hour when you were born;
Because of you the Ark must sail without the Unicorn.'

C.S. Lewis
1898–1963

The Donkey

When fishes flew and forests walked
    And figs grew upon thorn,
Some moment when the moon was blood
    Then surely I was born.

With monstrous head and sickening cry
    And ears like errant wings,
The devil's walking parody
    On all four-footed things.

The tattered outlaw of the earth,
    Of ancient crooked will;
Starve, scourge, deride me: I am dumb,
    I keep my secret still.

Fools! For I also had my hour;
    One far fierce hour and sweet:
There was a shout about my ears,
    And palms about my feet.

G.K. Chesterton
1874–1936

In the Wilderness

Christ of his gentleness
Thirsting and hungering
Walked in the wilderness;
Soft words of grace he spoke
Unto lost desert-folk
That listened wondering.
He heard the bitterns call
From ruined palace-wall,
Answered them brotherly.
He held communion
With the she-pelican
Of lonely piety.
Basilisk, cockatrice,
Flocked to his homilies,
With mail of dread device,
With monstrous barbed stings,
With eager dragon-eyes;
Great rats on leather wings
And poor blind broken things,
Foul in their miseries.
And ever with him went,
Of all his wanderings
Comrade, with ragged coat,
Gaunt ribs—poor innocent—
Bleeding foot, burning throat,
The guileless old scape-goat;
For forty nights and days
Followed in Jesus' ways,
Sure guard behind him kept,
Tears like a lover wept.

Robert Graves
1895–1985

Good-Nature to Animals

The man of Mercy (says the Seer)
    Shows mercy to his beast;
Learn not of churls to be severe,
    But house and feed at least.

Shall I melodious prisoners take
    From out the linnet's nest,
And not keep busy care awake,
    To cherish every guest?

What, shall I whip in cruel wrath
    The steed that bears me safe,
Or 'gainst the dog, who plights his troth,
    For faithful service chafe? . . .

Let thine industrious silk-worms reap
    Their wages to the full,
Nor let neglected dormice sleep
    To death within thy wool.

Know when the frosty weather comes,
    'Tis charity to deal
To wren and redbreast all thy crumbs,
    The remnant of thy meal.

Tho' these some spirits think but light,
    And deem indifferent things;
Yet they are serious in the sight
    Of CHRIST, the King of kings.

Christopher Smart
1722–71

At the Last Judgment

A dog starved at his master's gate
Predicts the ruin of the state.

A horse misused upon the road
Cries to Heaven for human blood.

Each outcry of the hunted hare
A fibre from the brain does tear.

Kill not the moth nor butterfly;
For the Last Judgment draweth nigh.

William Blake
1757–1827

The Exile

The fool said to the animals:
'You are merely my chattels,
With one lesson to learn—
That what happens to you is not your concern
But mine; for a just God has set
You on earth for my profit.'

The animals answered the fool
Nothing at all,
But for a single moment
Turned on him their wild, true, innocent
Eyes, where an Angel of the Lord
Holds Eden's flaming sword.

Frances Bellerby
20th century

Times and Seasons

Wishes for the Months

I wish you, in January, the swirl of blown snow—
A green January makes a full churchyard;

Thrushes singing through the February rain; in March
The clarion winds, the daffodils;

April, capricious as an adolescent girl,
With cuckoo-song, and cuckoo-flowers;

May with a dog rose, June with a musk rose; July
Multi-foliate, with all the flowers of summer;

August—a bench in the shade, and a cool tankard;
September golden among his sheaves;

In October, apples; in grave November
Offerings for the beloved dead;

And, in December, a midwinter stillness,
Promise of new life, incarnation.

John Heath-Stubbs 20th century

The Pear Tree

The weathered pear, four generations old
My window-meditation, lives in peace.
Rough boughs, pale clouds of fragile blossom hold
Where slim bees hover. Tender leaves increase,
Light-fringed, to cup the summer sky and move
In gentle lifting through blue-dappled shade.
So may I ponder on such kindly Love
Which keeps in beauty every shining blade
Destined so soon to drift through Autumn air
Towards winter dissolution: Glory lost
Reveals new grandeur of trimmed branches, bare
To the gale's strength, crisp outlined in chaste frost.
So wondering, I dream through the tree's year
Learning acceptance of God's Order here.

Clare Girling 20th century

For Everything There is a Season

(ECCLESIASTES 3)

The time to weep is in the heart's winter.
  Grief is the grip of ice and silence,
snow and vast grey skies. Bending under
  tree-caught snow, nerves hold the sad immense.

The time to laugh is when new is sprung
  suddenly. Renewal—new love, new
light, new green, new morning, blossom-hung
  delight—makes the Spring of the heart due.

There is a time for living. Into
  a wide green under a thoughtful sun
we move and struggle. Who is the True
  must reach here, must judge what we have done.

There is also a time for dying.
  The green leaves become brown, the grass fades,
the unplucked fruit drops and rots. Sighing
  tree-sung rain makes cold decaying shades.

Colin Duriez
20th century

SPRING AND SUMMER

Kindly Spring

Kindly spring again is here,
Trees and fields in bloom appear;
Hark! the birds with artless lays
Warble their creator's praise.

Where in winter all was snow,
Now the flowers in clusters grow;
And the corn, in green array,
Promises a harvest-day.

Lord, afford a spring to me,
Let me feel like what I see;
Speak, and by thy gracious voice,
Make my drooping soul rejoice.

On thy garden deign to smile,
Raise the plants, enrich the soil;
Soon thy presence will restore
Life to what seemed dead before.

John Newton
1725–1807

The Flower

How fresh, O Lord, how sweet and clean
Are thy returns! E'en as the flowers in Spring,
  To which, besides their own demesne,
The late-past frosts tributes of pleasure bring;
    Grief melts away
    Like snow in May,
  As if there were no such cold thing.

  Who would have thought my shrivelled heart
Could have recovered greenness? It was gone
  Quite under ground; as flowers depart
To see their mother-root, when they have blown,
    Where they together
    All the hard weather,
  Dead to the world, keep house unknown.

These are thy wonders, Lord of power,
Killing and quickening, bringing down to Hell
   And up to Heaven in an hour;
Making a chiming of a passing-bell.
      We say amiss
      This or that is;
   Thy word is all, if we could spell.

O that I once past changing were,
Fast in thy Paradise, where no flower can wither;
   Many a spring I shoot up fair,
Offering at Heaven, growing and groaning thither;
      Nor doth my flower
      Want a spring-shower,
   My sins and I joining together.

But while I grow in a straight line,
Still upwards bent, as if Heaven were mine own,
   Thy anger comes, and I decline:
What frost to that? what pole is not the zone
      Where all things burn,
      When thou dost turn,
   And the least frown of thine is shown?

And now in age I bud again,
After so many deaths I live and write;
   I once more smell the dew and rain,
And relish versing: O, my only Light,
      It cannot be
      That I am he
   On whom thy tempests fell at night.

These are thy wonders, Lord of love,
To make us see we are but flowers that glide;
   Which when we once can find and prove,
Thou hast a garden for us where to bide;
      Who would be more,
      Swelling through store,
   Forfeit their Paradise by their pride.

George Herbert
1593–1633

The Green Lane

A little lane—the brook runs close beside,
And spangles in the sunshine,
   while the fish glide swiftly by;
And hedges leafing with the green springtide;
From out their greenery the old birds fly,
And chirp and whistle in the morning sun;
The pilewort glitters 'neath the pale blue sky,
The little robin has its nest begun,
And grass-green linnets round the bushes fly.
How mild the spring comes in! the daisy buds
Lift up their golden blossoms to the sky.
How lovely are the pingles and the woods.
Here a beetle runs—and there a fly
Rests on the arum leaf in bottle-green,
And all the spring in this sweet lane is seen.

John Clare
1793–1864

Spring Flowers

Bowing adorers of the gale,
Ye cowslips delicately pale,
   Upraise your loaded stems,
Unfold your cups in splendour; speak!
Who decked you with that ruddy streak,
   And gilt your golden gems?

Violets, sweet tenants of the shade,
In purple's richest pride arrayed,
   Your errand here fulfil!
Go, bid the artist's simple stain
Your lustre imitate, in vain,
   And match your Maker's skill.

Daisies, ye flowers of lowly birth,
Embroiderers of the carpet earth,
   That stud the velvet sod;
Open to spring's refreshing air,
In sweetest smiling bloom declare
   Your Maker and my God.

John Clare
1793–1864

Spring Sonnet

The lilac bush puts forth its purple spikes
and pink-tipped blossom decks the apple tree,
while on the ground the bright-faced primrose likes
to highlight shaded violet's modesty;
and on the cherry bough full-throated thrush
sings out in answer to the cuckoo's call,
and over all the earth the first fair flush
of Spring unfolds its beauty to enthral.
In full accord but by more wondrous means
the Holy Spirit quickens all that lives
and like Spring's sun on many-shaded greens
new Life to people's varied natures gives.
And as Spring blooms are rendered safe from frost
may God save us from sin, else we are lost.

Cyril Lloyd
20th century

Virtue

Sweet day, so cool, so calm, so bright,
The bridal of the earth and sky,
The dew shall weep thy fall tonight;
    For thou must die.

Sweet rose, whose hue angry and brave
Bids the rash gazer wipe his eye,
Thy root is ever in its grave,
    And thou must die.

Sweet spring, full of sweet days and roses,
A box where sweets compacted lie,
My music shows ye have your closes,
    And all must die.

Only a sweet and virtuous soul,
Like seasoned timber, never gives;
And though the whole world turn to coal,
    Then chiefly lives.

George Herbert
1593–1633

After the Winter

As spring the winter doth succeed
And leaves the naked trees do dress,
The earth all black is clothed in green.
At sunshine each their joy express.

My sun's returned with healing wings,
My soul and body doth rejoice,
My heart exults and praises sings
To him that heard my wailing voice.

My winter's past, my storms are gone,
And former clouds seem now all fled,
But if they must eclipse again,
I'll run where I was succourèd.

I have a shelter from the storm,
A shadow from the fainting heat,
I have access unto his throne,
Who is a God so wondrous great.

O hath thou made my pilgrimage
Thus pleasant, fair, and good,
Blessed me in youth and elder age,
My Baca* made a springing flood.

O studious am what I shall do
To show my duty with delight;
All I can give is but thine own
And at the most a simple mite.

Anne Bradstreet
1612–72

* *Baca*: valley of weeping

fenscape

after winter rain the enormous sky
opens blue eyes in wet-lashed wonder

at its own shattered reflection
a blink a breath caught held in

cracked ice mirrors, thin light
fingering heaven's seamless hem of

broken clouds spilling colour into
painted pools of living moving water

shining turquoise puddles scooped from
pumpernickel earth's harsh richness of

clumbered furrows, black bones converging
to a narrow ribbed sharp-cut perspective

hardly peopled or housed this iron bleakness
broken tree scarecrow-man land taut to

time's horizon: mocked pecked he stands
dumb wooden guardian of all our innocences

as a man once swung between the heavens
and all the frozen darkened earth

Jan Godfrey
20th century

The Revival

Unfold, unfold! take in his light,
Who makes thy cares more short than night.
The joys, which with his day-star rise,
He deals to all but drowsy eyes;
And what the men of this world miss,
Some drops and dews of future bliss.
Hark how his winds have changed their note,
And with warm whispers call thee out.
The frosts are past, the storms are gone;
And backward life at last comes on.
The lofty groves in express joys
Reply unto the turtle's voice,
And here in dust and dirt, O here
The lilies of his love appear!

Henry Vaughan
1622–95

Spring

Nothing is so beautiful as spring—
When weeds, in wheels, shoot long and lovely and lush;
Thrush's eggs look little low heavens, and thrush
Through the echoing timber does so rinse and wring
The ear, it strikes like lightnings to hear him sing;
The glassy peartree leaves and blooms, they brush
The descending blue; that blue is all in a rush
With richness; the racing lambs too have fair their fling.
What is all this juice and all this joy?
A strain of the earth's sweet being in the beginning
In Eden garden.—Have, get, before it cloy,
Before it cloud, Christ, lord, and sour with sinning,
Innocent mind and Mayday in girl and boy,
Most, O maid's child, thy choice and worthy the winning.

Gerard Manley Hopkins
1844–89

Lenten Signs

Here in the city
where impassive pavements
light no signals for seasons,
fingers of woodland
point to the river.

Mottled ivy
wipes off winter dust,
burns greener: a thorn tree
is beginning to sweat
white tears.

Gnarled japonica
bursts into globules of blood,
beading leafless bones;
sunshots dazzle
through crossed boughs

of park lopped trees
and tearing nails of briars.
Robins extemporise
red warnings
of outrageous spring.

Joyce Weldom-Searle
20th century

Lent

Lent is a tree without blossom, without leaf,
Barer than blackthorn in its winter sleep,
All unadorned. Unlike Christmas which decrees
The setting-up, the dressing-up of trees,
Lent is a taking down, a stripping bare,
A starkness after all has been withdrawn
Of surplus and superfluous,
Leaving no hiding-place, only an emptiness
Between black branches, a most precious space
Before the leaf, before the time of flowers;
Lest we should see only the leaf, the flower,
Lest we should miss the stars.

Jean M. Watt
20th century

Knoxville, Tennessee

I always like summer
best
you can eat fresh corn
from daddy's garden
and okra
and greens
and cabbage
and lots of
barbecue
and buttermilk
and homemade ice-cream
at the church picnic
and listen to
gospel music
outside
at the church
homecoming
and go to the mountain with
your grandmother
and go barefooted
and be warm
all the time
not only when you go to bed
and sleep

Nikki Giovanni
20th century

AUTUMN

Villanelle for a Season's End

Autumn is here and summer will not stay
The season cuts a bloodline on the land
And all earth's singing green is stripped away.

Our parting drains the colour from the day.
The oak leaves' red is clotting in your hand.
Autumn is here and summer will not stay.

The sea fog settles. Even noon is grey.
The light recedes as though this dusk were planned.
The green of field and tree is stripped away.

We shiver on the beach and watch the way
The berries' blood is spilled along the sand.
The green of all our fields is stripped away.

See how the wind has scattered the salt hay
Across the dunes! Too well we understand:
Autumn is here, bright summer will not stay
And all earth's love and green are stripped away.

Luci Shaw
20th century

Falling Leaves

Fall, leaves, fall; die, flowers, away;
Lengthen night and shorten day;
Every leaf speaks bliss to me
Fluttering from the autumn tree.
I shall smile when wreaths of snow
Blossom where the rose should grow;
I shall sing when night's decay
Ushers in a drearier day.

Emily Brontë
1818–48

The Song of the Reapers

We know a field.
A sheltered, fertile ground,
Well-favoured by the sun.
    There the first yield
Of corn is reaped and bound
Before the harvest is begun.

    It is a sheaf
Of whitest gold, the green
Half-fainted from the stem.
    Upon the leaf
Spring's last veins are seen.
Each ear is a Jerusalem.

    Now from this first
Pure sheaf the bread is baked.
And offered, fragrant, fresh,
    To God.—Who thirst
And hunger shall be slaked
By holy wine, fed by this flesh.

    For when we eat
This bread that is new-made
We take into our blood
    His grace, our meat.
By faith, the earth is fed
And by His love we have our bread.

James Kirkup
20th century

The Burning of the Leaves

Now is the time for the burning of the leaves.
They go to the fire; the nostril pricks with smoke
Wandering slowly into a sweeping mist.
Brittle and blotched, ragged and rotten sheaves!
A flame seizes the smouldering ruin and bites
On stubborn stalks that crackle as they resist.

The last hollyhock's falled tower is dust;
All the spices of June are a bitter reek,
All the extravagant riches spent and mean.
All burns! The reddest rose is a ghost;
Sparks whirl up, to expire in the mist: the wild
Fingers of fire are making corruption clean.

Now is the time for stripping the spirit bare,
Time for the burning of days ended and done,
Idle solace of things that have gone before:
Rootless hopes and fruitless desires are there;
Let them go to the fire, with never a look behind.
The world that was ours is a world that is ours no more.

They will come again, the leaf and the flower, to arise
From squalor of rottenness into the old splendour,
And magical scents to a wondering memory bring;
The same glory, to shine upon different eyes.
Earth cares for her own ruins, naught for ours.
Nothing is certain, only the certain spring.

Laurence Binyon
1869–1943

Harvest Moon

The swaying aspen glides before our eyes.
Entranced,
    Unaware of snapping twigs,
    Ignoring whipping branches,
We gaze at the orb:
    The hanging harvest moon,
Orange and glowing in an October sky.

Partners in a cosmic dance,
    We creak across hoary grass
As the moon hovers, a fingertip away.

Our steps sing, gravel-throated,
    As we crunch along the moon-lit path,
Wrapped in the frost-scented evening.

A crust of light; the oak door swings:
    We stand inside a cornucopia,
Bearing our muddy potatoes and runner beans.

Lights flicker, spinning out from the cross,
    Glancing off ruddy apples.
Scented sweet-peas overpower, mingling with crumbly earth.

Our voices rise in praise and thanks.
Spiralling upwards,
    To float to the moon.

Sian Midgley
20th century

The Golden Boy

In March he was buried
    And nobody cried
Buried in the dirt
    Nobody protested
Where grubs and insects
    That nobody knows
With outer-space faces
    That nobody loves
Can make him their feast
    As if nobody cared.

But the Lord's mother
    Full of her love
Found him underground
    And wrapped him with love
As if he were her baby
    Her own born love
She nursed him with miracles
    And starry love
And he began to live
    And to thrive on her love

He grew night and day
    And his murderers were glad
He grew like a fire
    And his murderers were happy
He grew lithe and tall
    And his murderers were joyful
He toiled in the fields
    And his murderers cared for him
He grew a gold beard
    And his murderers laughed.

With terrible steel
    They slew him in the furrow
With terrible steel
    They beat his bones from him
With terrible steel
    They ground him to powder
They baked him in ovens
    They sliced him on tables
They ate him they ate him
    They ate him they ate him

Thanking the Lord
Thanking the Wheat
Thanking the Bread
For bringing them Life
Today and Tomorrow
Out of the dirt.

Ted Hughes
20th century

Broad Autumn

True faith matures without discarding.
All I unearthed, each sky-sign crudely mapped
On the white rasped hills of youth,
Warms me still by rowan-tapped crags,
Far up the autumnal mountain,
Incredibly remote in climate, texture, weathering
Of bare stones, from my first insights:
I leave no wreckage on those low rasped cones.

There is no snarl of tools
Where broad wisdom calls across the cordial heather,
But the hacked glints my young heart stored
Still tone the subtle comforts and the sharp
Fearful shifts of shade as the blood cools
To admit, and clarify, the expanding mental range.

No pestilence of proud ripeness,
Urbane, agnostic, cankers the wide braes
Which my spirit, eagle-keen now, calls native
In the pale sun's gloss. The spikes of raw praise,
Sparse once on the white hills,
Glow ruddier here against the thinned
Thieving of the schooled foreign crows.

I have not changed my country; I have grown and explored
In my faith's undivided world.
I discard no primal certainty, no rasped
Sky-sign of the Cross;
But now in broad autumn, feeling a new peace
And the old poise of defence,
I accept the pure trysting lochs,
The full antler in the glens.

Jack Clemo
20th century

WINTER

Winter Woe

Winter wakens all my care,
Now the leaves are waxing bare;
Oft I sigh and mourn sare*
When it come in my thought
Of this world's joy, how it goes all to nought.

Anonymous
about 1300

* *sare:* sore

A Better Resurrection

I have no wit, no words, no tears;
   My heart within me like a stone
Is numbed too much for hopes or fears;
   Look right, look left, I dwell alone;
I lift mine eyes, but dimmed with grief
     No everlasting hills I see;
My life is in the falling leaf
     O Jesus, quicken me.

My life is like a faded leaf,
   My harvest dwindled to a husk;
Truly my life is void and brief
   And tedious in the barren dusk;
My life is like a frozen thing,
     No bud nor greenness can I see:
Yet rise it shall—the sap of Spring;
     O Jesus, rise in me.

My life is like a broken bowl,
   A broken bowl that cannot hold
One drop of water for my soul
   Or cordial in the searching cold;
Cast in the fire the perished thing,
     Melt and remould it, till it be
A royal cup for him my King:
     O Jesus, drink of me.

Christina Rossetti
1830–94

November Sonnet

Spirit of place. Spirit of time. Re-form
The rugged oaks and chestnuts. Now they stand
Naked and pallid giants out of storm
And out of sorts. It is the Autumn's end

And this is Winter brought in by All Saints
Fast followed by All Souls to keep us in
Touch with chill and death. Each re-acquaints
Us with the year's end. Yet we now begin

A life of realism, watching out
For a red sunset, grateful for a dawn
Of rich light now. Tall shadows step and strut

Facing the big wind daily coming on
Faster. This is the season of right doubt
While that elected child waits to be born.

Elizabeth Jennings
20th century

Winter Now

'Tis winter now; the fallen snow
    Has left the heavens all coldly clear;
Through leafless boughs the sharp winds blow,
    And all the earth lies dead and drear.

And yet God's love is not withdrawn;
    His life within the keen air breathes;
His beauty paints the crimson dawn,
    And clothes the boughs with glittering wreaths.

And though abroad the sharp winds blow,
    And skies are chill, and frosts are keen,
Home closer draws her circle now,
    And warmer glows her light within.

O God! who giv'st the winter's cold,
    As well as summer's joyous rays,
Us warmly in thy love enfold,
    And keep us through life's wintry days.

Samuel Longfellow
1819–92

Shadows

And if to-night my soul may find her peace
in sleep, and sink in good oblivion,
and in the morning wake like a new-opened flower
then I have been dipped again in God, and new-created.

And if, as weeks go round, in the dark of the moon
my spirit darkens and goes out, and soft strange gloom
pervades my movements and my thoughts and words
then I shall know that I am walking still
with God, we are close together now the moon's in shadow.

And if, as autumn deepens and darkens
I feel the pain of falling leaves, and stems that break in storms
and trouble and dissolution and distress
and then the softness of deep shadows folding,
    folding around my soul and spirit, around my lips
so sweet, like a swoon, or more like the drowse of a low, sad song
singing darker than the nightingale, on, on to the solstice
and the silence of short days, the silence of the year, the shadow,
then I shall know that my life is moving still
with the dark earth, and drenched
with the deep oblivion of earth's lapse and renewal.

And if, in the changing phases of man's life
I fall in sickness and in misery
my wrists seem broken and my heart seems dead
and strength is gone, and my life
is only the leavings of a life:

and still, among it all, snatches of lovely oblivion, and snatches
    of renewal
odd, wintry flowers upon the withered stem, yet new, strange flowers
such as my life has not brought forth before, new blossoms of me:

then I must know that still
I am in the hands of the unknown God,
he is breaking me down to his own oblivion
to send me forth on a new morning, a new man.

D.H. Lawrence
1885–1930

Flos Campi

The rooftree of the year is fallen, fallen
and fallen is the splendour of the grass.
The great trees, barebone senators, observe
gravely the crepuscular season pass.

Here in the stripped pathology of winter
time's bleak agenda lately comes to light;
Summer's fluorescence now, and the autumn idyll
matters for hindsight, else an oversight.

This iron season, cloaked in fictive beauty,
the icefield's glory and the blizzard's pride;
and which of us at length has his desire?
or which in having it, is satisfied?

New rose, effulgent, out of time and season
flower of grace on Jesse's ancient tree,
Ah, be the benison of all beginnings,
the steadfast root in our declension be.

Kevin Nichols
20th century

Dance of the Months

January comes with his ice-crown.
February spilling thaw and snowdrops.
March, bursting loud cheeks!
Then April, with a troop of lambs and daffodils.
May, keeper of peat-hill and cuithe-stream.
June, covering the night fire in the north.
July, tall and blue as lupins.
August with the cut cornstalks.
September, dusting cobwebs from the lamp.
October, good witch, with apples and nuts.
November, host to shades and hallows.
December, with snowflake and star.

In the inn of December, a fire.
A loaf, a bottle of wine.
Travellers, rich and poor, are on the roads.

George Mackay Brown
20th century

THE PILGRIM'S WAY

From: The Lord of the Rings

The Road goes ever on and on
    Down from the door where it began.
Now far ahead the Road has gone,
    And I must follow, if I can,
Pursuing it with eager feet,
    Until it joins some larger way
Where many paths and errands meet.
    And whither then? I cannot say.

J.R.R. Tolkien
1892–1973

The Journey

The Pilgrim's Song

Who would true valour see
Let him come hither;
One here will constant be,
Come wind, come weather.
There's no discouragement
Shall make him once relent
His first avowed intent,
To be a pilgrim.

Who so beset him round
With dismal stories,
Do but themselves confound;
His strength the more is.
No lion can him fright,
He'll with a giant fight,
But he will have a right
To be a pilgrim.

Hobgoblin, nor foul fiend
Can daunt his spirit:
He knows he, at the end,
Shall life inherit.
Then fancies flee away,
He'll fear not what men say,
He'll labour night and day
To be a pilgrim.

John Bunyan 1628–88

Vox Ultima Crucis

Tarry no longer; toward thine heritage
Haste on thy way, and be of right good cheer.
Go each day onward on thy pilgrimage;
Think how short time thou hast abiden here.
Thy place is built above the starès clear,
No earthly palace wrought in so stately wise.
Come on, my friend, my brother may enter!
For thee I offered my blood in sacrifice.

John Lydgate 1370?–1450?

Uphill

Does the road wind uphill all the way?
  Yes, to the very end.
Will the day's journey take the whole long day?
  From morn to night, my friend.

But is there for the night a resting-place?
  A roof for when the slow, dark hours begin.
May not the darkness hide it from my face?
  You cannot miss that inn.

Shall I meet other wayfarers at night?
  Those who have gone before.
Then must I knock, or call when just in sight?
  They will not keep you waiting at that door.

Shall I find comfort, travel-sore and weak?
  Of labour you shall find the sum.
Will there be beds for me and all who seek?
  Yes, beds for all who come.

Christina Rossetti
1830–94

The Pilgrim's Aiding

God be with thee in every pass,
Jesus be with thee on every hill,
Spirit be with thee on every stream,
  Headland and ridge and lawn;

Each sea and land, each moor and meadow,
Each lying down, each rising up,
In the trough of the waves, on the crest of the billows,
  Each step of the journey thou goest.

Traditional Celtic
Collected by Alexander Carmichael
19th century

From: The Wanderer

Often the wanderer pleads for pity
and mercy from the Lord; but for a long time,
sad in mind, he must dip his oars
into icy waters, the lanes of the sea;
he must follow the paths of exile: fate is inflexible ...
A wise man must fathom how eerie it will be
when all the riches of the world stand waste,
as now in diverse places in this middle-earth
walls stand, tugged at by winds
and hung with hoar-frost, buildings in decay.
The wine-halls crumble, lords lie dead ...
'Here possessions are fleeting, here friends are fleeting,
here man is fleeting, here kinsman is fleeting,
the whole world becomes a wilderness.'
So spoke the wise man in his heart as he sat apart in thought.
Brave is the man who holds to his beliefs; nor shall he ever
show the sorrow in his heart before he knows how he
can hope to heal it. It is best for a man to seek
mercy and comfort from the Father in heaven where
security stands for us all.

Anonymous
about 850
translated by Kevin Crossley-Holland

Seek the Lord

Seek the Lord, and in his ways persever.
　　O faint not, but as eagles fly;
　　For his steep hill is high;
Then striving gain the top, and triumph ever.

When with glory there thy brows are crowned,
　　New joys so shall abound in thee,
　　Such sights thy soul shall see,
That worldly thoughts shall by their beams be drownèd.

Farewell, World, thou mass of mere confusion,
　　False light, with many shadows dimmed,
　　Old witch, with new foils trimmed,
Thou deadly sleep of soul, and charmed illusion.

I the King will seek, of kings adorèd;
　　Spring of light, tree of grace and bliss,
　　Whose fruit so sovereign is
That all who taste it are from death restorèd.

Thomas Campion
1567–1620

Road of my Desire

O thou who dost direct my feet
　　To right or left where pathways part,
Wilt thou not, faithful Paraclete
　　Direct the journeying of my heart?

Into the love of God, I pray,
　　Deeper and deeper let me press,
Exploring all along the way
　　Its secret strength and tenderness.

Into the steadfastness of one
　　Who patiently endured the cross.
Of him who, though he were a Son,
　　Came to his crown through bitter loss.

This is the road of my desire—
　　Learning to love as God loves me,
Ready to pass through flood or fire
　　With Christ's unwearying constancy.

Frank Houghton
1894–1972

From: To her Lord

Alas, how hard a thing
It is to bring
Into a true subjection flesh and blood,
Quietly to entertain
(And not complain)
Those exercises that attend for good!

My Life, my Joy, my Love,
If thus thou please to prove
And exercise my poor perplexèd mind,
Teach me to wait in fear,
That I may learn to hear
What trials may attend, of any kind:

And, guarded by thy ray,
Walk in the way,
That leads directly to the throne of grace;
Where in humility,
Poor I may be
Admitted to sit down in the heavenly place.

And there to thee discharge
My griefs at large,
As to a Bosom-Friend, that bears with me,
And often passes by
Faults of infirmity:
Alas! I cannot bear too much for thee!

Mary Mollineux   1648?–95

Prayer for the Journey

Here I am and forth I must,
And in Jesus Christ is all my trust.
No wicked thing do me no dere*,
Neither here nor elleswhere.
The Father with me, the Son with me,
The Holy Ghost, and the Trinity,
Be betwixt my ghostly enemy and me.
   In the name of the Father and the Son
   And the Holy Ghost, Amen.

Anonymous   Medieval

* *do me no dere*: do me any harm

~ 186 ~

A Journey Spell

I guard myself with this rod and give myself into God's protection,
Against the painful stroke, against the grievous stroke,
Against the grim dread,
Against the great terror which is hateful to each
And against all evil which may enter the land.
I chant a charm of victory, I bear a rod of victory,
Word-victory, work-victory. May they be of power for me ...
I pray now to the God of victory, to the mercy of God,
For a good journey, a mild and gentle
Wind from these shores. I have heard of winds
Which rouse whirling waters. Thus ever preserved
From all fiends may I meet friends,
So that I may dwell in the Almighty's protection,
Guarded from the enemy who seeks my life,
Set amid the glory of the angels,
And in the holy hand of the mighty one of heaven,
Whilst I may live in this life. Amen.

Anonymous
From a selection of Charms in the Anglo-Saxon Exeter Book *about 800*
translated by Ruth Etchell

From: The Growth of Love

3

Eternal Father, who didst all create,
In whom we live, and to whose bosom move,
To all men be thy name known, which is love,
Till its loud praises sound at heaven's high gate.
Perfect thy kingdom in our passing state,
That here on earth thou may'st as well approve
Our service, as thou ownest theirs above,
Whose joy we echo and in pain await.

Grant body and soul each day their daily bread:
And should in spite of grace fresh woe begin,
Even as our anger soon is past and dead
Be thy remembrance mortal of our sin:
By thee in paths of peace thy sheep be led,
And in the vale of terror comforted.

Robert Bridges
1844–1930

The Passionate Man's Pilgrimage

THOUGHT TO BE WRITTEN WHILE RALEGH WAS UNDER SENTENCE OF DEATH
IN THE TOWER OF LONDON IN 1603 OR JUST BEFORE HIS DEATH.

Give me my scallop-shell* of quiet,
My staff of faith to walk upon,
My scrip of joy, immortal diet,
My bottle of salvation,
My gown of glory, hope's true gage,
And thus I'll take my pilgrimage.

Blood must be my body's balmer,
No other balm will there be given,
While my soul like a white palmer
Travels to the land of heaven,
Over the silver mountains,
Where spring the nectar fountains;
And there I'll kiss
The bowl of bliss,
And drink my eternal fill
On every milken hill.
My soul will be a-dry before,
But after it will ne'er thirst more.

And by that happy blissful way
More peaceful pilgrims I shall see,
That have shook off their gowns of clay
And go apparelled fresh like me.
I'll bring them first
To slake their thirst,
And then to taste those nectar suckets*
At the clear wells
Where sweetness dwells,
Drawn up by saints in crystal buckets...

And this is my eternal plea
To him that made heaven, earth and sea:
Seeing my flesh must die so soon,
And want a head to dine next noon,
Just at the stroke when my veins start and spread,
Set on my soul an everlasting head.
Then am I ready, like a palmer fit,
To tread those blest paths which before I writ.

Sir Walter Ralegh
about 1552–1618

* *scallop shell*: a pilgrim's badge; *suckets*: sweetmeats, usually fruit candied in syrup.

'I Am the Way'

Thou art the Way
Hadst thou been nothing but the goal
    I cannot say
If thou hadst ever met my soul.

    I cannot see—
I, child of process—if there lies
    An end for me
Full of repose, full of replies.

    I'll not reproach
The road that winds, my feet that err.
    Access, Approach
Art thou, Time, Way, and Wayfarer.

Alice Meynell
1847–1922

From: Paradise Lost

ADAM AND EVE ARE BANISHED FROM PARADISE

They, looking back, all the eastern side beheld
Of Paradise, so late their happy seat,
Waved over by that flaming brand, the gate
With dreadful faces thronged and fiery arms.
Some natural tears they dropped, but wiped them soon;
The world was all before them, where to choose
Their place of rest, and Providence their guide:
They hand in hand, with wandering steps and slow,
Through Eden took their solitary way.

John Milton
1608–74

Restlessness

Weighing the steadfastness and state
Of some mean things which here below reside,
Where birds like watchful clocks the noiseless date
    And intercourse of times divide,
Where bees at night get home and hive, and flowers
    Early as well as late,
Rise with the sun, and set in the same bowers;

I would (said I) my God would give
The staidness of these things to man! for these
To his divine appointments ever cleave,
    And no new business breaks their peace;
The birds nor sow, nor reap, yet sup and dine,
    The flowers without clothes live,
Yet Solomon was never dressed so fine.

Man hath still either toys, or care,
He hath no root, nor to one place is tied,
But ever restless and irregular
    About this earth doth run and ride,
He knows he hath a home, but scarce knows where,
    He says it is so far
That he hath quite forgot how to go there.

He knocks at all doors, strays and roams,
Nor hath not so much wit as some stones have
Which in the darkest nights point to their homes,
    By some hid sense their Maker gave;
Man is the shuttle, to whose winding quest
    And passage through these looms
God ordered motion, but ordained no rest.

Henry Vaughan
1622–95

Faith and Doubt

Prayer

We doubt the Word that tells us: Ask,
And ye shall have your prayer:
We turn our thoughts as to a task,
With will constrained and rare.

And yet we have; these scanty prayers
Yield gold without alloy:
O God, but he that trusts and dares
Must have a boundless joy!

George MacDonald
1824–1905

From: Samson Agonistes

All is best, though we oft doubt,
What the unsearchable dispose
Of highest wisdom brings about,
And ever best found in the close.
Oft he seems to hide his face,
But unexpectedly returns
And to his faithful Champion hath in place
Bore witness gloriously; whence Gaza mourns
And all that band them to resist
His uncontrollable intent.
His servants he with new acquist
Of true experience from this great event
With peace and consolation hath dismissed,
And calm of mind all passion spent.

John Milton
1608–74

Agnosticism

It doesn't come easy.

In spite of it all,
I can't help pushing open
the doors of country churches;
shoving a coin or two
in the box on the wall,
paying twice over
for the leaflet I take.

It doesn't come easy.

Wandering among gravestones
is irresistible;
departure is almost
impossible. I delay
it over and over
to hear once more the song of the blackbird.

It doesn't come easy.

As I race back
into the modern
rationalistic world,
I think of cathedral towns
and country rectories
and gentle rectors' wives
arranging the flowers.

John Tatum
20th century

Adrift

Unto my faith as to a spar, I bring
   My love—and Faith and Love adrift I cast
   On a dim sea. I know not if at last
They the eternal shore of God shall find.

I know that neither waves nor wind
   Can sunder them, the cords are tied so fast
   That faith shall never—doubts and dangers past—
Come safe to land and Love be left behind.

By the wife of Edward Dowden
1843–1913
(Possibly his second wife, Elizabeth Dickinson)

Death on a Crossing

What he never thought to consider was whether
the thing was true. What bewildered him, mostly,
was the way that the rumours had of reaching him
from such improbable sources—illiterate pamphlets
pressed in his hand, the brash or the floundering stranger
who came to his door, the proclamations, among
so many others, on hoardings

        though sometimes waking
a brief dismay, that never quite prodded him
to the analyst's couch.

        But annunciations, he thought,
should come to a rational man in a rational way.
He walked between a skyful of midnight angels
and a patch on somebody's jeans, both saying
the same thing to his stopped ears

        till the day
when he stepped on a crossing with not enough conviction
to get him safe to the other side, and he lay
among strangers' feet, and the angels lowered their trumpets
and no sweet chariot swung, to carry him home.

Evangeline Paterson
20th century

Creation

This Chinese bowl
is barely tangible,
thin-skinned
as if spun from light.

Poised between
form and disintegration,
it almost breaks
at the edge of vision;

a taut perfection.

We whisper
lest our voices turn
it to dust,
know tenderness at
the passion of its survival.

It's the tremor
we feel when children
in cardboard crowns
tell the Christmas story.

This is our faith;
worked clay defeating death.

Isobel Thrilling 20th century

Story

For us there are no certainties, no star
blazing our journey, no decisive dream
to reassure hurt hearts or warn us when
it's time to move. The shepherds, harassed men,
are given answers to the questions they
have never thought to ask. Told where to go
and what to look for. We try out our way
unlit with angels, wondering 'How far?'
Yet in the story we find who we are:
the baby is told nothing, left to grow
slowly to vision through the coloured scheme
of touch, taste, sound; by needing learns to pray,
and makes the way of the flesh, dark strategem
by which God is and offers all we know.

Jennifer Dines 20th century

Thanksgiving

We give thanks for St Thomas
   All we who have known
   The darkness of disbelief,
The hollowness at the heart of Christmas,
The intolerable emptiness of Easter,
   The grief of separation.

With thy great mercy thou dost enfold us,
The waverers, the aliens, who stood apart, alone.
   For the impoverishments of our barren years
     Thou wilt atone.

Now with the faithful company we bring,
From depths of thankfulness
   Our adoration
    To thee,
O, Christ our King.

Edith Forrest
20th century

Paradox

Mild yoke of Christ, most harsh to me not bearing,
You bruise the neck that balks, the hands that break you;
Sweet bread and wine, bitter to me not sharing,
You scar and scorch the throat that will not take you;
Mount where he taught, you cripple feet not bloody
From your sharp flints of eight-fold benediction;
Bright cross, most shameful stripped of the stripped body,
You crucify me safe from crucifixion:
Yet I, who am my own dilemma, jolting
My mind with thought lest it unthink its stiffness,
Rise to revolt against my own revolting
Blind me to blindness, deafen me to deafness.
So will your gifts of sight and hearing plunder
My eyes with lightning and my ears with thunder.

Vassar Miller
20th century

From: Lord of the Rings

In western lands beneath the Sun
   the flowers may rise in Spring,
the trees may bud, the waters run,
   the merry finches sing.
Or there maybe 'tis cloudless night
   and swaying beeches bear
the Elven-stars as jewels white
   amid their branching hair.

Though here at journey's end I lie
   in darkness buried deep,
beyond all towers strong and high,
   beyond all mountains steep,
above all shadows rides the Sun
   and Stars for ever dwell:
I will not say the Day is done,
   nor bid the Stars farewell.

J.R.R. Tolkien
1892–1973

Mock on! Mock on!

Mock on, mock on, Voltaire, Rousseau;
Mock on, mock on: 'tis all in vain!
You throw the sand against the wind,
And the wind blows it back again.

And every sand becomes a gem
Reflected in the beams divine;
Blown back they blind the mocking eye,
But still in Israel's path they shine.

The atoms of Democritus
And Newton's particles of light
Are sands upon the Red Sea shore,
Where Israel's tents do shine so bright.

William Blake
1757–1827

E Tenebris

Come down, O Christ, and help me! reach thy hand,
For I am drowning in a stormier sea
Than Simon on the lake of Galilee:
The wine of life is spilt upon the sand,
My heart is as some famine-murdered land
Whence all good things have perished utterly,
And well I know my soul in Hell must lie
If I this night before God's throne should stand.
'He sleeps perchance, or rideth to the chase,
Like Baal, when his prophets howled that name
From morn to noon on Carmel's smitten height.'
Nay, peace, I shall behold, before the night,
The feet of brass, the robe more white than flame,
The wounded hands, the weary human face.

Oscar Wilde
1856–1900

After reading the life of Mrs Catherine Stubbs, in Isaac Ambrose's *War with the Devils*

Devil! I tell thee without nubbs or jubbs.
Thou wert no match at all for Catherine Stubbs,
And if her God give grace to play the man,
Thou wilt come off as bad with Isaac Hann.
For all the arguments she used shall be
The arguments which he will use with thee:
And when thou canst those arguments repel
He must submit to go with thee to hell;
But while his Saviour God doth live and reign
He is secure—gang off with thy cracked brain!
God is a sun and shield to every saint,
A cordial to their souls whene'er they faint;
He will give grace and glory we are told
And no good thing will he from them withhold.

Isaac Hann
1690–1778

Dover Beach

The sea is calm to-night,
The tide is full, the moon lies fair
Upon the Straits;—on the French coast, the light
Gleams and is gone; the cliffs of England stand,
Glimmering and vast, out in the tranquil bay.
Come to the window, sweet is the night air!
Only, from the long line of spray
Where the ebb meets the moon-blanched sand,
Listen! you hear the grating roar
Of pebbles which the waves suck back, and fling,
At their return, up the high strand,
Begin, and cease, and then again begin,
With tremulous cadence slow, and bring
The eternal note of sadness in.

　　Sophocles long ago
Heard it on the Aegean, and it brought
Into his mind the turbid ebb and flow
Of human misery; we
Find also in the sound a thought,
Hearing it by this distant northern sea.

The sea of faith
Was once, too, at the full, and round earth's shore
Lay like the folds of a bright girdle furled;
But now I only hear
Its melancholy, long, withdrawing roar,
Retreating to the breath
Of the night-wind down the vast edges drear
And naked shingles of the world.

Ah, love, let us be true
To one another! for the world, which seems
To lie before us like a land of dreams,
So various, so beautiful, so new,
Hath really neither joy, nor love, nor light,
Nor certitude, nor peace, nor help for pain;
And we are here as on a darkling plain
Swept with confused alarms of struggle and flight,
Where ignorant armies clash by night.

Matthew Arnold
1822–88

Tidal

The waves run up the shore
and fall back. I run
up the approaches of God
and fall back. The breakers return
reaching a little further,
gnawing away at the main land.
They have done this thousands
of years, exposing little by little
the rock under the soil's face.
I must imitate them only
in my return to the assault,
not in their violence. Dashing
my prayers at him will achieve
little other than the exposure
of the rock under the surface.
My returns must be made
on my knees. Let despair be known
as my ebb-tide; but let prayer
have its springs, too, brimming,
disarming him; discovering somewhere
among his fissures deposits of mercy
where trust may take root and grow.

R.S. Thomas
20th century

Amor Dei

Give me to be thy child, and learn for ever at thy knee.
Give me to grow weak and grey-headed, since thou willst it so.
Bid me aside
Lay all the pleasures of my youth and pride,
Gladness as well,
Sweet ardours and bright hopes—I'll not rebel.

Only, I pray, keep me beside thee all the night and day,
Only for all thou takest give thyself and past recall!
And when youth's gone
As men count going, twixt us two alone
Still let me be
Thy little child, left learning at thy knee.

Anonymous

From: The Eternal Goodness

I know not what the future hath
Of marvel or surprise,
Assured alone that life and death
His mercy underlies.

And if my heart and flesh are weak
To bear an untried pain,
The bruised reed he will not break,
But strengthen and sustain.

No offering of my own I have,
Nor works my faith to prove;
I can but give the gifts he gave,
And plead his love for love.

And so beside the silent sea
I wait the muffled oar;
No harm from him can come to me
On ocean or on shore.

I know not where his islands lift
Their fronded palms in air;
I only know I cannot drift
Beyond his love and care.

John Greenleaf Whittier 1807–92

No Worst

No worst, there is none. Pitched past pitch of grief,
More pangs will, schooled at forepangs, wilder wring.
Comforter, where, where is your comforting?
Mary, mother of us, where is your relief?
My cries heave, herds-long; huddle in a main, a chief-
woe, world-sorrow; on an age-old anvil wince and sing—
Then lull, then leave off. Fury had shrieked 'No linge-
ring! Let me be fell: force I must be brief'.
O the mind, mind has mountains; cliffs of fall
Frightful, sheer, no-man-fathomed. Hold them cheap
May who ne'er hung there. Nor does long our small
Durance deal with that steep or deep. Here! creep,
Wretch, under a comfort serves in a whirlwind: all
Life death does end and each day dies with sleep.

Gerard Manley Hopkins 1844–89

Latter Day Psalms

2

The tree waves in the wind
But does not break unless
The bough is over-burdened.
When spring disrupts the dead days
Buds, leaves, and birds praise God
In song and silent sound.

The dead dock, stiff
With last year's pride,
Leans unwillingly in the gale.

My heart, Lord, is unyielding.
My joints are stiff
The knuckles of my knees
Refuse to bend.
The knife is at my neck,
My back breaks.

I will say my matutinal prayers
From a crippled position,
Perhaps the Lord will hear?

4

On the estate, Lord, the people
Take counsel one with another
And in the public house
There is lamentation.
The cost of living soars
Like wild duck rising
After morning feed.
Man has neither means nor meaning.
The cry of the young in the street
Rouses a protest in the market place.
    What shall I do, Lord?
Though I bring my sad soul
And place it at your feet,
My mouth is bitter, for fear
Infects my hand and heart.
The pit of hell yawns wide
Before my floundering feet,
I slip, I slide, I fall,
I try to grasp a skylark
But it flies south for summer.
    My mind is melancholic,
    I cannot praise my maker.

Cliff Ashby 20th century

From: Abt Vogler

IX

Therefore to whom turn I but to thee, the ineffable Name?
Builder and maker, thou, of houses not made with hands!
What, have fear of change from thee who art ever the same?
Doubt that thy power can fill the heart that thy power expands?
There shall never be one lost good! What was, shall live as before;
The evil is null, is nought, is silence implying sound;
What was good shall be good, with, for evil, so much good more;
On the earth the broken arcs; in the heaven, a perfect round.

X

All we have willed or hoped or dreamed of good shall exist;
Not its semblance, but itself; no beauty, nor good, nor power
Whose voice has gone forth, but each survives for the melodist
When eternity affirms the conception of an hour.
The high that proved too high, the heroic for earth too hard,
The passion that left the ground to lose itself in the sky,
Are music sent up to God by the lover and the bard;
Enough that he heard it once: we shall hear it by-and-by.

Robert Browning
1812–89

Aridity

O soul, canst thou not understand
Thou art not left alone,
As a dog to howl and moan
His master's absence? Thou art as a book
Left in a room that he forsook,
But returns to by and by,
A book of his dear choice,—
That quiet waiteth for his Hand,
That quiet waiteth for his Eye,
That quiet waiteth for his Voice.

Michael Field
(Katharine Bradley 1846–1914
and Edith Cooper 1862–1913)

Many As Two

'Where there is the green thing
life springs clean.'
   Yes. There is blessed life, in
   bywaters; and in pondslime
   but not for your drinking.
'Where the heart's room
deepens, and the thrum
of the touched heartstrings reverberates——*vroom*—
there I am home.'
   Yes. And the flesh's doom
   is—a finally welcome going out on a limb?
   or a terror you who love dare not name?
   (No thing abiding.)
No sign, no magic, no roadmap, no
pre-tested foothold. 'Only that you know
there is the way, plain,
and the home-going.'

Outside the heartbreak home I know, I can own
no other.
   'The brokenness. I know.
   Alone.'
(Go with us, then?)

      Margaret Avison
      20th century

Faith Unfaithful

   Mute, with signs I speak:
   Blind, by groping seek:
   Heed; yet nothing hear:
   Feel; find no one near.

   Deaf, eclipsed, and dumb,
   Through this gloom I come
   On the time-path trod
   Towards ungranted God.

   Carnal, I can claim
   Only his known name
   Dying, can but be
   One with him in me.

      Siegfried Sassoon
      1886–1967

Last Lines

('THE FOLLOWING ARE THE LAST LINES MY SISTER EMILY EVER WROTE.'
CHARLOTTE BRONTË)

No coward soul is mine,
No trembler in the world's storm-troubled sphere:
I see Heaven's glories shine,
And faith shines equal, arming me from fear.

O God within my breast,
Almighty, ever-present Deity!
Life—that in me has rest,
As I—undying Life—have power in thee!

Vain are the thousand creeds
That move men's hearts: unutterably vain;
Worthless as withered weeds,
Or idlest froth amid the boundless main,

To waken doubt in one
Holding so fast by thine infinity;
So surely anchored on
The steadfast rock of immortality.

With wide-embracing love
Thy spirit animates eternal years,
Pervades and broods above,
Changes, sustains, dissolves, creates and rears.

Though earth and man were gone,
And suns and universes ceased to be,
And thou wert left alone,
Every existence would exist in thee.

There is not room for Death,
Nor atom that his might could render void:
Thou—THOU art Being and Breath,
And what THOU art may never be destroyed.

Emily Brontë
1818–48

Auguries of Innocence

To see a World in a grain of sand,
And a Heaven in a wild flower,
Hold Infinity in the palm of your hand,
And Eternity in an hour...

The bat that flits at close of eve
Has left the brain that won't believe.
The owl that calls upon the night
Speaks the unbeliever's fright...

Joy and woe are woven fine,
A clothing for the soul divine;
Under every grief and pine
Runs a joy with silken twine...

He who doubts from what he sees
Will ne'er believe, do what you please.
If the Sun and Moon should doubt,
They'd immediately go out...

God appears and God is Light,
To those poor souls who dwell in Night;
But does a Human Form display
To those who dwell in realms of Day...

William Blake
1757–1827

Abdication of Belief

Those—dying then,
Knew where they went—
They went to God's Right Hand
That Hand is amputated now
And God cannot be found—

The abdication of Belief
Makes the Behaviour small—
Better an ignis fatuus
Than no illume at all—

Emily Dickinson
1830–86

From: Bishop Blougram's Apology

Why first, you don't believe, you don't and can't,
(Not statedly, that is, and fixedly
And absolutely and exclusively)
In any revelation called divine.
No dogmas nail your faith; and what remains
But say so, like the honest man you are?
First, therefore, overhaul theology!
Nay, I too, not a fool, you please to think,
Must find believing every whit as hard:
And if I do not frankly say as much,
The ugly consequence is clear enough.

Now wait, my friend: well, I do not believe—
If you'll accept no faith that is not fixed,
Absolute and exclusive, as you say.
You're wrong—I mean to prove it in due time.
Meanwhile, I know where difficulties lie
I could not, cannot solve, nor ever shall,
So give up hope accordingly to solve—
(To you, and over the wine). Our dogmas then
With both of us, though in unlike degree,
Missing full credence—overboard with them!
I mean to meet you on your own premise:
Good, there go mine in company with yours!

And now what are we? unbelievers both,
Calm and complete, determinately fixed
Today, to-morrow and for ever, pray?
You'll guarantee me that? Not so, I think!
In no wise! All we've gained is, that belief,
As unbelief before, shakes us by fits,
Confounds us like its predecessor. Where's
The gain? how can we guard our unbelief,
Make it bear fruit to us—the problem here.
Just when we are safest, there's a sunset-touch,
A fancy from a flower-bell, someone's death,
A chorus-ending from Euripides,—
And that's enough for fifty hopes and fears
As old and new at once as nature's self,
To rap and knock and enter in our soul,
Take hands and dance there, a fantastic ring,
Round the ancient idol, on his base again,—
The grand Perhaps! We look on helplessly.
There the old misgivings, crooked questions are—
This good God,—what he could do if he would,

Would if he could—then must have done long since:
If so, when, where and how? some way must be,—
Once feel about, and soon or late you hit
Some sense, in which it might be, after all.
Why not, 'The Way, the Truth, the Life'?

Robert Browning
1812–89

Adam in the Garden

Adam in the suburban garden
Among the television trees,
Tasting the fruit of the Tree of Knowledge,
Carelessly tosses the core over his shoulder.

It explodes, brilliant as a million acetylene torches,
Deafening as a million sonic booms.
It shatters the picture windows and knocks
The cross of First Church out of the sky.

The sun hides his face behind a mushroom cloud.
The clock on the Federal Building and Loan Office
No longer reports the interest rate
Or flashes the time and temperature.

The net alert station is silent,
Huntley and Brinkley fail to report the flash,
Church bells are silent. Sermons on
Unilateral disarmament have been cancelled.

God, abandoned, lonely, obscured by smoke,
Stubs his toe on a steeple
Buried in the ashes of the garden and
Calls, 'Adam, where are you?'

Elmer F. Suderman
20th century

The Slip

The river takes the land and leaves nothing.
Where the great slip gave way in the bank
and an acre disappeared, all human plans
dissolve. An aweful clarification occurs
where a place was. Its memory breaks
from what is known now, and begins to drift.
Where cattle grazed and trees stood, emptiness
widens the air for birdflight, wind, and rain.
As before the beginning, nothing is there.
Human wrong is in the cause, human
ruin in the effect—but no matter;
all will be lost, no matter the reason.
Nothing, having arrived, will stay.
The earth, even, is like a flower, so soon
passeth it away. And yet this nothing
is the seed of all—heaven's clear
eye, where all the worlds appear.
Where the imperfect has departed, the perfect
begins its struggle to return. The good gift
begins again its descent. The maker moves
in the unmade, stirring the water until
it clouds, dark beneath the surface,
stirring and darkening the soul until pain
perceives new possibility. There is nothing
to do but learn and wait, return to work
on what remains. Seed will sprout in the scar.
Though death is in the healing, it will heal.

Wendell Berry 20th century

The Journey

And if you go up that way, you will meet with a man
Leading a horse, whose eyes declare:
There is no God. Take no notice.
There will be other roads and other men
With the same creed, whose lips yet utter
Friendlier greeting, men who have learned
To pack a little of the sun's light
In their cold eyes, whose hands are waiting
For your hand. But do not linger.
A smile is payment; the road runs on
With many turnings towards the tall
Tree to which the believer is nailed.

R.S. Thomas 20th century

A Highland Testimony

We had our ritual too. Down the long glen
While startled curlews cried on ebb-tide sands,
We all would walk, our Bibles in our hands,
And winter sunshine turned to rain again.

The crisp and cutting edge of our dark suits
Served as a weekly penance. We, in turn
Would kick some chuckies into ditch or burn,
And scuff the polish on our Sunday boots.

The church bell spread its iron news abroad,
Dull through the trees or clear across the bay.
With quickened step we hastened on our way.
And so we entered in the house of God.

Thus went the ritual of that far-off day.
The creak of bell and bell-rope clanged and jarred.
The psalms were dignified. The pews were hard.
The rain was soft. The lowering skies were grey.

Grey too the tenor of our world today.
The death of humanism, sick and sad.
And I could wish that once again we had
That child's acceptance of the Christian way.

Faith of my fathers. If it came again,
I would not change a moment of my youth,
The grey kirk and the straight unflinching truth,
Clean as the stones at the burn-side in the glen.

Alistair Halden
20th century

From: On Exodus 3:14 'I am that I am'

AN ODE

Man! Foolish Man!
Scarce know'st thou how thy self began;
Scarce hast thou thought enough to prove thou art;
Yet steeled with studied boldness, thou dar'st try
To send thy doubting reason's dazzled eye
Through the mysterious gulf of vast immensity.
Much thou canst there discern, much thence impart.
   Vain wretch! Suppress thy knowing pride
      Mortify thy learned lust:
Vain are thy thoughts, while thou thyself art dust...

Let cunning earth her fruitful wonders hide;
And only lift thy staggering Reason up
To trembling Calvary's astonished top;
Then mock thy knowledge, and confound thy pride,
Explaining how Perfection suffered pain,
Almighty languished, and Eternal died:
How by her patient victor Death was slain;
And Earth profaned, yet blessed, with deicide.
Then down with all thy boasted volumes, down;
   Only reserve the sacred one:
      Low, reverently low,
Make thy stubborn knowledge bow:
Weep out thy Reason's, and thy body's, eyes;
Deject thyself, that thou may'st rise;
To look to Heaven, be blind to all below.

Then Faith, for Reason's glimmering light, shall give
   Her immortal perspective;
And grace's presence nature's loss retrieve:
Then thy enlivened soul shall see
That all the volumes of philosophy,
With all their comments, never could invent
   So politic an instrument
To reach the Heaven of Heavens, the high abode
Where Moses places his mysterious God,
As was that ladder which old Jacob reared,
When light divine had human darkness cleared;
And his enlarged Ideas found the road
Which Faith had dictated, and angels trod.

Matthew Prior
1664–1721

From: In Memoriam

Strong Son of God, immortal Love,
    Whom we, that have not seen thy face,
    By faith, and faith alone, embrace,
Believing where we cannot prove;

Thine are these orbs of light and shade;
    Thou madest life in man and brute;
    Thou madest death; and lo, thy foot
Is on the skull which thou hast made.

Thou wilt not leave us in the dust:
    Thou madest man, he knows not why,
    He thinks he was not made to die;
And thou hast made him: thou art just.

Thou seemest human and divine,
    The highest, holiest manhood, thou:
    Our wills are ours, we know not how;
Our wills are ours, to make them thine.

Our little systems have their day;
    They have their day and cease to be:
    They are but broken lights of thee,
And thou, O Lord, art more than they.

We have but faith: we cannot know;
    For knowledge is of things we see;
    And yet we trust it comes from thee,
A beam in darkness: let it grow...

Forgive these wild and wandering cries,
    Confusion of a wasted youth;
    Forgive them where they fail in truth,
And in thy wisdom make me wise.

Alfred, Lord Tennyson
1809–92

Light Shining out of Darkness

God moves in a mysterious way
    His wonders to perform;
He plants his footsteps in the sea,
    And rides upon the storm.

Deep in unfathomable mines
    Of never-failing skill
He treasures up his bright designs
    And works his sovereign will.

Ye fearful saints, fresh courage take:
    The clouds ye so much dread
Are big with mercy, and shall break
    In blessings on your head.

Judge not the Lord by feeble sense,
    But trust him for his grace;
Behind a frowning providence
    He hides a smiling face.

His purposes will ripen fast,
    Unfolding every hour;
The bud may have a bitter taste,
    But sweet will be the flower.

Blind unbelief is sure to err,
    And scan his work in vain;
God is his own interpreter,
    And he will make it plain.

William Cowper
1731–1800

The Struggle of Good and Evil

The Harrowing of Hell

Love asks to penetrate
The hot dark place,
The place of pain,
From which the sons of light
Hide their modest faces.
Love is allowed.
And oh! what gnashing of teeth
Among the demons
Who thought it was their own!

D.M. Lewis   20th century

The Coronet

When for the thorns with which I long, too long,
   With many a piercing wound,
   My Saviour's head have crowned,
I seek with garlands to redress that wrong,
   Through every garden, every mead,
I gather flowers (my fruits are only flowers)
   Dismantling all the fragrant towers*
That once adorned my Shepherdess's head.
And now when I have summoned up all my store,
   Thinking (so I myself deceive)
   So rich a chaplet thence to weave
As never yet the King of Glory wore,
   Alas, I find the Serpent old
   That, twining in his speckled breast,
   About the flowers disguised does fold,
   With wreaths of fame and interest.
Ah, foolish man, that would'st debase with them,
And mortal glory, Heaven's diadem!
But thou who only could'st the Serpent tame,
Either his slippery knots at once untie,
And disentangle all his winding snare,
Or shatter too with him my curious* frame;
And let these wither, so that he may die,
Though set with skill and chosen out with care.
That they, while thou on both their spoils dost tread,
May crown thy feet, that could not crown thy head.

Andrew Marvell   1621–78
* *towers*: high head-dresses; *curious*: elaborately wrought

The Crucifixion

'String him up,' some repoman shouted,
'He's a weirdo.' 'In the bin, in the bin,'
Yelled another and grabbed some thorns,
Sharp as needles, twisting them round
A fresh-cut thorn branch. He made
A wreath and forced it down on his head,
The pain piercing his flesh. 'Morning, vicar,'
This comedian said and darted twigs
At him, aiming at his eyes. With three
Nails, he nailed him naked to a cross,
Lifted bitter drink to his lips, telling
Him drink and stop dropping off, hang
On a bit longer. 'Now if he's really something,'
He said, 'He'll get himself out of this one.
If you're Christ, and if Christ is God's
Son, come on down, off that cross.
We'll believe it then, you've got life
On a string, you're never going to be
            A goner.'
            'That's it,'
            Christ said,
            'That's it.'

            His senses
            Began to fade
            Pale and piteous
            Like a prisoner
            In death, the lord
            Of life and light
            Closed his eyes, day
            Shrank back, appalled,
            And the sun darkened.
            The Temple wall
            Shattered and split,
            The solid rocks
            Of earth ruptured.
            It was dark
            As thickest night,
            Earth convulsed,
            Quaked like a live thing.
            The noise brought
            Dead men clambering up
            From the coffined depths
            Who told why the tempest
            Raged so long.

One corpse said,
'There is in darkness
Here a bitter fight.
Life and Death
Destroy each other.
None can know
For sure who wins
Till Sunday
As the sun rises,'
And with these words
Sank back in earth.

From Piers Plowman, *by William Langland*
1330?–1400?
translated by Ronald Tamplin

Retreat

The enclosed garden, sensuous and chaste;
darkly, through bars, perceive angelic bees
dusting with gilded fur the flowers' lips.
The calf and the young lion lying down
beneath the laden, scented shade of trees
and guards with flaming swords at the east gates.

Outside, never enough to storm them,
never one enough. Heroic sacrifice
brings babel siege-towers down about our ears;
scapegoats and saboteurs are freighted out
on dwindling rails that meet the wilderness;
gardens of wire and huts with floors of blood.

The blood for milk and tears for honeydew
and smoke which never palls, always disperses
under heaven like perjurious prayers;
strong fingers dip into torn carcasses
and tongues lap sweetness hid in hives of bone.

There is a way, retreat. A swathe runs back
through thistles to skull-hill; one bare tree's shade
cast in the rocks' arena of defeat.
Deserted now, through-route when stone rolls back,
the tomb, unstoppered, spills the garden's light.

Paul Hyland
20th century

Hope in the Darkness

Say not the struggle naught availeth,
   The labour and the wounds are vain,
The enemy faints not, nor faileth,
   And as things have been they remain.

If hopes were dupes, fears may be liars;
   It may be, in yon smoke concealed,
Your comrades chase e'en now the fliers,
   And, but for you, possess the field.

For while the tired waves, vainly breaking,
   Seem here no painful inch to gain,
Far back, through creeks and inlets making,
   Comes silent, flooding in, the main.

And not by eastern windows only,
   When daylight comes, comes in the light;
In front the sun climbs slow, how slowly!
   But westward, look, the land is bright!

Arthur Hugh Clough
1819–61

Psalm 62 Nonne Deo

Yet shall my soul in silence still
   On God, my help, attentive stay:
Yet he my fort, my health, my hill,
   Remove I may not, move I may.
How long then shall your fruitless will
   An enemy so far from fall,
With weak endeavour strive to kill,
   You rotten hedge, you broken wall?

Forsooth, that he no more may rise,
   Advanced again to throne and crown:
To headlong him their thoughts devise,
   And, past relief, to tread him down.
Their love is only love of lies:
   Their words and deeds dissenting so,
When from their lips most blessing flies,
   Then deepest curse in heart doth grow.

Yet shall my soul in silence still
   On God, my hope, attentive stay:
Yet he my fort, my health, my hill,
   Remove? O no: not move I may.
My God doth me with glory fill,
   Not only shield me safe from harm:
To shun distress, to conquer ill,
   To him I climb, in him I arm.

O then, on God, our certain stay,
   All people in all times rely,
Your hearts before him naked lay:
   To Adam's sons 'tis vain to fly,
So vain so false, so frail are they;
   E'en he that seemeth most of might
With lightness' self if him you weigh,
   Then lightness' self will weigh more light.

In fraud, and force, no trust repose:
   Such idle hopes from thoughts expel,
And take good heed, when riches grows
   Let not your heart on riches dwell.
All power is God's, his own word shows,
   Once said by him, twice heard by me:
Yet from thee, Lord, all mercy flows,
   And each man's work is paid by thee.

Mary Herbert, Countess of Pembroke
1562–1621

From: To Keep the Cold Wind Away

There blows a cold wind today, today,
   The wind blows cold today;
Christ suffered his passion for man's salvation,
   To keep the cold wind away.

This wind by reason is called temptation
   It rages both night and day.
Remember, man, how the Saviour was slain
   To keep the cold wind away.

Pride and presumption and false extortion,
   That many man doth betray—
Man, come to contrition and ask confession
   To keep the cold wind away.

O Mary mild, for love of the child
   That died on Good Friday,
Be our salvation from mortal damnation
   To keep the cold wind away.

He was nailed, his blood was haled*,
   Our remission for to buy;
And for our sins all he drank both eisel* and gall
   To keep the cold wind away

Sloth, envy, covetousness and lechery
   Blow the cold wind, as I dare say;
Against such poison he suffered his passion
   To keep the cold wind away.

Anonymous
about 1500

* *haled:* drawn; *eisel:* vinegar

From: Samson Agonistes

O how comely it is and how reviving
To the spirits of just men long oppressed,
When God into the hands of their deliverer
Puts invincible might
To quell the mighty of the earth, the oppressor,
The brute and boisterous force of violent men,
Hardy and industrious to support
Tyrannic power, but raging to pursue
The righteous and all such as honour truth!
He all their ammunition
And feats of war defeats
With plain heroic magnitude of mind
And celestial vigour armed;
Their armouries and magazines contemns,
Renders them useless, while
With winged expedition
Swift as the lightning glance he executes
His errand on the wicked, who surprised,
Lose their defence, distracted and amazed.
       But patience is more oft the exercise
Of saints, the trial of their fortitude,
Making them each his own deliverer,
And victor over all
That tyranny or fortune can inflict;
Either of these is in thy lot,
Samson, with might endued
Above the sons of men; but sight bereaved
May chance to number thee with those
Whom patience finally must crown.

John Milton
1608–74

'Faint Yet Pursuing'

Heroic Good, target for which the young
Dream in their dreams that every bow is strung,
And, missing, sigh
Unfruitful, or as disbelievers die,
Thee having missed, I will not so revolt,
But lowlier shoot my bolt,
And lowlier still, if still I may not reach,
And my proud stomach teach
That less than highest is good, and may be high,
An even walk in life's uneven way,
Though to have dreamt of flight and not to fly
Be strange and sad,
Is not a boon that's given to all who pray.
If this I had
I'd envy none!
Nay, trod I straight for one
Year, month or week,
Should Heaven withdraw, and Satan me amerce
Of power and joy, still would I seek
Another victory with a like reverse;
Because the good of victory does not die,
As dies the failure's curse,
And what we have to gain
Is, not one battle, but a weary life's campaign.
Yet meaner lot being sent
Should more than me content;
Yea, if I lie
Among vile shards, though born for silver wings,
In the strong flight and feathers gold
Of whatsoever heavenward mounts and sings
I must by admiration so comply
That there I should my own delight behold.
Yea, though I sin each day times seven,
And dare not lift the fearfullest eyes to Heaven,
Thanks must I give
Because that seven times are not eight or nine,
And that my darkness is all mine,
And that I live
Within this oak-shade one more minute even,
Hearing the winds their Maker magnify.

Coventry Patmore
1823–96

Hymn for the Church Militant

Great God, that bowest sky and star
Bow down our towering thoughts to thee,
And grant us in a faltering war
   The firm feet of humility.

Lord, we that snatch the swords of flame,
Lord, we that cry about thy ear,
We too are weak with pride and shame,
   We too are as our foemen are.

Yea, we are mad as they are mad,
Yea, we are blind as they are blind,
Yea, we are very sick and sad
   Who bring good news to all mankind.

The dreadful joy thy Son has sent
Is heavier than any care;
We find, as Cain his punishment,
   Our pardon more than we can bear.

Lord, when we cry thee far and near
And thunder through all lands unknown
The gospel into every ear,
   Lord, let us not forget our own.

Cleanse us from ire of creed or class,
The anger of the idle kings;
Sow in our hearts, like living grass,
   The laughter of all lowly things.

G.K. Chesterton
1874–1936

St Patrick's Hymn before Tara

Christ, as a light,
Illumine and guide me!
Christ, as a shield, o'ershadow and cover me!
Christ be under me! Christ be over me!
Christ be beside me
On left hand and right!
Christ be before me, behind me, about me!
Christ this day be within and without me!

Christ, the lowly and meek,
Christ, the All-powerful, be
In the heart of each to whom I speak,
In the mouth of each who speaks to me!
In all who draw near me,
Or see me or hear me!

At Tara to-day, in this awful hour,
I call on the Holy Trinity!
Glory to him who reigneth in power,
The God of the elements, Father, and Son,
And Paraclete Spirit, which Three are in One,
The ever-existing Divinity!

Salvation dwells with the Lord,
With Christ, the Omnipotent Word.
From generation to generation
Grant us, O Lord, thy grace and salvation!

St Patrick
about 372–466
translated from the Irish by James Mangan

Be Thou my Vision

Be thou my vision, O Lord of my heart,
Naught be all else to me save that thou art;
Be thou my best thoughts in the day and night,
Waking and sleeping thy presence my light.

Be thou my wisdom, be thou my true word,
I ever with thee and thou with me, Lord;
Thou my great Father, and I thy true son;
Thou in me dwelling, and I with thee one.

Be thou my breast-plate, my sword for the fight,
Be thou my armour, and be thou my might,
Thou my soul's shelter, and thou my high tower,
Raise thou me heavenward, O Power of my power.

Riches I heed not, nor man's empty praise,
Thou mine inheritance through all my days;
Thou, and thou only, the first in my heart,
High King of heaven, my treasure thou art!

High King of heaven, when battle is done,
Grant heaven's joy to me O bright heaven's sun,
Christ of my own heart, whatever befall,
Still be my vision, O Ruler of all.

Gaelic
8th century
translated by Eleanor Hull

Battle Hymn of the Republic

Mine eyes have seen the glory of the coming of the Lord:
He is trampling out the vintage where the grapes of wrath are stored:
He has loosed the fateful lightning of his terrible swift sword:
    His truth is marching on.

I have seen him in the watch-fires of a hundred circling camps;
They have builded him an altar in the evening dews and damps;
I can read his righteous sentence by the dim and flaring lamps:
    His day is marching on.

I have read a fiery gospel, writ in burnished rows of steel:
'As ye deal with my contemners, so with you my grace shall deal;
Let the Hero, born of woman, crush the serpent with his heel!
    Since God is marching on.'

He has sounded forth the trumpet that shall never call retreat;
He is sifting out the hearts of men before his Judgement Seat;
O, be swift, my soul, to answer him, be jubilant my feet!
    Our God is marching on.

In the beauty of the lilies Christ was born, across the sea,
With a glory in his bosom that transfigures you and me:
As he died to make men holy, let us die to make men free,
    While God is marching on.

Julia Ward Howe
1819–1910

The Harrowing of Hell

'Hold still,'
Truth said: 'I hear some spirit
Speaking to the guards of hell,
And see him too, telling them
Unbar the gates. "Lift your heads
    You gates."'
  And from the heart
  of light
A loud voice spoke.
  'Open
These gates, Lucifer,
Prince of this land: the king of glory
  A crown upon his head
    Comes,'

Satan groaned and said to his hell's angels,
'It's that sort of light sprung Lazarus.
Unstoppable. This'll be big, big
Trouble, I mean all sorts of bother
For the lot of us . . .

    Again
The light said, 'Unlock.'
  Said Lucifer, 'Who
    Goes there?'

A huge voice replied, 'The lord
Of power, of strength, that made
All things. Dukes of this dark place
Undo these gates so Christ come
In, the son of heaven's King.'
With that word, hell split apart,
Burst its devil's bars; no man
Nor guard could stop the gates swing
Wide. The old religious men,
Prophets, people who had walked
In darkness, 'Behold the Lamb
Of God,' with Saint John sang now.
But Lucifer could not look
At it, the light blinding him.
And along that light all those
Our Lord loved came streaming out.

'Body and soul,' Christ said,
'I am here. Look on me.
I come for all sinners,
To give both the devil
His due and claiming mine…

'So, Lucifer, don't let yourself think
I'm bringing any of these sinners
Out illegally, by power alone.
I ransom my people in justice
And in law. I come not to destroy
The law but to fulfil it. And so
    What a trick
      Took
      Grace
    Has regained.

    As Adam
And all his people
    Died
Through a tree
    So
Through a tree
    Adam
And all his people
    Shall
Rise again.

Your tricks begin to turn upon you.
My grace, everywhere, spreads wider,
Wider. The bitter drink you have brewed,
Taste it yourself. Doctor of Death, drink
The prescription you have made. I am
Lord of life and so love is my drink.'

From Piers Plowman, *by William Langland*
1330?–1400?
translated by Ronald Tamplin

Sickness and Suffering

Prayer

God stir the soil,
Run the ploughshare deep,
Cut the furrows round and round,
Overturn the hard, dry ground,
Spare no strength nor toil,
Even though I weep.
In the loose, fresh mangled earth
Sow new seed.
Free of withered vine and weed
Bring fair flowers to birth.

Anonymous

A Hymn to my God in a Night of my Late Sickness

O thou great Power, in whom I move,
For whom I live, to whom I die,
Behold me through thy beams of love,
Whilst on this couch of tears I lie,
    And cleanse my sordid soul within
    By thy Christ's blood, the bath of sin.

No hallowed oils, no grains I need,
No rags of saints, no purging fire,
One rosy drop from David's seed
Was worlds of seas to quench thine ire.
    O precious ransom, which once paid
    That *Consummatum Est* was said;

And said by him that said no more,
But sealed it with his sacred breath.
Thou then, that has dispunged my score,
And dying was the death of Death,
    Be to me now—on thee I call—
    My Life, my Strength, my Joy, my All.

Sir Henry Wotton
1568–1639

From: Litany to the Holy Spirit

In the hour of my distress,
When temptations me oppress,
And when I my sins confess,
  Sweet Spirit comfort me!

When I lie within my bed,
Sick in heart, and sick in head,
And with doubts discomforted,
  Sweet Spirit comfort me!

When the house doth sigh and weep,
And the house is drowned in sleep,
Yet mine eyes the watch do keep;
  Sweet Spirit comfort me!

When the artless doctor sees
Not one hope, but of his fees,
And his skill runs on the lees;
  Sweet Spirit comfort me!

When his potion and his pill,
Has, or none, or little skill,
Meet for nothing, but to kill;
  Sweet Spirit comfort me!

When the passing-bell doth toll,
And the furies in a shoal
Come to fright a parting soul;
  Sweet Spirit comfort me!...

When the flames and hellish cries
Fright mine ears, and fright mine eyes,
And all terrors me surprise;
  Sweet Spirit comfort me!

When the judgement is revealed,
And that opened which was sealed,
When to thee I have appealed;
  Sweet Spirit comfort me!

              Robert Herrick
              1591–1674

Hymn to God, my God, in my Sickness

Since I am coming to that holy room,
   Where, with thy choir of saints for evermore,
I shall be made thy music; as I come
     I tune the instrument here at the door,
     And what I must do then, think here before.

Whilst my physicians by their love are grown
   Cosmographers, and I their map, who lie
Flat on this bed, that by them may be shown
     That this is my south-west discovery
     Per fretum febris, by these straits to die,

I joy, that in these straits, I see my west;
   For, though their currents yield return to none,
What shall my west hurt me? As west and east
     In all flat maps (and I am one) are one,
     So death doth touch the resurrection.

Is the pacific sea my home? Or are
   The eastern riches? Is Jerusalem?
Anyan, and Magellan, and Gibraltar,
     All straits, and none but straits, are ways to them,
     Whether where Japhet dwelt, or Cham, or Sem.

We think that Paradise and Calvary,
   Christ's Cross, and Adam's tree, stood in one place;
Look Lord, and find both Adams met in me;
     As the first Adam's sweat surrounds my face,
     May the last Adam's blood my soul embrace.

So, in his purple wrapped receive me, Lord,
   By these his thorns give me his other crown;
And as to others' souls I preached thy word,
     Be this my text, my sermon to mine own,
     Therefore that he may raise the Lord throws down.

John Donne
1572–1631

Before the Anaesthetic

OR
A REAL FRIGHT

Intolerably sad, profound
St. Giles's bells are ringing round,
They bring the slanting summer rain
To tap the chestnut boughs again
Whose shadowy cave of rainy leaves
The gusty belfry-song receives.
Intolerably sad and true,
Victorian red and jewel blue,
The mellow bells are ringing round
And charge the evening light with sound,
And I look motionless from bed
On heavy trees and purple red
And hear the midland bricks and tiles
Throw back the bells of stone St. Giles,
Bells, ancient now as castle walls,
Now hard and new as pitchpine stalls,
Now full with help from ages past,
Now dull with death and hell at last.
Swing up! and give me hope of life,
Swing down! and plunge the surgeon's knife.
I, breathing for a moment, see
Death wing himself away from me
And think, as on this bed I lie,
Is it extinction when I die?
I move my limbs and use my sight;
Not yet, thank God, not yet the Night.
Oh better far those echoing hells
Half-threaten'd in the pealing bells
Than that this 'I' should cease to be—
Come quickly, Lord, come quick to me.
St. Giles's bells are asking now
'And hast thou known the Lord, hast thou?'
St. Giles' bells, they richly ring
'And was that Lord our Christ the King?'
St. Giles's bells they hear me call
I never knew the Lord at all.
Oh not in me your Saviour dwells
You ancient, rich St.Giles's bells.
Illuminated missals—spires—
Wide screens and decorated quires—
All these I loved, and on my knees
I thanked myself for knowing these
And watched the morning sunlight pass
Through richly stained Victorian glass

And in the colour-shafted air
I, kneeling, thought the Lord was there.
Now, lying in the gathering mist
I know that Lord did not exist;
Now, lest this 'I' should cease to be,
Come, real Lord, come quick to me.
With every gust the chestnut sighs,
With every breath, a mortal dies;
The man who smiled alone, alone,
And went his journey on his own
With 'Will you give my wife this letter,
In case, of course, I don't get better?'
Waits for his coffin lid to close
On waxen head and yellow toes.
Almighty Saviour, had I Faith
There'd be no fight with kindly Death.
Intolerably long and deep
St. Giles's bells swing on in sleep:
'But still you go from here alone'
Say all the bells about the Throne.

John Betjeman 20th century

Healing

Sick wards. The sailed beds
becalmed. The nurses tack
hither and fro. The chloroform
breeze rises and falls.
Hospitals are their own
weather. The temperatures
have no relation
to the world outside. The surgeons,
those cunning masters
of navigation, follow
their scalpels' compass through
hurricanes of pain to a calm
harbour. Somewhere far down
in the patient's darkness,
where faith died, like a graft
or a transplant prayer
gets to work, repairing
the soul's tissue, leading
the astonished self between
twin pillars, where life's angels
stand wielding their bright swords of flame.

R.S. Thomas 20th century

Intercession Against the Plague

Set free thy people, set free thy servants,
Lighten thine anger, Ruler most holy;
Look on their anguish, bitter their weeping,
    Christ, in thy mercy.

Thou art our Father, Master exalted,
We are thy servants, thou the Good Shepherd,
Bearing thy token of blood and of crimson
    Marked on our foreheads.

Deep in thy hell who then shall confess thee?
Yea, shall the dead give praise to thy name?
Judge of our dread, thy rod is of iron,
    Spare us, we pray thee.

Bring not so near to thy people, thy servants,
The cup of thine anger, thy merited wrath:
Lighten upon us thine ancient compassion.
    We cry. Do thou hear!

Loosen, we pray thee, our load of transgression.
Vouchsafe to keep us, Prince ever blessed.
Vanquish the shadow that darkens our spirits,
    Light of the world.

Saint of all saints and king of all kingships,
Visit thy people with thy right hand.
Lift up the light of thy countenance upon us,
    Lord, or we perish.

Sedulius Scottus
about 848–74
translated by Helen Waddell

OUT OF THE DEPTHS:
PSALMS OF SUFFERING

Psalm 6

Lord, in thine anger do not reprehend me,
  Nor in thy hot displeasure me correct;
Pity me, Lord, for I am much deject,
  Am very weak and faint; heal and amend me,
For all my bones, that even with anguish ache,
  Are troubled, yea, my soul is troubled sore.
And thou, O Lord, how long? turn, Lord, restore
  My soul, O save me for thy goodness sake,
For in death no remembrance is of thee;
  Who in the grave can celebrate thy praise?
Wearied I am with sighing out my days,
  Nightly my couch I make a kind of sea;
My bed I water with my tears; mine eye
  Through grief consumes, is waxen old and dark
I' the midst of all mine enemies that mark.
  Depart, all ye that work iniquity,
Depart from me, for the voice of my weeping
  The Lord hath heard; the Lord hath heard my prayer;
My supplication with acceptance fair
  The Lord will own, and have me in his keeping.
Mine enemies shall all be blank and dashed
  With much confusion; then grow red with shame;
They shall return in haste the way they came
  And in a moment shall be quite abashed.

John Milton
1608–74

Lord, Hear my Prayer

A PARAPHRASE OF PSALM 102

Lord, hear my prayer when trouble glooms,
Let sorrow find a way,
And when the day of trouble comes,
Turn not thy face away:
My bones like hearthstones burn away,
My life like vapoury smoke decays.

My heart is smitten like the grass,
That withered lies and dead,
And I, so lost to what I was,
Forget to eat my bread.
My voice is groaning all the day,
My bones prick through this skin of clay.

The wilderness's pelican,
The desert's lonely owl—
I am their like, a desert man
In ways as lone and foul.
As sparrow on the cottage top
I wait till I with fainting drop.

I hear my enemies reproach,
All silently I mourn;
They on my private peace encroach,
Against me they are sworn.
Ashes as bread my trouble shares,
And mix my food with weeping cares.

Yet not for them is sorrow's toil,
I fear no mortal frowns—
But thou hast held me up awhile
And thou hast cast me down.
My days like shadows waste from view,
I mourn like withered grass in dew.

But thou, Lord, shalt endure for ever,
All generations through;
Thou shalt to Zion be the giver
Of joy and mercy too.
Her very stones are in thy trust,
Thy servants reverence her dust.

Heathens shall hear and fear thy name,
All kings of earth thy glory know
When thou shalt build up Zion's fame
And live in glory there below.
He'll not despise their prayers, though mute,
But still regard the destitute.

John Clare
1793–1864

Psalm 13

How long, O Lord, shall I forgotten be?
  What? Ever?
How long wilt thou thy hidden face from me
  Dissever?

How long shall I consult with careful sprite*
  In anguish?
How long shall I with foes triumphant might
  Thus languish?

Behold me, Lord; let to thy hearing creep
  My crying;
Nay, give me eyes and light, lest that I sleep
  In dying:

Lest my foe brag, that in my ruin he
  Prevailed;
And at my fall they joy that, troublous, me
  Assailed.

No! no! I trust on thee, and joy in thy
  Great pity:
Still, therefore, of thy graces shall be my
  Song's ditty.

Mary Herbert, Countess of Pembroke
1561–1621

* *sprite*: spirit

DISTRESS OF MIND AND SPIRIT

'Wherefore hidest thou thy face, and holdest me for thy enemy?'

(JOB 13:24)

Why dost thou shade thy lovely face? O, why
Does that eclipsing hand so long deny
The sunshine of thy soul-enlivening eye?

Without that Light, what light remains in me?
Thou art my Life, my Way, my Light; in thee
I live, I move, and by thy beams I see.

Thou art my Life; if thou but turn away,
My life's a thousand deaths. Thou art my Way;
Without thee, Lord, I travel not but stray.

My Light thou art; without thy glorious sight
Mine eyes are darkened with perpetual night.
My God, thou art my Way, my Life, my Light.

Thou art my Way; I wander if thou fly:
Thou art my Light; if hid, how blind am I!
Thou art my Life; if thou withdraw, I die ...

Thou art the pilgrim's path, the blind man's eye,
The dead man's Life; on thee my hopes rely.
If thou remove, I err, I grope, I die.

Disclose thy sunbeams; close thy wings and stay;
See, see, how I am blind, and dead, and stray,
O thou, that art my Light, my Life, my Way.

Francis Quarles
1592–1644

The Fell of Dark

I wake and feel the fell of dark, not day.
What hours, O what black hours we have spent
This night! What sights you, heart, saw; ways you went!
And more must, in yet longer light's delay.

With witness I speak this. But where I say
Hours I mean years, mean life. And my lament
Is cries countless, cries like dead letters sent
To dearest him that lives alas! away.

I am gall, I am heartburn. God's most deep decree
Bitter would have me taste: my taste was me;
Bones built in me, flesh filled, blood brimmed the curse.

Selfyeast of spirit a dull dough sours. I see
The lost are like this, and their scourge to be
As I am mine, their sweating selves; but worse.

Gerard Manley Hopkins   1844–89

I Am

I am—yet what I am none cares or knows,
My friends forsake me like a memory lost;
I am the self-consumer of my woes,
They rise and vanish in oblivions host,
Like shadows in love—frenzied stifled throes
And yet I am, and live like vapours tossed.

Into the nothingness of scorn and noise,
Into the living sea of waking dreams,
Where there is neither sense of life or joys,
But the vast shipwreck of my life's esteems;
And e'en the dearest—that I love the best—
Are strange—nay, rather stranger than the rest.

I long for scenes where man has never trod,
A place where woman never smiled or wept;
There to abide with my Creator, God,
And sleep as I in childhood sweetly slept:
Untroubling and untroubled where I lie,
The grass below—above the vaulted sky.

John Clare   1793–1864

Remorse

Remorse is memory awake,
Her parties all astir,
A presence of departed acts
At window and at door.

It's past set down before the soul
And lighted with a match,
Perusal to facilitate
And help belief to stretch.

Remorse is cureless—the disease
Not even God can heal,
For 'tis his institution and
The adequate of Hell.

Emily Dickinson
1830–86

Lines Written During a Period of Insanity

Hatred and vengeance, my eternal portion
Scarce can endure delay of execution,
Wait, with impatient readiness, to seize my
    Soul in a moment.

Damned below Judas: more abhorred than he was
Who for a few pence sold his holy Master.
Twice betrayed Jesus me, the last delinquent,
    Deems the profanest.

Man disavows, and Deity disowns me:
Hell might afford my miseries a shelter;
Therefore hell keeps her ever hungry mouths all
    Bolted against me.

Hard lot! encompassed with a thousand dangers;
Weary, faint, trembling with a thousand terrors;
I'm called, if vanquished, to receive a sentence
    Worse than Abiram's.

Him the vindictive rod of angry justice
Sent quick and howling to the centre headlong;
I, fed with judgement, in a fleshly tomb, am
    Buried above ground.

William Cowper
1731–1800

GLEAMS OF LIGHT

Anguish

I shall know why, when time is over,
And I have ceased to wonder why;
Christ will explain each separate anguish
In the fair schoolroom of the sky.

He will tell me what Peter promised,
And I, for wonder at his woe,
I shall forget the drop of anguish
That scalds me now, that scalds me now.

Emily Dickinson
1830–86

Casting all your Care upon God, for he careth for you

Come, heavy souls, oppressed that are
With doubts, and fears, and carking care.
Lay all your burdens down, and see
There's one that carried once a tree
Upon his back, and, which is more,
A heavier weight, your sins, he bore.
Think then how easily he can
Your sorrows bear that's God and man;
Think too how willing he's to take
Your care on him, who for your sake
Sweat bloody drops, prayed, fasted, cried,
Was bound, scourged, mocked and crucified.
He that so much for you did do,
Will do yet more, and care for you.

Thomas Washbourne
1606–87

To Heaven

Good and great God, can I not think of thee
    But it must straight my melancholy be?
Is it interpreted in me disease
    That, laden with my sins, I seek for ease?
O be thou witness, that the reins dost know
    And hearts of all, if I be sad for show,
And judge me after, if I dare pretend
    To aught but grace, or aim at other end.
As thou art all, so be thou all to me,
    First, midst, and last, converted, one and three;
My faith, my hope, my love; and in this state
    My judge, my witness, and my advocate.
Where have I been this while exiled from thee,
    And whither raped, now thou but stoop'st to me?
Dwell, dwell here still. O, being everywhere,
    How can I doubt to find thee ever, here?
I know my state, both full of shame and scorn,
    Conceived in sin, and unto labour born,
Standing with fear, and must with horror fall,
    And destined unto judgement, after all.
I feel my griefs too, and there scarce is ground
    Upon my flesh to inflict another wound.
Yet dare I not complain, or wish for death
    With holy Paul, lest it be thought the breath
Of discontent; or that these prayers be
    For weariness of life, not love of thee.

Ben Jonson 1572?–1637

God our Help

With floods and storms thus we be tossed,
Awake, good Lord, to thee we cry.
Our ship is almost sunk and lost.
Thy mercy help our misery.
    Man's strength is weak: man's wit is dull:
Man's reason's blind. These things to amend,
Thy hand, O Lord, of might is full;
Awake betime, and help us send.
    In thee we trust, and in no wight:
Save us as chickens under the hen.
Our crookedness thou canst make right
Glory to thee for aye. Amen.

Anonymous 17th century

PEACE AND ACCEPTANCE

From: The Brewing of Soma

Drop thy still dews of quietness,
 Till all our strivings cease;
Take from our souls the strain and stress,
And let our ordered lives confess
 The beauty of thy peace.

John Greenleaf Whittier
1807–92

Quiet Peace

O Lord, my heart is all a prayer,
 But it is silent unto thee;
I am too tired to look for words,
 I rest upon thy sympathy
To understand when I am dumb;
 And well I know thou hearest me.

I know thou hearest me because
 A quiet peace comes down to me,
And fills the places where before
 Weak thoughts were wandering wearily;
And deep within me it is calm,
 Though waves are tossing outwardly.

Amy Carmichael
1867–1951

God, the Port of Peace

Now come all you who have been brought
In bondage full of busy bitterness,
Earthly desire abiding in your thought!
Here is the rest from all your busyness,
Here is the port of peace and restfulness
To those who stand in storms and in dis-ease,
Open refuge to wretches in distress,
And all comfort from trouble and mis-ease.

Adapted from John Walton
about 1410

From: The Thoughts of God

They say there is a hollow, safe and still,
A point of coolness and repose
Within the centre of a flame, where life might dwell
Unharmed and unconsumed, as in a luminous shell,
Which the bright walls of fire enclose
In breachless splendour, barrier that no foes
    Could pass at will.

    There is a point of rest
At the great centre of the cyclone's force
    A silence at its secret source;—
A little child might slumber undistressed,
Without the ruffle of one fairy curl,
In that strange central calm amid the mighty whirl.

So in the centre of these thoughts of God,
Cyclones of power, consuming glory-fire,
    As we fall o'erawed
Upon our faces, and are lifted higher
By his great gentleness, and carried nigher
Than unredeemèd angels, till we stand
    Even in the hollow of his hand,—
    Nay more! we lean upon his breast—
There, there we find a point of perfect rest
    And glorious safety. There we see
    His thoughts to us-ward, thoughts of peace
That stoop to tenderest love; that still increase
With increase of our need; that never change,
That never fail, or falter, or forget.
    O pity infinite!
    O royal mercy free!
    O gentle climax of the depth and height
Of God's most precious thoughts, most wonderful, most strange
    'For I am poor and needy, yet
The Lord himself, Jehovah, *thinketh upon me!'*

Frances Ridley Havergal
1836–79

The Good Shepherd

Christ who knows all his sheep
Will all in safety keep;
He will not lose his blood,
    Nor intercession:
Nor we the purchased good
    Of his dear passion.

I know my God is just,
To him I wholly trust
All that I have and am,
    All that I hope for.
All's sure and seen to him,
    Which I here grope for.

Lord Jesus, take my spirit:
I trust thy love and merit:
Take home this wandering sheep,
    For thou hast sought it:
This soul in safety keep,
    For thou hast bought it.

Richard Baxter
1615–91

Intimations

Henry Vaughan saw eternity
and far beyond star countries;
Blake met angels in the garden
pleasantly building green Jerusalem.

I border bred, London extended,
little matchstick man
for whom the sparrows do not care two farthings,
remain untutored by exceptions

Lord keep us in our proper stations.

If the communion of saints
is not only the shining ones
but the incompetent and ineffective,
let grace sidle down the repeated street
and a wing flash in ambiguous sunlight

Raymond Chapman
20th century

Thy Way, not Mine

Thy way, not mine, O Lord,
   However dark it be!
Lead me by thine own hand,
   Choose out the path for me.

Smooth let it be or rough,
   It will be still the best;
Winding or straight, it leads
   Right onward to thy rest.

I dare not choose my lot;
   I would not, if I might;
Choose thou for me, my God;
   So shall I walk aright.

The kingdom that I seek
   Is thine; so let the way
That leads to it be thine;
   Else I must surely stray.

Take thou my cup, and it
   With joy or sorrow fill,
As best to thee may seem;
   Choose thou my good and ill;

Choose thou for me my friends,
   My sickness or my health;
Choose thou my cares for me,
   My poverty or wealth.

Not mine, not mine the choice,
   In things or great or small;
Be thou my guide, my strength,
   My wisdom, and my all!

Horatius Bonar
1808–89

City of God

Glorious things of thee are spoken,
    Zion, city of our God;
He, whose word cannot be broken,
    Formed thee for his own abode:
On the Rock of Ages founded,
    What can shake thy sure repose?
With salvation's walls surrounded,
    Thou mayst smile at all thy foes.

See, the streams of living waters,
    Springing from eternal love,
Well supply thy sons and daughters,
    And all fear of want remove:
Who can faint, while such a river
    Ever flows their thirst to assuage—
Grace, which like the Lord the giver,
    Never fails from age to age.

Blest inhabitants of Zion,
    Washed in the Redeemer's blood;
Jesus, whom their souls rely on,
    Makes them kings and priests to God.
'Tis his love his people raises
    Over self to reign as kings;
And as priests, his solemn praises
    Each for a thankoffering brings.

Saviour, if of Zion's city
    I, through grace, a member am,
Let the world deride or pity,
    I will glory in thy name:
Fading is the worldling's pleasure,
    All his boasted pomp and show;
Solid joys and lasting treasure
    None but Zion's children know.

John Newton
1725–1807

Deep-sea Soundings

Mariner, what of the deep?
      This of the deep:
Twilight is there, and solemn, changeless calm;
Beauty is there, and tender healing balm—
Balm with no root in earth, or air, or sea,
Poised by the finger of God, it floateth free,
And, as it threads the waves, the sound doth rise,—
Hither shall come no further sacrifice;
Never again the anguished clutch at life,
Never again great Love and Death in strife;
He who hath suffered all, need fear no more,
Quiet his portion now, for evermore.

Mariner, what of the deep?
      This of the deep:
Solitude dwells not there, though silence reign;
Mighty the brotherhood of loss and pain;
There is communion past the need of speech,
There is a love no words of love can reach;
Heavy the waves that superincumbent press,
But as we labour here with constant stress,
Hand doth hold out to hand not help alone,
But the deep bliss of being fully known.
There are no kindred like the kin of sorrow,
There is no hope like theirs who fear no morrow.

Mariner, what of the deep?
      This of the deep:
Though we have travelled past the line of day,
Glory of night doth light us on our way,
Radiance that comes we know not how nor whence,
Rainbows without the rain, past duller sense,
Music of hidden reefs and waves long past,
Thunderous organ tones from far-off blast,
Harmony, victrix, throned in state sublime,
Couched on the wrecks be-gemmed with pearls of time;
Never a wreck but brings some beauty here;
Down where the waves are stilled the sea shines clear;
Deeper than life the plan of life doth lie,
He who knows all, fears naught. Great Death shall die.

Sarah Williams
1841–68

St Peter

St Peter once: 'Lord, dost thou wash my feet?'—
   Much more I say: Lord dost thou stand and knock
   At my closed heart more rugged than a rock,
Bolted and barred, for thy soft touch unmeet,
Nor garnished nor in any wise made sweet?
      Owls roost within and dancing satyrs mock.
      Lord, I have heard the crowing of the cock
And have not wept: ah, Lord, thou knowest it.
Yet still I hear thee knocking, still I hear:
      'Open to me, look on me eye to eye,
That I may wring thy heart and make it whole;
And teach thee love because I hold thee dear
      And sup with thee in gladness soul with soul,
      And sup with thee in glory by and by.'

Christina Rossetti
1830–94

The Hands of God

It is a fearful thing to fall into the hands of the living God.
But it is a much more fearful thing to fall out of them.

Did Lucifer fall through knowledge?
oh then, pity him, pity him that plunge!

Save me, O God, from falling into the ungodly knowledge
of myself as I am without God.

Let me never know, O God
let me never know what I am or should be
when I have fallen out of your hands, the hands of the living God.

That awful and sickening endless sinking, sinking
through the slow corruptive levels of disintegrative knowledge
when the self has fallen from the hands of God
and sinks, seething and sinking, corrupt
and sinking still, in depth after depth of disintegrative consciousness
sinking in the endless undoing, the awful katabolism into the abyss!
even of the soul, fallen from the hands of God!

Save me from that, O God!
Let me never know myself apart from the living God!

D.H. Lawrence *1885–1930*

The Waiting

I wait and watch: before my eyes
Methinks the night grows thin and grey;
I wait and watch the eastern skies
To see the golden spears uprise
Beneath the oriflamme of day!

Like one whose limbs are bound in trance
I hear the day-sounds swell and grow,
And see across the twilight glance,
Troop after troop, in swift advance,
The shining ones with plumes of snow!

I know the errand of their feet,
I know what mighty work is theirs;
I can but lift up hands unmeet
The threshing-floors of God to beat,
And speed them with unworthy prayers.

I will not dream in vain despair
The steps of progress wait for me:
The puny leverage of a hair
The planet's impulse well may spare,
A drop of dew the tided sea.

The loss, if loss there be, is mine,
And yet not mine if understood;
For one shall grasp and one resign,
One drink life's rue, and one its wine,
And God shall make the balance good.

O power to do! O baffled will!
O prayer and action! ye are one.
Who may not strive, may yet fulfil
The harder task of standing still,
And good but wished with God is done!

John Greenleaf Whittier
1807–92

Quickness

False life! a foil and no more, when
    Wilt thou be gone?
Thou foul deception of all men
That would not have the true come on.

Thou art a moonlike toil; a blind
    Self-posing state;
A dark contest of waves and wind;
A mere tempestuous debate.

Life is a fixed, discerning light,
    A knowing joy;
No chance, or fit: but ever bright,
And calm and full, yet doth not cloy.

'Tis such a blissful thing, that still
    Doth vivify,
And shine and smile, and hath the skill
To please without Eternity.

Thou art a toilsome mole, or less,
    A moving mist,
But life is, what none can express,
A quickness, which my God hath kissed.

Henry Vaughan
1622–95

Dum vivimus, vivamus

Live while you live, the Epicure would say,
And seize the pleasures of the present day.
Live while you live, the sacred Preacher cries,
And give to God each moment as it flies.
Lord, in my view, let both united be,
I live in pleasure if I live to thee.

Philip Doddridge
1702–51

On His Blindness

When I consider how my light is spent,
  Ere half my days, in this dark world and wide,
  And that one talent which is death to hide
  Lodged with me useless, though my soul more bent
To serve therewith my Maker, and present
  My true account, lest he returning chide,
  'Doth God exact day-labour, light denied?'
  I fondly ask. But Patience, to prevent
That murmur, soon replies: 'God does not need
  Either man's work or his own gifts; who best
  Bear his mild yoke, they serve him best. His state
  Is kingly: thousands at his bidding speed,
And post o'er land and ocean without rest;
They also serve who only stand and wait.'

John Milton
1608–74

True Felicity

Contentment is a sleepy thing!
If it in death alone must die;
A quiet mind is worse than poverty!
  Unless it from enjoyment spring!
That's blessedness alone that makes a king!
Wherein the joys and treasures are so great,
They all the powers of the soul employ,
    And fill it with a work complete,
      While it doth all enjoy.
True joys alone contentment do inspire,
Enrich content, and make our courage higher.
      Content alone's a dead and silent stone:
        The real life of bliss
        Is glory reigning in a throne,
          Where all enjoyment is
The soul of man is so inclined to see,
Without his treasures no man's soul can be,
        Nor rest uncrowned!
        Desire and love
Must in the height of all their rapture move,
      Where there is true felicity.

Thomas Traherne
1636?–74

The Pulley

When God at first made man,
Having a glass of blessings standing by,
'Let us,' said he, 'pour on him all we can;
Let the world's riches, which dispersèd lie,
    Contract into a span.'

So strength first made a way;
Then beauty flowed, then wisdom, honour, pleasure;
When almost all was out, God made a stay,
Perceiving that, alone of all his treasure,
    Rest in the bottom lay.

'For if I should,' said he,
'Bestow this jewel also on my creature,
He would adore my gifts instead of me,
And rest in Nature, not the God of Nature:
    So both should losers be.

'Yet let him keep the rest,
But keep them with repining restlessness;
Let him be rich and weary, that at least,
If goodness lead him not, yet weariness
    May toss him to my breast.'

George Herbert   1593–1633

The Holy Man

A trapped bird
A wrecked ship
An empty cup
A withered tree
Is he
Who scorns the will of the King above.

Pure gold
Bright sun
Filled wine-cup
Happy beautiful holy
Is he
Who does the will of the King of love.

Brendan Kennelly   20th century

Faith's Review and Expectation

Amazing grace! how sweet the sound
  That saved a wretch like me!
I once was lost, but now am found,
  Was blind, but now I see.

'Twas grace that taught my heart to fear,
  And grace my fears relieved;
How precious did that grace appear
  The hour I first believed.

Through many dangers, toils, and snares
  I have already come;
'Tis grace has brought me safe thus far
  And grace will lead me home.

The Lord has promised good to me,
  His word my hope secures;
He will my shield and portion be
  As long as life endures.

John Newton
1725–1807

The Shepherd's Song

He that is down needs fear no fall,
  He that is low no pride;
He that is humble ever shall
  Have God to be his guide.

I am content with what I have,
  Little be it or much:
And, Lord, contentment still I crave,
  Because thou savest such.

Fulness to such a burden is
  That go on pilgrimage:
Here little, and hereafter bliss,
  Is best from age to age.

John Bunyan
1622–88

Shadow and Coolness

Shadow and coolness, Lord, art thou to me;
Cloud of my soul, lead on, I follow thee.
What though the hot winds blow,
Fierce heat beat up below,
Fountains of water flow—
    Praise, praise to thee.

Clearness and glory, Lord, art thou to me;
Light of my soul, lead on, I follow thee.
All through the moonless night,
Making its darkness bright,
Thou art my heavenly light—
    Praise, praise to thee.

Shadow and shine art thou, dear Lord, to me;
Pillar of cloud and fire, I follow thee.
What though the way be long,
In thee my heart is strong,
Thou art my joy, my song—
    Praise, praise to thee.

Amy Carmichael
1867–1951

The Garden

I saw the spot where our first parents dwelt;
And yet it wore to me no face of change,
For while amid its fields and groves, I felt
As if I had not sinned, nor thought it strange;
My eye seemed but a part of every sight,
My ear heard music in each sound that rose;
Each sense forever found a new delight,
Such as the spirit's vision only knows;
Each act some new and ever-varying joy
Did by my Father's love for me prepare;
To dress the spot my ever fresh employ,
And in the glorious whole with him to share;
No more without the flaming gate to stray,
No more for sin's dark stain the debt of death to pay.

Jones Very
1813–80

Character of a Happy Life

How happy is he born and taught
That serveth not another's will;
Whose armour is his honest thought
And simple truth his utmost skill!

Whose passions not his masters are,
Whose soul is still prepared for death,
Not tied unto the world with care
Of public fame, or private breath;

Who envies none that chance doth raise,
Or vice; who never understood
How deepest wounds are given by praise;
Nor rules of state, but rules of good:

Who hath his life from rumours freed,
Whose conscience is his strong retreat;
Whose state can neither flatterers feed,
Nor ruin make oppressors great;

Who God doth late and early pray
More of his gifts than grace to lend;
And entertains the harmless day
With a well-chosen book or friend;

—This man is freed from servile bands
Of hope to rise, or fear to fall;
Lord of himself, though not of lands;
And having nothing, yet hath all.

Henry Wotton
1568–1639

Ballade of Good Counsel

Flee from the crowd and dwell with truthfulness:
　　Suffice thee with thy goods, tho' they be small:
To hoard brings hate, to climb brings giddiness;
　　The crowd has envy, and success blinds all;
　　Desire no more than to thy lot may fall;
Work well thyself to counsel others clear,
And Truth shall make thee free, there is no fear!

Torment thee not all crooked to redress,
　　Nor put thy trust in fortune's turning ball;
Great peace is found in little busy-ness;
　　And war but kicks against a sharpened awl;
Strive not, thou earthen pot, to break the wall;
Subdue thyself, and others thee shall hear;
And Truth shall make thee free, there is no fear!

What God doth send, receive in gladsomeness;
　　To wrestle for this world foretells a fall.
Here is no home, here is but wilderness:
　　Forth, pilgrim, forth; up, beast, and leave thy stall!
　　Know thy country, look up, thank God for all:
Hold the high way, thy soul the pioneer,
And Truth shall make thee free, there is no fear!

ENVOY

Therefore, poor beast, forsake thy wretchedness;
　　No longer let the vain world be thy stall.
His mercy seek who in his mightiness
　　Made thee of naught but not to be a thrall.
　　Pray freely for thyself and pray for all
Who long for larger life and heavenly cheer;
And Truth shall make thee free, there is no fear!

Geoffrey Chaucer
1343?–1400
translated by Henry Van Dyke

With Christ

Lord, it belongs not to my care,
   Whether I die or live;
To love and serve thee is my share,
   And this thy grace must give.

If life be long I will be glad,
   That I may long obey;
If short—yet why should I be sad
   To soar to endless day?

Christ leads me through no darker rooms
   Than he went through before;
He that unto God's kingdom comes,
   Must enter by this door.

Come, Lord, when grace has made me meet
   Thy blessed face to see;
For if thy work on earth be sweet,
   What will thy glory be!

Then I shall end my sad complaints,
   And weary, sinful days,
And join with the triumphant saints,
   To sing Jehovah's praise.

My knowledge of that life is small,
   The eye of faith is dim,
But 'tis enough that Christ knows all,
   And I shall be with him.

Richard Baxter
1615–91

JESUS THE CHRIST

Wit Wonders

A God and yet a man,
A maid and yet a mother:
Wit wonders what wit can
Conceive this or the other.

A God and can he die?
A dead man, can he live?
What wit can well reply?
What reason reason give?

God, Truth itself, doth teach it.
Man's wit sinks too far under
By reason's power to reach it:
Believe and leave to wonder.

Anonymous
15th century

Christ the Child:
Christmas Nativity

THE ANNUNCIATION

The annunciation

The angel and the girl are met.
Earth was the only meeting place.
For the embodied never yet
Travelled beyond the shore of space.
The eternal spirits in freedom go.

See, they have come together, see,
While the destroying minutes flow,
Each reflects the other's face
Till heaven in hers and earth in his
Shine steady there. He's come to her
From far beyond the farthest star,
Feathered through time. Immediacy
Of strangest strangeness is the bliss
That from their limbs all movement takes.
Yet the increasing rapture brings
So great a wonder that it makes
Each feather tremble on his wings.

Outside the window footsteps fall
Into the ordinary day
And with the sun along the wall
Pursue their unreturning way.
Sounds perpetual roundabout
Rolls its numbered octaves out
And hoarsely grinds its battered tune.

But through the endless afternoon
These neither speak nor movement make,
But stare into their deepening trance
As if their gaze would never break.

Edwin Muir
1887–1959

'I Sing of a Maiden'

I sing of a maiden
  That is matchless:
King of all kings
  For her son she ches*.

He came all so stillè
  Where his mother was,
As dew in Aprillè
  That falls on the grass.

He came all so stillè
  To his mother's bower,
As dew in Aprillè
  That falls on the flower.

He came all so stillè
  Where his mother lay,
As dew in Aprillè
  That falls on the spray.

Mother and maiden
  Was never none but she
Well may such a lady
  God's mother be.

Anonymous
15th century

* ches: chose

THE SAVIOUR COMES

From: Messiah

The Saviour comes! by ancient bards foretold:
Hear him, ye deaf, and all ye blind, behold!
He from thick films shall purge the visual ray,
And on the sightless eyeball pour the day:
'Tis he the obstructed paths of sound shall clear,
And bid new music charm the unfolding ear:
The dumb shall sing, the lame his crutch forego,
And leap exulting like the bounding roe.
No sigh, no murmur the wide world shall hear,
From every face he wipes off every tear.
In adamantine chains shall Death be bound,
And hell's grim tyrant feel the eternal wound.
As the good shepherd tends his fleecy care,
Seeks freshest pasture and the purest air,
Explores the lost, the wandering sheep directs,
By day o'ersees them, and by night protects,
The tender lambs he raises in his arms,
Feeds from his hand, and in his bosom warms;
Thus shall mankind his guardian care engage,
The promised father of the future age.

Alexander Pope
1688–1744

Salus Mundi

I saw a stable, low and very bare,
  A little child in a manger.
The oxen knew him, had him in their care,
  To men he was a stranger.
The safety of the world was lying there,
  And the world's danger.

Mary Coleridge
1861–1907

Joy to the World

Joy to the world! the Lord is come;
Let earth receive her King.
Let every heart prepare him room
And heaven and nature sing.

Joy to the earth! the Saviour reigns;
Let men their songs employ,
While fields and floods, rocks, hills, and plains
Repeat the sounding joy.

No more let sins and sorrows grow,
Nor thorns infest the ground;
He comes to make his blessings flow
Far as the curse is found.

He rules the world with truth and grace
And makes the nations prove
The glories of his righteousness
And wonders of his love.

Isaac Watts
1674–1748

Noel: Christmas Eve, 1913

PAX HOMINIBUS BONAE VOLUNTATIS

A frosty Christmas Eve
   when the stars were shining
Fared I forth alone
   where westward falls the hill,
And from many a village
   in the water'd valley
Distant music reach'd me
   peals of bells aringing:
The constellated sounds
   ran sprinkling on earth's floor
As the dark vault above
   with stars was spangled o'er.
Then sped my thoughts to keep
   that first Christmas of all
When the shepherds watching
   by their folds ere the dawn
Heard music in the fields
   and marvelling could not tell
Whether it were angels
   or the bright stars singing.
Now blessed be the tow'rs
   that crown England so fair
That stand up strong in prayer
   unto God for our souls:
Blessed be their founders
   (said I) an' our country folk
Who are ringing for Christ
   in the belfries tonight
With arms lifted to clutch
   the rattling ropes that race
Into the dark above
   and the mad romping din.

But to me heard afar
   it was starry music
Angels' song, comforting
   as the comfort of Christ
When he spake tenderly
   to his sorrowful flock:
The old words came to me
   by the riches of time
Mellow'd and transfigured
   as I stood on the hill
Heark'ning in the aspect
   of th'eternal silence.

Robert Bridges   *1844–1930*

Chanticleer

All this night shrill chanticleer,
Day's proclaiming trumpeter,
  Claps his wings and loudly cries,
  Mortals, mortals, wake and rise!
    See a wonder
    Heaven is under;
  From the earth is risen a Sun
  Shines all night, though day be done.

Wake, O earth, wake everything!
Wake and hear the joy I bring;
  Wake and joy; for all this night
  Heaven and every twinkling light,
    All amazing,
    Still stand gazing.
  Angels, powers, and all that be,
  Wake, and joy this Sun to see.

Hail, O Sun, O blessed light,
Sent into the world by night!
  Let thy rays and heavenly powers
  Shine in these dark souls of ours;
    For most duly
    Thou art truly
  God and man, we do confess:
  Hail, O Sun of righteousness!

William Austin
1587–1634

The Oxen

Christmas Eve, and twelve of the clock,
  'Now they are all on their knees,'
An elder said as we sat in a flock
  By the embers in hearthside ease.

We pictured the meek mild creatures where
  They dwelt in their strawy pen,
Nor did it occur to one of us there
  To doubt they were kneeling then.

So fair a fancy few would weave
  In these years! Yet, I feel,
If someone said on Christmas Eve,
  'Come, see the oxen kneel

In the lonely barton by yonder coomb
  Our childhood used to know,'
I should go with him in the gloom,
  Hoping it might be so.

Thomas Hardy
1840–1928

All in Tune

All in tune to William's flute
Now is Robin's tabor,
Dance tonight and sing high praise
As they did in other days,
Every kindly neighbour.
All in tune, all in tune,
Are the flute and tambourine,
All in tune, all in tune,
Heaven and earth tonight are seen.

God and man are in accord,
More than flute or tabor,
Dance for joy and sing with awe,
For the child upon the straw
Is our God and neighbour.
God and man, God and man,
Are like flute and tambourine,
God and man, God and man,
As true neighbours here are seen.

Anonymous

CHRISTMAS DAY: THE INCARNATION

From: Ode on the Morning of Christ's Nativity

COMPOSED 1629

This is the month, and this the happy morn,
Wherein the Son of heaven's eternal King,
Of wedded maid and virgin mother born,
Our great redemption from above did bring;
For so the holy sages once did sing,
   That he our deadly forfeit should release,
And with his Father work us a perpetual peace.

That glorious form, that light insufferable,
And that far-beaming blaze of majesty,
Wherewith he wont at heaven's high council-table
To sit the midst of trinal unity,
He laid aside; and here with us to be,
   Forsook the courts of everlasting day,
And chose with us a darksome house of mortal clay.

Say, heavenly muse, shall not thy sacred vein
Afford a present to the infant God?
Hast thou no verse, no hymn, or solemn strain,
To welcome him to this his new abode,
Now while the heaven, by the sun's team untrod,
   Hath took no print of the approaching light,
And all the spangled host keep watch in squadrons bright?

See how from far upon the eastern road
The star-led wizards haste with odours sweet!
O run, prevent them with thy humble ode,
And lay it lowly at his blessed feet;
Have thou the honour first thy Lord to greet,
   And join thy voice unto the angel quire,
From out his secret altar touched with hallowed fire.

John Milton
1608–74

Psalm for Christmas Day

Fairest of morning lights appear,
　　Thou blest and gaudy day*,
On which was born our Saviour dear;
　　Arise and come away!

This day prevents his day of doom;
　　His mercy now is nigh;
The mighty God of love is come,
　　The dayspring from on high!

Behold the great Creator makes
　　Himself a house of clay,
A robe of virgin-flesh he takes
　　Which he will wear for aye.

Hark, hark, the wise eternal Word
　　Like a weak infant cries:
In form of servant is the Lord,
　　And God in cradle lies.

This wonder struck the world amazed,
　　It shook the starry frame;
Squadrons of spirits stood and gazed,
　　Then down in troops they came.

Glad shepherds ran to view this sight;
　　A quire of angels sings;
And eastern sages with delight
　　Adore this King of kings.

Join them all hearts that are not stone,
　　And all our voices prove,
To celebrate this holy one,
　　The God of peace and love.

Thomas Pestel
1584?–1659?

* *gaudy day:* festival

A Christmas Carol

In the bleak mid-winter
  Frosty wind made moan,
Earth stood hard as iron,
  Water like a stone;
Snow had fallen, snow on snow,
  Snow on snow,
In the bleak mid-winter
  Long ago.

Our God, heaven cannot hold him,
  Nor earth sustain;
Heaven and earth shall flee away
  When he comes to reign:
In the bleak mid-winter
  A stable-place sufficed
The Lord God Almighty
  Jesus Christ.

Enough for him whom cherubim
  Worship night and day,
A breastful of milk
  And a mangerful of hay;
Enough for him whom angels
  Fall down before,
The ox and ass and camel
  Which adore.

Angels and archangels
  May have gathered there,
Cherubim and seraphim
  Thronged the air,
But only his mother
  In her maiden bliss
Worshipped the Beloved
  With a kiss.

What can I give him,
  Poor as I am?
If I were a shepherd
  I would bring a lamb,
If I were a wise man
  I would do my part,—
Yet what I can I give him,
  Give my heart.

Christina Rossetti
1830–94

Christmas Bells

I heard the bells on Christmas day
Their old familiar carols play,
   And wild and sweet
   The words repeat,
Of 'Peace on earth, good will to men!'

And thought how, as the day had come,
The belfries of all Christendom
   Had rolled along
   The unbroken song,
Of 'Peace on earth, good will to men!'

Till ringing, singing on its way,
The world revolved from night to day—
   A voice, a chime,
   A chant sublime,
Of 'Peace on earth, good will to men!'

And in despair I bowed my head;
'There is no peace on earth,' I said,
   'For hate is strong
   And mocks the song
Of peace on earth, good will to men!'

Then pealed the bells more loud and deep:
'God is not dead; nor doth he sleep!
   The wrong shall fail,
   The right prevail,
With peace on earth, good will to men!'

Henry Wadsworth Longfellow
1807–82

The Birth

at zero hour God came
a baby on the bloody thirsty earth
with vernix on its skin
little sheep in a sundown pasture
and wrinkles on its face
little year rings of untimeliness
like summer wood in a balsam fir
and twenty billion invisible nerve cells
with a live reminiscence of heaven
and more knowledge than
100 volumes of encyclopaedia Britannica
in the dna molecules of one cell string

when shepherds knocked noisily at the door
of the sepulchral-sounding cave
his arms and legs swung out with a jerk
and he cried an earthly roar of flesh and blood
a simple startle reaction

God spoke one small creative word
a benediction for creation

at 33 expansive wide his hands spread all around
arms thrown out wide to embrace the universe
purple of passion in a sunset sky
day without end

the Word has reached the beach, the field, the town,
bloodthirsty earth of men to retrieve
chief sinners and braves
break out of your crust
it is time to be born.

Cor W. Barendrecht
20th century

Song for a Winter Birth

Under the watchful lights
  A child was born
From a mortal house of flesh
  Painfully torn.

And we, who later assembled
  To praise or peer,
Saw merely an infant boy
  Soft sleeping there;

Till he awoke and stretched
  Small arms wide
And, for food or comfort,
  Quavering cried.

A cry and attitude
  Rehearsing, in small,
The deathless death still haunting
  The Place of the Skull.

Outside, in the festive air,
  We lit cigars;
The night was nailed to the sky
  With hard bright stars.

Vernon Scannell
20th century

Mangers

Who knows the name and country now
  Of that rich man who lived of old;
Whose horses fed at silver mangers,
  And drank of wine from troughs of gold?

He who was in a manger born,
  By gold and silver undefiled—
Is known as Christ to every man
  And Jesus to a little child.

W.H. Davies
1871–1940

From: The Nativity of our Lord and Saviour Jesus Christ

Where is this stupendous stranger?
   Swains of Solyma, advise,
Lead me to my Master's manger,
   Show me where my Saviour lies.

O most Mighty! O most Holy!
   Far beyond the seraph's thought
Art thou then so mean and lowly,
   As unheeded prophets taught?

O the magnitude of meekness!
   Worth from worth immortal sprung;
O the strength of infant weakness,
   If eternal is so young!...

Nature's decorations glisten
   Far above their usual trim;
Birds on box and laurel listen,
   As so near the cherubs hymn.

Boreas now no longer winters
   On the desolated coast;
Oaks no more are riven in splinters
   By the whirlwind and his host.

Spinks and ouzels sing sublimely
   'We too have a Saviour born';
Whiter blossoms burst untimely
   On the blest Mosaic thorn.

God all-bounteous, all creative,
   Whom no ills from good dissuade,
Is incarnate and a native
   Of the very world he made.

Christopher Smart
1722–71

At the Manger Mary Sings

O shut your bright eyes that mine must endanger
With their watchfulness; protected by its shade
Escape from my care: what can you discover
From my tender look but how to be afraid?
Love can but confirm the more it would deny.
    Close your bright eye.

Sleep. What have you learned from the womb that bore you
But an anxiety your Father cannot feel?
Sleep. What will the flesh that I gave do for you,
Or my mother love, but tempt you from his will?
Why was I chosen to teach his Son to weep?
    Little One, sleep.

Dream. In human dreams earth ascends to Heaven
Where no one need pray nor ever feel alone.
In your first few hours of life here, O have you
Chosen already what death must be your own?
How soon will you start on the Sorrowful Way?
    Dream while you may.

W.H. Auden
20th century

Balulalow

O my dear heart, young Jesus sweet,
Prepare thy cradle in my spirit,
And I shall rock thee in my heart
And never more from thee depart.

But I shall praise thee evermore
With songs sweet to thy glory;
The knees of my heart shall I bow,
And sing that right *Balulalow!*

James, John and Robert Wedderburn
about 1567

Joseph's Lullaby

Sleep now, little one.
I will watch while you and your mother sleep.
I wish I could do more.
This straw is not good enough for you.
Back in Nazareth I'll make a proper bed for you
Of seasoned wood, smooth, strong, well-pegged.
A bed fit for a carpenter's son.

Just wait till we get back to Nazareth.
I'll teach you everything I know.
You'll learn to use the cedarwood, eucalyptus and fir.
You'll learn to use the drawshave, axe, and saw.
Your arms will grow strong, your hands rough—like these.
You will bear the pungent smell of new wood
and wear shavings and sawdust in your hair.

You'll be a man whose life centres
on hammer and nails and wood.
But for now,
sleep, little Jesus, sleep.

Ron Klug
20th century

The Burning Babe

As I in hoary winter's night stood shivering in the snow,
Surprised I was with sudden heat which made my heart to glow;
And lifting up a fearful eye to view what fire was near,
A pretty Babe all burning bright did in the air appear;
Who scorchèd with excessive heat, such floods of tears did shed,
As though his floods should quench his flames which with his tears
    were fed.
'Alas!' quoth he, 'but newly born in fiery heats I fry,
Yet none approach to warm their hearts or feel my fire but I.
My faultless breast the furnace is, the fuel wounding thorns;
Love is the fire, and sighs the smoke, the ashes shame and scorns;
The fuel justice layeth on, and mercy blows the coals;
The metal in this furnace wrought are men's defilèd souls:
For which, as now on fire I am to work them to their good,
So will I melt into a bath to wash them in my blood.'
With this he vanished out of sight and swiftly shrunk away,
And straight I callèd unto mind that it was Christmas day.

Robert Southwell
1561–95

A Christmas Carol

The other night
I saw a light!
   A star as bright as day!
And ever among
A maiden sung:
   'By-by, baby, lullay.'

This virgin clear
Who had no peer
   Unto her son did say,
'I pray thee, son,
Grant me a boon
   To sing by-by, lullay.

'Let child or man,
Whoever can
   Be merry on this day,
And blessings bring—
So I shall sing
   "By-by, baby, lullay." '

Anonymous
about 1500

The Wonder of the Incarnation

To spread the azure canopy of heaven,
And make it twinkle with those spangs of gold,
To stay the ponderous globe of earth so even,
That it should all, and nought should it uphold;
To give strange motions to the planets seven,
Or Jove to make so meek, or Mars so bold,
To temper what is moist, dry, hot, and cold,
Of all their jars that sweet accords are given:
Lord, to thy wisdom's nought; nought to thy might.
But that thou shouldst (thy glory laid aside)
Come meanly in mortality to bide,
And die for those deserved eternal plight,
   A wonder is so far above our wit,
   That angels stand amazed to muse on it.

William Drummond
1585–1649

At Christmas

Always
in the dark centre
of this season
the birth occurs
noiseless and marvellous
the seers
move on their journeys
there are gestures
of wonder, and at midnight
a resting star.
Always
it is amazing
that the mountains
do not relinquish
their momentary grandeur,
bend to the stable,
let the ermine tremble
there
where the oxen
and the angels are.

Jean Kenward
20th century

It is as if Infancy were the Whole of Incarnation

One time of the year
the new-born child
is everywhere,
planted in madonnas' arms
hay mows, stables,
in palaces or farms,
or quaintly, under snowed gables,
gothic angular or baroque plump,
naked or elaborately swathed,
encircled by Della Robbia wreaths,
garnished with whimsical
partridges and pears,
drummers and drums,
lit by oversize stars,
partnered with lambs,
peace doves, sugar plums,
bells, plastic camels in sets of three
as if these were what we need
for eternity.

But Jesus the Man is not to be seen.
We are too wary, these days,
of beards and sandalled feet.

Yet if we celebrate, let it be
that he
has invaded our lives with purpose,
striding over our picturesque traditions,
our shallow sentiment,
overturning our cash registers,
wielding his peace like a sword,
rescuing us into reality,
demanding much more
than the milk and the softness
and the mother warmth

of the baby in the storefront creche,
(only the Man would ask
all, of each of us)
reaching out
always, urgently, with strong
effective love
(only the Man would give
his life and live
again for love of us).

Oh come, let us adore him—
Christ—*the Lord.*

Luci Shaw
20th century

Unto Us a Son is Given

Given, not lent,
And not withdrawn—once sent,
This Infant of mankind, this One,
Is still the little welcome Son.

New every year,
New born and newly dear,
He comes with tidings and a song,
The ages long, the ages long;

Even as the cold
Keen winter grows not old,
As childhood is so fresh, foreseen,
And spring in the familiar green.

Sudden as sweet
Come the expected feet.
All joy is young, and new all art,
And he, too, whom we have by heart.

Alice Meynell
1847–1922

On the Infancy of our Saviour

Hail, blessed Virgin, full of heavenly grace,
Blest above all that sprang from human race;
Whose heaven-saluted womb brought forth in one,
A blessed Saviour, and a blessed son:
Oh! what a ravishment it had been to see
Thy little Saviour perking on thy knee!
To see him nuzzle in thy virgin breast,
His milk-white body all unclad, undressed!
To see thy busy fingers clothe and wrap
His spradling limbs in thy indulgent lap!
To see his desperate eyes, with childish grace,
Smiling upon his smiling mother's face!
And, when his forward strength began to bloom,
To see him diddle up and down the room!
Oh, who would think so sweet a babe as this
Should e'er be slain by a false-hearted kiss!
Had I a rag, if sure thy body wore it,
Pardon, sweet Babe, I think I should adore it:
Till then, O grant this boon (a boon far dearer),
The weed not being, I may adore the wearer.

Francis Quarles
1592–1644

Judah's Lion

Where does the lion, Judah's lion walk?
Stealthy under star by winter night his soft paws stalk.
Out on lonely hills a cold wind howls and darkness scowls;
Shepherds shiver—danger in the dark!—some wild beast prowls.
Suddenly up springs a light; a voice rings like a bell;
'Joy, O men of Judah! Come and see! Noel! Noel!'
Where lies Judah's longed-for lion? 'Come and see the sight!
Fear not—your golden one is couched among the lambs tonight.'

Keith Patman
20th century

A Meditation for Christmas

Consider, O my soul, what morn is this!
　Whereon the eternal Lord of all things made,
For us poor mortals, and our endless bliss,
　　Came down from heaven; and, in a manger laid
　　The first, rich, offerings of our ransom paid:
Consider, O my soul, what morn is this!

Consider what estate of fearful woe
　Had then been ours, had he refused this birth;
From sin to sin tossed vainly to and fro,
　　Hell's playthings, o'er a doomed and helpless earth!
　　Had he from us withheld his priceless worth,
Consider man's estate of fearful woe!

Consider to what joys he bids thee rise,
　Who comes, himself, life's bitter cup to drain!
Ah! look on this sweet Child, whose innocent eyes
　　Ere all be done, shall close in mortal pain,
　　That thou at last Love's Kingdom may'st attain:
Consider to what joys he bids thee rise!

Consider all this wonder, O my soul;
　And in thine inmost shrine make music sweet!
Yea, let this world, from furthest pole to pole,
　　Join in thy praises this dread birth to greet;
　　Kneeling to kiss thy Saviour's infant feet!
Consider all this wonder, O my soul.

Selwyn Image
1849–1930

Kid Stuff

The wise guys
tell me
that Christmas
is Kid Stuff...
Maybe they've got
something there—
Two thousand years ago
three wise guys
chased a star
across a continent
to bring
frankincense and myrrh
to a Kid
born in a manger
with an idea in his head...
And as the bombs
crash
all over the world today
the real wise guys know
that we've all got to go
chasing stars
again
in the hope
that we can get back
some of that
Kid Stuff
born two thousand years ago.

Frank Horne
20th century

THE SHEPHERDS

For the Nativity

Shepherds, I sing you, this winter's night
Our Hope new-planted, the womb'd, the buried Seed:
For a strange Star has fallen, to blossom from a tomb,
And infinite Godhead circumscribed, hangs helpless at the breast.
Now the cold airs are musical, and all the ways of the sky
Vivid with moving fires, above the hills where tread
The feet—how beautiful!—of them that publish peace.

The sacrifice, which is not made for them,
The angels comprehend, and bend to earth
Their worshipping way. Material kind Earth
Gives him a Mother's breast, and needful food.

A Love, shepherds, most poor,
And yet most royal, kings,
Begins this winter's night;
But oh, cast forth, and with no proper place,
Out in the cold he lies!

John Heath-Stubbs
20th century

From: A Christmas Sequence

IV THE SHEPHERDS

He is so small the stars bow down
    The fierce winds ease their breath,
And careful shepherds look upon
    The one unsullied birth.
They kneel and stare while time seems gone
    And goodness rules the earth.

The blight on man is all undone
    And there will be no death,
For though this child will be nailed on
    A cross, he'll be so since
He is the jewel of untold worth,
    For him all stars have shone.

Elizabeth Jennings
20th century

At Bethlehem

Come, we shepherds, whose blest sight
   Hath met Love's noon in nature's night;
Come, lift we up our loftier song,
And wake the sun that lies too long.

Gloomy night embraced the place
   Where the noble Infant lay:
The Babe looked up and showed his face;
   In spite of darkness, it was day:—
It was the Day, Sweet! and did rise
Not from the east, but from thine eyes.

We saw thee in thy balmy nest,
   Young dawn of our eternal day;
We saw thine eyes break from their east,
   And chase the trembling shades away;
   We saw thee, (and we bless the sight),
We saw thee by thine own sweet light.

Welcome, all wonders in one sight!
   Eternity shut in a span!
Summer in winter! Day in night!
Heaven in earth! and God in man!
Great Little One, whose all-embracing birth,
Lifts earth to heaven, stoops heaven to earth.

Richard Crashaw
1613–49

The Angels for the Nativity of our Lord

Run, shepherds, run, where Bethlem blest appears,
We bring the best of news, be not dismayed,
A Saviour there is born more old than years,
Amidst heaven's rolling heights this earth who stayed.
In a poor cottage inned, a virgin maid
A weakling did him bear, who all upbears;
There is he, poorly swaddled, in manger laid,
To whom too narrow swaddlings are our spheres:
Run, shepherds run, and solemnize his birth,
This is that night—no, day, grown great with bliss,
In which the power of Satan broken is;
In heaven be glory, peace unto the earth!
    Thus singing, through the air the angels swam,
    And cope of stars re-echoèd the same.

William Drummond of Hawthornden
1585–1649

The Shepherds' Carol

We stood on the hills, Lady,
Our day's work done,
Watching the frosted meadows
That winter had won.

The evening was calm, Lady,
The air so still,
Silence more lovely than music
Folded the hill.

There was a star, Lady,
Shone in the night,
Larger than Venus it was
And bright, so bright.

Oh, a voice from the sky, Lady,
It seemed to us then
Telling of God being born
In the world of men.

And so we have come, Lady,
Our day's work done,
Our love, our hopes, ourselves
We give to your son.

Clive Sansom

NEW YEAR: THE MAGI

The Blade of Grass

'A SWORD SHALL GO THROUGH THINE OWN HEART.'
PROPHECY OF SIMEON

Oh! little blade of grass,
    A little sword thou art,
That in thy haste to pass
    Hast pierced thy mother's heart!

Oh! little blade of grass,
    A little tongue thou art
Of cleaving flame,—alas!
    Thou hast cleft thy mother's heart.

Oh! little blade, upcurled
    Leaf, sword, or fiery dart,
To win thy Father's world
    Thou must break thy mother's heart!

Dora Greenwell
1821–82

The New-Year's Gift

Let others look for pearl and gold,
Tissues or tabbies* manifold;
One only look of that sweet hay
Whereon the blessed Baby lay,
Or one poor swaddling-clout, shall be
The richest New-Year's gift to me.

Robert Herrick
1591–1674

* *tabbies:* silks

Two Poems for the Epiphany

1

'This is your road,' sang the bright nova.
'This way, this way!' celestial birds
Shrilled inside their skulls.

Their paths converged before a gaping cave,
A makeshift shelter for cattle.
The Child—vulnerable, red,
Hairless, with pulsing fontanelle—
Received the unbidden gifts.

Three kings—one, blond and frosty eyed,
Chinked the gold coins; a second, yellow,
Long fingernails sheathed in jade, was grasping
A bundle of joss-sticks; while the third
Black-skinned and curly, offered
The bitter herb that's bred from servitude.

2

Winter, a cave, the glittering
Of an unnamed star, to bring
A yellow, a red, and a black king,
With fragrant gum, with gleaming awe,
And with that bitter herb of death:
'Come,' said the wind, with icy breath.
'Come, draw near: you touch, you see
The pivot of the galaxy,
The fire that kindles the sun's core—
God's, and man's epiphany.'

John Heath-Stubbs
20th century

From: Three Kings Came Riding

The Three Kings rode through the gate and the guard,
  Through the silent street, till their horses turned
And neighed as they entered the great inn-yard;
But the windows were closed, and the doors were barred,
  And only a light in the stable burned.

And cradled there in the scented hay,
  In the air made sweet by the breath of kine,
The little child in the manger lay,
The child that would be King one day
  Of a kingdom not human but divine.

His mother, Mary of Nazareth,
  Sat watching beside his place of rest,
Watching the even flow of his breath,
For the joy of life and the terror of death
  Were mingled together in her breast.

They laid their offerings at his feet:
  The gold was their tribute to a King,
The frankincense, with its odour sweet,
Was for the Priest, the Paraclete,
  The myrrh for the body's burying.

And the mother wondered and bowed her head,
  And sat as still as a statue of stone;
Her heart was troubled yet comforted,
Remembering what the angel had said,
  Of an endless reign and of David's throne.

Henry Wadsworth Longfellow
1807–82

Royal Presents

The off'rings of the Eastern kings of old
Unto our lord were incense, myrrh and gold;
Incense because a God; gold as a king;
And myrrh as to a dying man they bring.
Instead of incense (blessed Lord) if we
Can send a sigh or fervent prayer to thee,
Instead of myrrh if we can but provide
Tears that from penitential eyes do slide,
And though we have no gold; if for our part
We can present thee with a broken heart
Thou wilt accept: and say those Eastern kings
Did not present thee with more precious things.

Nathaniel Wanley
1634–80

The Offering

They gave to thee
Myrrh, frankincense and gold
But, Lord, with what shall we
Present ourselves before thy majesty,
Whom thou redeemedst when we were sold?
We've nothing but ourselves, and scarce that neither;
Vile dirt and clay;
Yet it is soft and may
Impression take.
Accept it, Lord, and say, this thou hadst rather;
Stamp it, and on this sordid metal make
Thy holy image, and it shall outshine
The beauty of the golden mine.

Jeremy Taylor
1613–67

Twelfth Night

No night could be darker than this night,
no cold so cold,
as the blood snaps like a wire,
and the heart's sap stills,
and the year seems defeated.

O never again, it seems, can green things run,
or sky birds fly,
or the grass exhale its humming breath
powdered with pimpernels,
from this dark lung of winter.

Yet here are lessons for the final mile
of pilgrim kings;
the mile still left when all have reached
their tether's end: that mile
where the Child lies hid.

For see, beneath the hand, the earth already
warms and glows;
for men with shepherd's eyes there are
signs in the dark, the turning stars,
the lamb's returning time.

Out of this utter death he's born again,
his birth our saviour;
from terror's equinox he climbs and grows,
drawing his finger's light across our blood
the son of heaven, and the son of God.

Laurie Lee
20th century

Hymn

Lord, when the wise men came from far
Led to thy cradle by a star,
Then did the shepherds too rejoice,
Instructed by thy angel's voice.
Blest were the wise men in their skill,
And shepherds in their harmless will.

Wise men, in tracing nature's laws,
Ascend unto the highest cause;
Shepherds with humble fearfulness
Walk safely, though their light be less.
Though wise men better know the way,
It seems no honest heart can stray.

There is no merit in the wise
But love, the shepherds' sacrifice.
Wise men, all ways of knowledge passed,
To the shepherds' wonder come at last.
To know can only wonder breed,
And not to know is wonder's seed.

A wise man at the altar bows,
And offers up his studied vows,
And is received. May not the tears,
Which spring too from a shepherd's fears,
And sighs upon his frailty spent,
Though not distinct, be eloquent?

'Tis true, the object sanctifies
All passions which within us rise,
But since no creature comprehends
The cause of causes, end of ends,
He who himself vouchsafes to know
Best pleases his creator so.

When then our sorrows we apply
To our own wants and poverty,
When we look up in all distress,
And our own misery confess,
Sending both thanks and prayers above,
Then, though we do not know, we love.

Sidney Godolphin
1610–43

The Star of the Heart

The star has risen in the heart,
The sweet light flushes every part.
The shepherds of the body know,
The rumour reached them long ago,
Abiding in the field were they
When deity informed the clay.
The wise kings of the mind bow down,
They yield the wiser king his crown;
Before a cradle they unfold
The myrrh and frankincense and gold.

Susan Mitchell
1866–1926

Epiphany

('... ANGELS BENDING NEAR THE EARTH
TO TOUCH THEIR HARPS OF GOLD.'
Edmund Hamilton Sears 1810–76)

Thank you
Edmund Hamilton Sears
for your carol about the angels,
Thank you, Fra Angelico
for the feather detail of their wings.

Were your pipes frozen
Christina Georgina Rossetti
that you wrote of bleak mid-winter,
earth like iron, snow on snow
and water like a stone. Gas-fired
my central heating keeps the ice out.

Who's that knocking?
A king with a gift of aromatic herbs.
The stick insects, for whom parthenogenesis
is a fact of daily life, sway hopefully
on the drying privet in their tank.
We offer wine. His camel chews the roses.

He insists there is a miracle
In this untidy house.

Jeffery Wheatley
20th century

Words for the Magi

'Shall I bring you wisdom, shall I bring you power?'
The first great stranger said to the child.
Then he noticed something he'd never felt before—
A wish in himself to be innocent and mild.

'Shall I bring you glory, shall I bring you peace?'
The second great stranger said when he saw
The star shine down on entire helplessness.
The gift that he offered was his sense of awe.

'Shall I show you riches' the third one began
Then stopped in terror because he had seen
A God grown-up and a tired tempted man.
'Suffering's my gift' he said
'That is what I mean.'

Elizabeth Jennings
20th century

Rich Man

Rich man, rich man, who are you?
Do you seek the Christ Child, too?
In your palace and your court,
Life is busy, life is short.
Have you time to go away
To find a baby in the hay?
Can you get your camel through
The needle's eye, as you must do?

Rich man, rich man, you've come far.
Where did you learn to trust a star
Instead of turning to a king
To guide you in your wandering?
Rich man, how did you grow wise
In spite of all your kingly guise?
Who taught you to play your part,
To bring an educated heart
To the stable in the west
So you could kneel there and be blessed?

Elizabeth Rooney
20th century

The Journey of the Magi

'A cold coming we had of it,
Just the worst time of the year
For a journey, and such a long journey:
The ways deep and the weather sharp,
The very dead of winter.'
And the camels galled, sore-footed, refractory,
Lying down in the melting snow.
There were times we regretted
The summer palaces on slopes, the terraces,
And the silken girls bringing sherbet.
Then the camel men cursing and grumbling
And running away, and wanting their liquor and women,
And the night-fires going out, and the lack of shelters,
And the cities hostile and the towns unfriendly
And the villages dirty and charging high prices:
A hard time we had of it.
At the end we preferred to travel all night,
Sleeping in snatches,
With the voices singing in our ears, saying
That this was all folly.
Then at dawn we came down to a temperate valley,
Wet, below the snow line, smelling of vegetation,
With a running stream and a water-mill beating the darkness,
And three trees on the low sky.
And an old white horse galloped away in the meadow.
Then we came to a tavern with vine-leaves over the lintel,
Six hands at an open door dicing for pieces of silver,
And feet kicking the empty wine-skins.
But there was no information, and so we continued
And arrived at evening, not a moment too soon
Finding the place; it was (you may say) satisfactory.

All this was a long time ago, I remember,
And I would do it again, but set down
This set down
This; were we led all that way for
Birth or Death? There was a Birth, certainly,
We had evidence and no doubt. I had seen birth and death,
But had thought they were different; this Birth was
Hard and bitter agony for us, like Death, our death.
We returned to our places, these Kingdoms,
But no longer at ease here, in the old dispensation,
With an alien people clutching their gods.
I should be glad of another death.

T.S. Eliot   1888–1965

The Southern Cross

Three ancient men in Bethlehem's cave,
  With awful wonder stand:
A voice had called them from their grave,
  In some far Eastern land.

They lived: they trod the former earth,
  When the old waters swelled,
The ark, that womb of second birth,
  Their house and lineage held.

Pale Japhet bows the knee with gold,
  Bright Sem sweet incense brings,
And Cham the myrrh his fingers hold:
  Lo! the three Orient kings.

Types of the total earth, they hailed
  The signal's starry frame;
Shuddering with second life, they quailed
  At the Child Jesu's Name.

Then slow the Patriarchs turned and trod,
  And this their parting sigh:
'Our eyes have seen the living God,
  And now—once more to die.'

Robert Stephen Hawker
1804–75

Desert Rose

No one will sing your beauty, the poet said—
You must live and die alone.

Three travellers out of the morning rode.
They lingered.
They stirred my incense. They journeyed on.

No shower or shade—
I suffered all day the barren gold of the sun.

A star lifted its head
And seemed to murmur to me alone.

All beyond time are made
star and poem, cornstalk and stone.

Now to the House-of-Bread
I guide three hungry gold-burdened men.

Midnight, rejoicing, shed
Dew in my cup like wine.

George Mackay Brown
20th century

HEROD'S SLAUGHTER
OF THE CHILDREN

Innocent's Song

Who's that knocking on the window,
Who's that standing at the door,
What are all those presents
Lying on the kitchen floor?

Who is the smiling stranger
With hair as white as gin,
What is he doing with the children
And who could have let him in?

Why has he rubies on his fingers,
A cold, cold crown on his head,
Why, when he caws his carol,
Does the salty snow run red?

Why does he ferry my fireside
As a spider on a thread,
His fingers made of fuses
And his tongue of gingerbread?

Why does the world before him
Melt in a million suns,
Why do his yellow, yearning eyes
Burn like saffron buns?

Watch where he comes walking
Out of the Christmas flame,
Dancing, double-talking:

Herod is his name.

Charles Causley
20th century

Christ the Man:
Easter Death and Resurrection

The Call

My blood so red
For thee was shed,
Come home again, come home again:
My own sweet heart, come home again!
You've gone astray
Out of your way,
Come home again, come home again!

Anonymous
17th century

HOLY WEEK

Palm Sunday

Astride the colt and claimed as King
that Sunday morning in the spring,
He passed a thornbush flowering red
that one would plait to crown his head.

He passed a vineyard where the wine
was grown for men of royal line
and where the dregs were also brewed
into a gall for Calvary's rood.

A purple robe was cast his way,
then caught and kept until that day
when, with its use, a trial would be
profaned into a mockery.

His entourage was forced to wait
to let a timber through the gate,
a shaft that all there might have known
would be an altar and a throne.

Marie J. Post
20th century

Ride on!

Ride on! Ride on in majesty!
Hark, all the tribes hosanna cry;
Thy humble beast pursues his road
With palms and scattered garments strowed.

Ride on! Ride on in majesty!
In lowly pomp ride on to die;
O Christ, thy triumphs now begin
O'er captive death and conquered sin.

Ride on! Ride on in majesty!
The wingèd squadrons of the sky
Look down with sad and wondering eyes
To see the approaching sacrifice.

Ride on! Ride on in majesty!
Thy last and fiercest strife is nigh;
The Father on his sapphire throne
Expects his own anointed Son.

Ride on! Ride on in majesty!
In lowly pomp ride on to die;
Bow thy meek head to mortal pain,
Then take, O God, thy power, and reign.

Henry Hart Milman
1791–1868

Palm Sunday: Good Friday

It was but now their sounding clamours sung,
'Blessed is he that comes from the Most High',
And all the mountains with 'Hosanna' rung,
And now, 'Away with him, away,' they cry,
And nothing can be heard but 'Crucify!'
   It was but now the crown itself they save,
   And golden name of King unto him gave,
And now no King but only Caesar they will have.

It was but now they gathered blooming May,
And of his arms disrobed the branching tree,
To strew with boughs and blossoms all thy way,
And now, the branchless trunk a cross for thee,
And May, dismayed, thy coronet must be:
   It was but now they were so kind to throw
   Their own best garments where thy feet should go,
And now, thyself they strip, and bleeding wounds they show.

See where the author of all life is dying.
O fearful day! He dead, what hope of living?
See where the hopes of all our lives are buying*.
O cheerful day! They bought, what fear of grieving?
Love love for hate, and death for life is giving:
   Lo, how his arms are stretched abroad to grace thee,
   And, as they open stand, call to embrace thee.
Why stay'st thou then my soul; O fly, fly thither haste thee.

Giles Fletcher
1586–1623

* *buying*: being bought

A Psalm for Maundy Thursday

Tonight
Lord Jesus Christ
You sat at supper
with your friends.
It was a simple meal
that final one
of lamb
unleavened bread
and wine.
Afterward
You went out to die.
How many other meals you shared
beside the lake
fried fish and toasted bread
at Simon's banquet hall a feast
at Lazarus' home in Bethany
the meal that Martha cooked
on mountain slope
where you fed the hungry crowd
at close of tiring day.
Please sit with us tonight
at our small meal
of soup and rolls and tea.
Then go with us
to feast of bread and wine
that you provide
because afterward
you went out to die.

Joseph Bayly
20th century

A Ballad of Trees and the Master

Into the woods my Master went,
Clean forspent, forspent.
Into the woods my Master came,
Forspent with love and shame.
But the olives they were not blind to him,
The little grey leaves were kind to him:
The thorn-trees had a mind to him
   When into the woods he came.

Out of the woods my Master went,
And he was well content.
Out of the woods my Master came,
Content with death and shame.
When death and shame would woo him last,
From under the trees they drew him last:
'Twas on a tree they slew him—last
   When out of the woods he came.

Sidney Lanier
1842–81

GOOD FRIDAY: THE CRUCIFIXION

Good Friday

O heart, be lifted up; O heart be gay,
Because the Light was lifted up today—
Was lifted on the Rood, but did not die,
To shine eternally for such as I.

O heart, rejoice with all your humble might
That God did kindle in the world this Light,
Which stretching on the Cross could not prevent
From shining with continuous intent.

Why weep, O heart, this day? Why grieve you so?
If all the glory of the Light had lost its glow
Would the sun shine or earth put on her best—
Her flower-entangled and embroidered vest?

Look up, O heart; and then, O heart, kneel down
In humble adoration: give no crown
Nor golden diadem to your fair Lord,
But offer love and beauty by your word...

The everlasting fire of love, O heart,
Has blazed in you and it will not depart.
Wherefore, O heart, exult and praises sing:
Lift up your voice and make the echoes ring...

O heart, rise up: O heart be lifted high.
Rejoice; for Light was slain today, yet did not die.

Anonymous

The Saviour Speaks

Thou who createdst everything,
Sweet Father, heavenly King,
Hear me—I, thy son, implore:
For Man this flesh and bone I bore.

Clear and bright my breast and side,
Blood over whiteness spilling wide,
Holes in my body crucified.

Stiff and stark my long arms rise,
Dimness and darkness cloud my eyes;
Like sculpted marble hang my thighs.

Red my feet with the flowing blood,
Holes in them washed through with that flood.
Mercy on Man's sins, Father on high!
Through all my wounds to thee I cry!

Anonymous
13th century

Good Friday: the Third Nocturn

Alone to sacrifice thou goest, Lord,
Giving thyself to death whom thou hast slain.
For us thy wretched folk is any word,
Who know that for our sins this is thy pain?

For they are ours, O Lord, our deeds, our deeds,
Why must thou suffer torture for our sin?
Let our hearts suffer for thy passion, Lord,
That sheer compassion may thy mercy win.

This is that night of tears, the three days' space,
  Sorrow abiding of the eventide,
Until the day break with the risen Christ,
  And hearts that sorrowed shall be satisfied.

So may our hearts have pity on thee, Lord,
  That they may sharers of thy glory be:
Heavy with weeping may the three days pass,
  To win the laughter of thine Easter Day.

Peter Abelard
1079–1142
translated from Latin by Helen Waddell

Crucifixion to the World by the Cross of Christ

When I survey the wondrous Cross
　　Where the young Prince of Glory died,
My richest gain I count but loss,
　　And pour contempt on all my pride.

Forbid it, Lord, that I should boast
　　Save in the death of Christ my God;
All the vain things that charm me most,
　　I sacrifice them to his blood.

See from his head, his hands, his feet,
　　Sorrow and love flow mingled down;
Did e'er such love and sorrow meet,
　　Or thorns compose so rich a crown?

His dying crimson, like a robe,
　　Spreads o'er his body on the tree;
Then am I dead to all the globe,
　　And all the globe is dead to me.

Were the whole realm of nature mine
　　That were a present far too small;
Love so amazing, so divine,
　　Demands my soul, my life, my all.

Isaac Watts
1674–1748

From: The Dream of the Rood

Listen! I will describe the best of dreams
which I dreamed in the middle of the night
when, far and wide, all men slept.
It seemed that I saw a wondrous tree
soaring into the air, surrounded by light,
the brightest of crosses; that emblem was entirely
cased in gold; beautiful jewels
were strewn around its foot, just as five
studded the cross-beam. All the angels of God
fair creations, guarded it. That was no cross
of a criminal, but holy spirits and men on earth
watched over it there—the whole glorious universe ...

     Now I look day by day
for that time when the cross of the Lord,
which once I saw in a dream here on earth,
will fetch me away from this fleeting life
and lift me to the home of joy and happiness
where the people of God are seated at the feast
in eternal bliss, and set me down
where I may live in glory unending and share
the joy of the saints. May the Lord be a friend to me,
he who suffered once for the sins of men
here on earth on the gallows-tree.
He has redeemed us; he has given life to us,
and a home in heaven.

Anonymous
translated from Anglo-Saxon
by Kevin Crossley-Holland

Christ Crucified

Thy restless feet now cannot go
    For us and our eternal good,
As they were ever wont. What though
    They swim, alas! in their own flood?

Thy hands to give thou canst not lift,
    Yet will thy hand still giving be;
It gives, but O, itself's the gift!
    It gives tho' bound, tho' bound 'tis free!

Richard Crashaw
1613–49

The Crucifixion

    Oh, man's capacity
For spiritual sorrow, corporal pain!
Who has explored the deepmost of that sea,
With heavy links of a far-fathoming chain?

    That melancholy lead,
Let down in guilty and in innocent hold,
Yet into childish hands deliverèd,
Leaves the sequestered floor unreached, untold.

    One only has explored
The deepmost; but he did not die of it.
Not yet, not yet he died. Man's human Lord
Touched the extreme; it is not infinite.

    But over the abyss
Of God's capacity for woe he stayed
One hesitating hour; what gulf was this?
Forsaken he went down, and was afraid.

Alice Meynell
1847–1922

Good Friday, 1613. Riding Westward

Let man's soul be a sphere, and then, in this,
The intelligence that moves, devotion is,
And as the other Spheres, by being grown
Subject to foreign motions, lose their own,
And being by others hurried every day,
Scarce in a year their natural form obey:
Pleasure or business, so, our souls admit
For their first mover, and are whirl'd by it.
Hence is't, that I am carried towards the west
This day, when my soul's form bends toward the east.
There I should see a sun, by rising set,
And by that setting endless day beget;
But that Christ on this cross, did rise and fall,
Sin had eternally benighted all.
Yet dare I almost be glad, I do not see
That spectacle of too much weight for me.
Who sees God's face, that is self life, must die;
What a death were it then to see God die?
It made his own lieutenant, Nature, shrink,
It made his footstool crack, and the sun wink.
Could I behold those hands which span the poles,
And turn all spheres at once, pierced with those holes?
Could I behold that endless height which is
Zenith to us, and our Antipodes,
Humbled below us? or that blood which is
The seat of all our souls, if not of his,
Made dirt of dust, or that flesh which was worn
By God, for his apparel, ragg'd and torn?
If on these things I durst not look, durst I
Upon his miserable mother cast mine eye,
Who was God's partner here, and furnished thus
Half of that sacrifice, which ransomed us?
Though these things, as I ride, be from mine eye,
They are present yet to my memory,
For that looks towards them; and thou look'st towards me,
O Saviour, as thou hang'st upon the tree;
I turn my back to thee, but to receive
Corrections, till thy mercies bid thee leave.
O think me worth thine anger, punish me,
Burn off my rusts, and my deformity,
Restore thine image, so much, by thy grace,
That thou may'st know me, and I'll turn my face.

John Donne
1572–1631

A Quiet Roar

one

he lays his left hand along the beam
hand that moulded clay into fluttering birds
hand that cupped wild flowers to learn their peace
hand that stroked the bee's soft back and touched death's sting

two

he stretches his right hand across the grain
hand that blessed a dead corpse quick
hand that smeared blind spittle into sight
hand that burgeoned bread, smoothed down the rumpled sea

three

he stands laborious
sagging, split,
homo erectus, poor bare forked thing
hung on nails like a picture

he is not beautiful
blood sweats from him in rain

far off where we are lost, desert dry
thunder begins its quiet roar
the first drops startle us alive
the cloud no bigger
than a man's hand

Veronica Zundel
20th century

BURIAL: THE WAITING

Dead and Buried

And so we took him down
(Or thought we did),
Wiped off the sweat and spittle
From his face,
Washed the dried blood,
Threw out the crown of thorns,
And wrapped him once again
In swaddling clothes.

A tomb can be a cramped,
Confining place,
Far smaller than a stable.
We laid him there
(Or thought we did).
We were not able
To comprehend
The infinite contained.
For us it was the end.
Only the harsh realities
Of death and stone
Remained.

Elizabeth Rooney
20th century

Before Easter

Spring;
yet frost still builds
dead palaces.

We hear the crack from
icicles of bone,
snow crowns
have snapped the throats
of daffodils,
the ice-queen walks in
her brittle dress.

No rose-blood in the stem,
no cumulus
perfume in trees,
each day
is a coffin of glass.

The sun is turned
to crystal,
it is our alchemy of winter;
inner cold.

Christ sleeps
behind the quickening stone.

Isobel Thrilling
20th century

Poem for Easter

Wrapped in his shroud of wax, his swoon of wounds,
still as a winter's star he lies with death.

Still as a winter's lake his stark limbs lock
the pains that run in stabbing frosts about him.

Star in the lake, grey spark beneath the ice,
candle of love snuffed in its whitened flesh,

I, too, lie bound within your dawn of cold
while on my breath the serpent mortal moans.

O serpent in the egg, become a rod,
crack the stone shell that holds his light in coil.

O grief within the serpent sink your root
and bear the flower for which our forked tongues wail.

Cold in this hope our mortal eyes forgather
wandering like moths about the tomb's shut mouth;

Waiting the word the riven rock shall utter,
waiting the dawn to fly its bird of god.

Laurie Lee
20th century

Easter Saturday

A curiously empty day,
As if the world's life
Had gone underground.
The April sun
Warming dry grass
Makes pale spring promises
But nothing comes to pass.

Anger
Relaxes into despair
As we remember our helplessness,
Remember him hanging there.
We have purchased the spices
But they must wait for tomorrow.
We shall keep today
For emptiness and sorrow.

Elizabeth Rooney
20th century

Easter Midnight Service

A pagan fire to conjure in the spring—
But this fire we have lit to conjure out
The winter chill of all the pagan rout,
And conjure in the summer of the king.
Soon will the brazen bells of triumph ring,
And midnight dark be shaken by a shout
That death's cold chain that gripped the world about
Is broken link from link: and the links sing.

And fire from fire our candles take the light,
As we take fire from the eternal flame,
And flame from flame we walk down the dark aisle,
Each flame a glory gold against the night,
That trembles at the whisper of the name
That burns through all the empty halls of hell.

Marion Pitman
20th century

EASTER DAY:
THE RESURRECTION

There Was No

There was no grave grave enough
to ground me
to mound me
I broke the balm then slit the shroud
wound round me
that bound me

There was no death dead enough
to dull me
to cull me
I snapped the snake and waned his war
to lull me
to null me

there was no cross cross enough
to nil me
to still me
I hung as gold that bled, and bloomed
A rose that rose and prised the tomb
away from Satan's wilful doom
There was no cross, death, grave
or room
to hold me.

Stewart Henderson
20th century

Easter Night

All night had shout of men and cry
   Of woeful women filled his way;
Until that noon of sombre sky
   On Friday, clamour and display
Smote him; no solitude had he,
    No silence, since Gethsemane.

Public was Death; but Power, but Might,
   But Life again, but Victory,
Were hushed within the dead of night,
   The shuttered dark, the secrecy.
And all alone, alone, alone,
He rose again behind the stone.

Alice Meynell
1847–1922

Easter Hymn

Death and darkness get you packing,
Nothing now to man is lacking,
All your triumphs now are ended,
And what Adam marred is mended;
Graves are beds now for the weary,
Death a nap, to wake more merry;
Youth now, full of pious duty,
Seeks in thee for perfect beauty,
The weak, and agèd tired, with length
Of days, from thee look for new strength,
And infants with thy pangs contest
As pleasant, as if with the breast;
Then, unto him, who thus hath thrown
Even to contempt thy kingdom down,
And by his blood did us advance
Unto his own inheritance,
To him be glory, power, praise,
From this, unto the last of days.

Henry Vaughan
1622–95

Lord of Life

Most glorious Lord of life, that on this day
  Didst make thy triumph over death and sin;
  And having harrowed hell didst bring away
  Captivity thence captive, us to win:
This joyous day, dear Lord, with joy begin,
  And grant that we for whom thou didest die
  Being with thy dear blood clean washed from sin,
  May live for ever in felicity.
And that thy love we weighing worthily,
  May likewise love thee for the same again;
  And for thy sake that all like dear didst buy,
  With love may one another entertain.
So let us love, dear love, like as we ought.
Love is the lesson which the Lord us taught.

Edmund Spenser
1552–99

Glittering Morn

Light's glittering morn bedecks the sky;
Heaven thunders forth its victor-cry;
The glad earth shouts her triumph high,
And groaning hell makes wild reply;

While he, the King, the mighty King,
Despoiling death of all its sting,
And, trampling down the powers of night,
Brings forth his ransomed saints to light.

His tomb of late the threefold guard
Of watch and stone and seal had barred;
But now, in pomp and triumph high,
He comes from death to victory.

The pains of hell are loosed at last;
The days of mourning now are past;
An angel robed in light hath said,
'The Lord is risen from the dead.'

John Mason Neale
1818–66

Love is Come Again

Now the green blade riseth from the buried grain,
Wheat that in dark earth many days has lain;
Love lives again, that with the dead has been:

> *Love is come again,*
> *Like wheat that springeth green.*

In the grave they laid him, Love whom men had slain,
Thinking that never he would wake again,
Laid in the earth like grain that sleeps unseen:

Forth he came at Easter, like the risen grain,
He that for three days in the grave had lain,
Quick from the dead my risen Lord is seen:

When our hearts are wintry, grieving, or in pain,
Thy touch may call us back to life again,
Fields of our hearts that dead and bare have been.

J.M.C. Crum 1872–1958

Resurrection

Everything panicked. Trees shrieked
And withered in the moon's heat.
Birds rose like helium balloons.
Telephone poles popped like corks.
The night was brighter than
A hamburg stand.
The night was hotter than
A hamburg stand.

At last
There came a popping sound
And nails were popping off
The crazy iron armadillo
Like buttons. All the nails.
Fizzing high into the air
Like Roman candles,
Until the spread-eagled body
Once again lay white,
Rising like bread.
And the world and all the nations
Peeled away.

Randall Vander Mey 20th century

Hymn Written at the Holy Sepulchre in Jerusalem

Saviour of mankind, Man, Emmanuel!
Who sinless died for sin, who vanquished hell;
The first-fruits of the grave; whose life did give
Light to our darkness; in whose death we live:—
Oh! strengthen thou my faith, convert my will,
That mine may thine obey; protect me still,
So that the latter death may not devour
My soul, sealed with thy seal.—So, in the hour
When thou (whose body sanctified this tomb,
Unjustly judged), a glorious judge shall come
To judge the world with justice; by that sign
I may be known, and entertained for thine.

George Sandys 1577–1644

When Mary Thro' the Garden Went

When Mary thro' the garden went
    There was no sound of any bird,
And yet, because the night was spent,
    The little grasses lightly stirred,
    The flowers awoke, the lilies heard.

When Mary thro' the garden went,
    The dew lay still on flower and grass,
The waving palms about her sent
    Their fragrance out as she did pass,
    No light upon the branches was.

When Mary thro' the garden went,
    Her eyes, for weeping long, were dim,
The grass beneath her footsteps bent,
    The solemn lilies, white and slim,
    These also stood and wept for him.

When Mary thro' the garden went,
    She sought, within the garden ground,
One for whom her heart was rent,
    One who for her sake was bound,
    One who sought and she was found.

Mary Coleridge 1861–1907

Seven Stanzas at Easter

Make no mistake
if he rose at all
it was as his body;
if the cells' dissolution did not reverse, the
    molecules reknit, the amino acids rekindle,
        the church will fall.

It was not as the flowers,
each soft Spring recurrent;
it was not as his Spirit in the mouths and
    fuddled eyes of the eleven apostles;
it was as his flesh: ours.

The same hinged thumbs and toes,
the same valved heart
that—pierced—died, withered, decayed, and then
    regathered out of his Father's might
new strength to enclose.

Let us not mock God with metaphor,
analogy, sidestepping transcendence;
making of the event a parable, a sign painted in the
    faded credulity of earlier ages;
let us walk through the door.

The stone is rolled back, not papier-mâché,
not a stone in a story,
but the vast rock of materiality that in the slow
    grinding of time will eclipse each of us
the wide light of day.

And if we will have an angel at the tomb,
make it a real angel,
weighty with Max Planck's quanta, vivid with hair,
    opaque in the dawn light, robed in real linen
spun on a definite loom.

Let us not seek to make it less monstrous,
for our own convenience, our own sense of beauty,
lest, awakened in one unthinkable hour, we are
    embarrassed by the miracle,
and crushed by remonstrance.

John Updike
20th century

I Missed Your Resurrection

Left the golden city
by the wrong road.

Passed clacking women
weighted down with flowers
in first spring's colours
sulphur and bone-white

Pressed on to the palled
hills of dead Judaea
whence no help came

Smelt vinegar that one
had scattered there

Burned ass's turds

Light grew behind me
clapped the pale flames out.

Saw only shadows then
on the shining road—my own.

Never looked back.

Catherine Byron
20th century

THE HOLY SPIRIT AND THE CHURCH

From: The Rock

There shall always be the Church and the World
And the Heart of Man
Shivering and fluttering between them, choosing and chosen,
Valiant, ignoble, dark, and full of light
Swinging between Hell Gate and Heaven Gate.
And the Gates of Hell shall not prevail.
Darkness now, then
   Light.

T.S. Eliot
1888–1965

The Holy Spirit: Pentecost

Come Holy Ghost

Come, Holy Ghost, our souls inspire
And lighten with celestial fire;
Thou the anointing Spirit art,
Who dost thy sevenfold gifts impart.

Thy blessed unction from above
Is comfort, life, and fire of love;
Enable with perpetual light
The dulness of our blinded sight;

Anoint and cheer our soiled face
With the abundance of thy grace;
Keep far our foes; give peace at home:
Where thou art guide no ill can come.

Teach us to know the Father, Son,
And thee of both, to be but One,
That through the ages all along
This may be our endless song,
    Praise to thine eternal merit,
    Father, Son, and Holy Spirit.

Anonymous
9th century
translated by John Cosin

Veni Creator Spiritus

Creator Spirit, by whose aid
The world's foundations first were laid,
Come visit every pious mind;
Come pour thy joys on humankind;
From sin and sorrow set us free,
And make thy temples worthy thee.
   O source of uncreated light,
The Father's promised Paraclete!
Thrice holy fount, thrice holy fire,
Our hearts with heavenly love inspire;
Come, and thy sacred unction bring
To sanctify us while we sing!
   Plenteous of grace, descend from high,
Rich in thy sevenfold energy,
Thou strength of his almighty hand,
Whose power does heaven and earth command!
Proceeding Spirit, our defence,
Who dost the gift of tongues dispense,
And crownst thy gift with eloquence!
   Refine and purge our earthy parts;
But, O, inflame and fire our hearts!
Our frailties help, our vice control,
Submit the senses to the soul;
And when rebellious they are grown,
Then lay thy hand and hold them down.
   Chase from our minds the infernal foe,
And peace, the fruit of love, bestow;
And lest our feet should step astray,
Protect and guide us in the way.
   Make us eternal truths receive,
And practise all that we believe:
Give us thyself that we may see
The Father and the Son, by thee.
   Immortal honour, endless fame,
Attend the Almighty Father's Name:
The Saviour Son be glorified,
Who for lost man's redemption died;
And equal adoration be,
Eternal Paraclete, to thee.

John Dryden
1631–1700

Hymn to the Holy Spirit

Come, Holy Dove,
Descend on silent pinion,
Brood o'er my sinful soul with patient love,
Till all my being owns thy mild dominion.

Round yon sad Tree
With frequent circles hover,
That in my glorious Surety I may see
Grace to redeem and righteousness to cover.

On wings of peace
Bring from that precious altar
The blood which bids the storms of conscience cease,
And blots out all the debt of the defaulter.

Spirit of grace,
Reveal in me my Saviour,
That I may gaze upon his mirrored face,
Till I reflect it in my whole behaviour.

Oh, let me hear
Thy soft, low voice controlling
My devious steps with intimations clear,
With comforts manifold my heart consoling.

Let that sweet sound
To holy deeds allure me,
With heavenly echoes make my spirit bound,
And of my home in paradise assure me.

Come, Holy Dove,
Guide me to yon bright portal,
Where I shall see the Saviour whom I love,
And enter on the joys which are immortal.

Richard Wilton
1827–1903

Be the Power of All Things Within Us

O God the Holy Ghost who art Light unto thine elect,
  Evermore enlighten us.
Thou who art Fire of love,
  Evermore enkindle us.
Thou who art Lord and Giver of life,
  Evermore live in us.
Thou who bestowest sevenfold grace,
  Evermore replenish us.
As the wind is thy symbol,
  So forward our goings.
As the dove,
  So launch us heavenwards.
As water,
  So purify our spirits.
As a cloud,
  So abate our temptations.
As dew,
  So revive our languor.
As fire,
  So purge out our dross.

Christina Rossetti
1830–94

The Holy Spirit

Come with birds' voices when the light grows dim
Yet lovelier in departure and more dear:
While the warm flush hangs yet at heavens' rim,
And the one star shines clear.

Though the swift night haste to approaching day
Stay thou and stir not, brooding on the deep:
Thy secret love, thy silent word let say
Within the senses' sleep.

Softer than dew. But where the morning wind
Blows down the world, O Spirit! show thy power:
Quicken the dreams within the languid mind
And bring thy seed to flower!

Evelyn Underhill
1875–1941

Pentecost is Every Day

I share and share and share again
sometimes with a new language
which, if you are so open
will take you behind the sky
and award you cartwheels across the sun
I give and give and give again
not restricted by the church calendar
or concocted ritual
I have no need of anniversaries
for I have always been
I speak and speak and speak again
with the sting of purity
that can only be Me
causing joyous earthquakes in the mourning soul of man
I am and am and am again

Stewart Henderson
20th century

Breath of God

Breathe on me, breath of God
Fill me with life anew,
That I may love what thou dost love,
And do what thou wouldst do.

Breathe on me, breath of God,
Until my heart is pure:
Until with thee I have one will
To do and to endure.

Breathe on me, breath of God,
Till I am wholly thine,
Until this earthly part of me
Glows with thy fire divine.

Breathe on me, breath of God,
So shall I never die,
But live with thee the perfect life
Of thine eternity.

Edwin Hatch
1835–89

Pentecost

So free, so bright, so beautiful and fair,
the Holy Dove descends the earthly air:
in startling joyance come
from its immortal home,
it bears the Glory that all men may share.

Through ancient space and newest time, it brings
transcendent reason to a world of things:
it shows each mind and heart
how to assume its part
in dances born of God's imaginings.

On wings of subtlest flame, the Holy Dove
flies through the human world and offers love:
it teaches Heart and Mind
how to transcend their kind
and praise the God who lets all being move.

So free, so bright, so beautiful and fair,
the Holy Dove flies through the mortal air:
always there descending,
always there ascending,
it brings the Glory that all men may share.

John Bennett
20th century

The Church – and Churches

The Church the Garden of Christ

We are a Garden walled around,
Chosen and made peculiar Ground;
A little Spot enclosed by Grace
Out of the World's wide Wilderness.

Like Trees of Myrrh and Spice we stand,
Planted by God the Father's hand;
And all the Springs in Sion flow,
To make the young Plantation grow.

Awake, O heavenly Wind, and come,
Blow on this Garden of Perfume;
Spirit Divine, descend and breathe
A gracious Gale on Plants beneath.

Make our best Spices flow abroad
To entertain our Saviour-God:
And Faith, and Love, and Joy appear,
And every Grace be active here.

Let my Beloved come, and taste
His pleasant Fruits at his own Feast.
I come, my Spouse, I come, he cries,
With Love and Pleasure in his eyes.

Our Lord into his Garden comes,
Well pleased to smell our poor Perfumes,
And calls us to a Feast Divine,
Sweeter than Honey, Milk, or Wine.

Eat of the tree of Life, my Friends,
The Blessings that my Father sends;
Your taste shall all my Dainties prove,
And drink abundance of my Love.

Jesus, we will frequent thy Board,
And sing the Bounties of our Lord:
But the rich Food on which we live
Demands more Praise than Tongues can give.

Isaac Watts
1674–1748

The Winds

There is a tree grows upside down,
  Its roots are in the sky;
Its lower branches reach the earth
  When amorous winds are nigh.

On one lone bough there starkly hangs
  A Man just crucified,
And all the other branches bear
  The choice fruits of the Bride.

When Pleasure's wind goes frisking past,
  Unhallowed by a prayer,
It swirls dead leaves from earth-born trees,
  Old growths of pride and care.

The gracious fruits are hidden by
  These leaves of human stain;
The Crucified, beneath his load
  Shudders, as if in pain.

But swift springs down a credal wind,
  It thrills through all the boughs;
The dead leaves scatter and are lost;
  The Christ renews his vows.

His hands direct the Spirit's wind
  Branch after branch to shake;
The Bride's fruit drops, and at the touch
  Elected hearts awake.

Jack Clemo
20th century

The City of God

O thou not made with hands,
Not throned above the skies,
Nor walled with shining walls,
Nor framed with stones of price,
　　More bright than gold or gem,
　　God's own Jerusalem!

Where'er the gentle heart
Finds courage from above;
Where'er the heart forsook
Warms with the breath of love;
　　Where faith bids fear depart,
　　City of God! thou art.

Thou art where'er the proud
In humbleness melts down;
Where self itself yields up;
Where martyrs win their crown;
　　Where faithful souls possess
　　Themselves in perfect peace.

Where in life's common ways
With cheerful feet we go;
When in his steps we tread
Who trod the way of woe;
　　Where he is in the heart,
　　City of God! thou art.

Not throned above the skies,
Nor golden-walled afar,
But where Christ's two or three
In his name gathered are,
　　Be in the midst of them,
　　God's own Jerusalem!

Francis Palgrave
1825–97

The Kingdom of God

'IN NO STRANGE LAND'

O world invisible, we view thee,
O world intangible, we touch thee,
O world unknowable, we know thee,
Inapprehensible, we clutch thee!

Does the fish soar to find the ocean,
The eagle plunge to find the air—
That we ask of the stars in motion
If they have rumours of thee there?

Not where the wheeling systems darken,
And our benumbed conceiving soars!—
The drift of pinions, would we hearken,
Beats at our own clay-shuttered doors.

The angels keep their ancient places;—
Turn but a stone, and start a wing!
'Tis ye, 'tis your estranged faces,
That miss the many-splendoured thing.

But (when so sad thou canst not sadder)
Cry;—and upon thy so sore loss
Shall shine the traffic of Jacob's ladder
Pitched betwixt Heaven and Charing Cross.

Yea, in the night, my Soul, my daughter,
Cry;—clinging Heaven by the hems;
And lo, Christ walking on the water
Not of Gennesareth, but Thames!

Francis Thompson
1859–1907

The Belfry

I have seen it standing up grey,
Gaunt, as though no sunlight
Could ever thaw out the music
Of its great bell; terrible
In its own way, for religion
Is like that. There are times
When a black frost is upon
One's whole being, and the heart
In its bone belfry hangs and is dumb.

But who is to know? Always,
Even in winter in the cold
Of a stone church, on his knees
Someone is praying, whose prayers fall
Steadily through the hard spell
Of weather that is between God
And himself. Perhaps they are warm rain
That brings the sun and afterwards the flowers
On the raw graves and throbbing of bells.

R.S.Thomas 20th century

From: Il Penseroso

To walk the studious cloister's pale,
And love the high embowèd roof,
With antique pillars massy proof,
And storied windows richly dight,
Casting a dim religious light.
There let the pealing organ blow
To the full-voicèd quire below,
In service high and anthems clear,
As may with sweetness, through mine ear,
Dissolve me into ecstasies,
And bring all heaven before mine eyes.
And may at last my weary age
Find out the peaceful hermitage,
The hairy gown and mossy cell,
Where I may sit and rightly spell
Of every star that heaven doth shew,
And every herb that sips the dew,
Till old experience do attain
To something like prophetic strain.

John Milton 1608–74

Church Closed

(ST MATTHIAS' POPLAR: OCTOBER 24 1986,
THE 10TH ANNIVERSARY OF ITS LAST SERVICE)

Like some great barn grown old among the trees,
windblown and empty, broken and betrayed,
so slowly rots this consecrated place
where every week I preached, and daily prayed.

No hands now offer books or pull the bell;
silent except for pigeon-wings and rain
it speaks yet from the monuments that tell
'Here lies the body...' dust to dust again.

In sombre gloom, let us today aspire
to make one last procession, single file:
there hung the sailors' flags, here stood the choir
(step carefully as we tread the cratered aisle).

These vestries—dark and empty holes at best;
what chaplains, vicars, bishops passed this way?
What children sang their songs, souls found their rest?
If walls could speak, or bricked-up windows say!

Yes, gently walk, this earth, this pitted floor
was polished once with care, trodden with love;
these wooden pillars which the waves once saw—
how long before they creak, and crack, and move?

And here lies—half a font, beyond repair;
above, the pensioned bell-rope still hangs down:
here rose the gallery with curving stair—
how long before the roof is overthrown?

The organ's quiet now, scarcely a sign
of pipe or pedal, stops and console gone:
it sounded many a tuneful wedding-line,
but now its final funeral is done.

'With angels and archangels...' here we joined;
we broke the bread, and held the precious cup:
three centuries have heard the gospel's sound—
what message now of life, what word of hope?

Do angels weep at this—or have they seen
worse things to mourn than broken bricks and stones?
Even the tombs outside are crumbling in
as roots and branches overgrow old bones.

Stop! Let our solemn, silent progress cease;
I'll not sing Alleluia here again:
but let me pray 'Forgive our trespasses...'
before a foolish pilgrim's last Amen.

Christopher Idle
20th century

The Windows

Lord, how can man preach thy eternal word?
   He is a brittle, crazy glass;
Yet in thy temple thou dost him afford
   This glorious and transcendent place,
   To be a window, through thy grace.

But when thou dost anneal in glass thy story,
   Making thy life to shine within
The holy Preacher's, then the light and glory
   More rev'rend grows, and more doth win;
   Which else shows waterish, bleak, and thin.

Doctrine and life, colours and light, in one
   When they combine and mingle, bring
A strong regard and awe; but speech alone
   Doth vanish like a flaring thing,
   And in the ear, not conscience, ring.

George Herbert
1593–1633

The Porch

Do you want to know his name?
It is forgotten. Would you learn
what he was like? He was like
anyone else, a man with ears
and eyes. Be it sufficient
that in a church porch on an evening
in winter, the moon rising, the frost
sharp, he was driven
to his knees and for no reason
he knew. The cold came at him;
his breath was carved angularly
as the tombstones; an owl screamed.

He had no power to pray.
His back turned on the interior
he looked out on a universe
that was without knowledge
of him and kept his place
there for an hour on that lean
threshold, neither outside nor in.

R.S. Thomas
20th century

Divina Commedia

Oft have I seen at some cathedral door
    A labourer pausing in the dust and heat,
    Lay down his burden, and with reverent feet
Enter, and cross himself, and on the floor
Kneel to repeat his paternoster o'er;
    Far off the noises of the world retreat;
    The loud vociferations of the street
    Become an indistinguishable roar.
So, as I enter here from day to day,
    And leave my burden at this minster gate,
    Kneeling in prayer, and not ashamed to pray,
The tumult of the time disconsolate
    To inarticulate murmurs dies away,
    While the eternal ages watch and wait.

Henry Wadsworth Longfellow
1807–82

Thy Kingdom Come

The Lord's Prayer
  flows from facile worshippers
  like TV voices
  recounting the worries of the world
  and the wonders of anti-perspirants.

Lacking a congregation,
since all are
praying to themselves
or to impress the rest,
God seldom has a thing to do
or anyone to listen to.

Quietly he waits
to catch a man
who wants to find
but has not found
the meaning of
'Thy will be done.'
One such is worth
a thousand dissembling
'Thine be the glories'
to an idol god.

Patiently God listens
for a troubled saint
with nothing
but a sense of sin
to lean heavily
on his pew
praying 'Lord, have mercy!'
and yearning
for the Kingdom
that is yet to come.

Elmer F. Suderman
20th century

Compound Metaphors for Sunday Morning

No war of earth or heaven darkens
the stillness of this timely church.

Earth is ours:
It blusters against the windows
and shakes the panes
we eye the sky through.

And heaven too:
Falling, it intersects the wind,
cuts through all panes
and fills with light the eyes
we close to see.

The long division of the saints
is set aside.
In the mathematics of the cross
all products, sums, and quotients
equal one.

John Leax 20th century

Lavinia at Church

Lavinia is polite, but not profane;
To church as constant as to Drury Lane.
She decently, in form, pays heaven its due;
And makes a civil visit to her pew.
Her lifted fan, to give a solemn air,
Conceals her face, which passes for a prayer:
Curtsies to curtsies, then, with grace, succeed;
Not one the fair omits, but at the creed.
Or if she joins the service, 'tis to speak;
Through dreadful silence the pent heart might break;
Untaught to bear it, women talk away
To God himself, and fondly think they pray.
But sweet their accent, and the air refined;
For they're before their Maker—and mankind:
When ladies once are proud of praying well,
Satan himself will toll the parish bell.

Edward Young 1683–1765

Lambeth Lyric

Some seven score Bishops late at Lambeth sat,
Grey-whiskered and respectable debaters:
Each had on head a well-strung curly hat;
    And each wore gaiters.

And when these prelates at their talk had been
Long time, they made yet longer proclamation,
Saying: 'These creeds are childish! both Nicene,
    And Athanasian.

'True, they were written by the Holy Ghost;
So, to re-write them were perhaps a pity.
Refer we their revision to a most
    Select Committee!

'In ten years' time we wise Pan Anglicans
Once more around this Anglo Catholic table
Will meet, to prove God's word more weak than man's,
    His truth less stable.'

So saying homeward the good Fathers go;
Up Mississippi some and some up Niger.
For thine old mantle they have clearly no
    More use, Elijah!

Instead, an apostolic apron girds
Their loins, which ministerial fingers tie on:
And Babylon's songs they sing, new tune and words,
    All over Zion.

The Creeds, the Scriptures, all the Faith of old,
They hack and hew to please each bumptious German,
Windy and vague as mists and clouds that fold
    Tabor and Hermon.

Happy Establishment in this thine hour!
Behold thy bishops to their sees retreating!
'Have at the Faith!' each cries: 'good bye till our
    Next merry meeting!'

Lionel Johnson
1867–1902

The Evangelist

'My brethren...' And a bland, elastic smile
Basks on the mobile features of Dissent.
No hypocrite, you understand. The style
Befits a church that's based on sentiment.

Solicitations of a swirling gown,
The sudden vox humana, and the pause,
The expert orchestration of a frown
Deserve, no doubt, a murmur of applause.

The tides of feeling round me rise and sink;
Bunyan, however, found a place for wit.
Yes, I am more persuaded than I think;
Which is, perhaps, why I disparage it.

You round upon me, generously keen:
The man, you say, is patently sincere.
Because he is so eloquent, you mean?
That test was never patented, my dear.

If, when he plays upon our sympathies,
I'm pleased to be fastidious, and you
To be inspired, the vice in it is this:
Each does us credit, and we know it too.

Donald Davie
20th century

The Leader

He comes, The Leader, with much applause
and turning of heads and scraping—
bring out the candles and celebrity damask!
(Colour the carpet red,
the ride first class,
the bills paid.
Colour his face smiley in the morning papers.)
For He's here our great our only
our venerated Christian VIP!
So spread the banquet rich and pungent
and politely munch and listen
to his poised and perpendicular words
on world poverty the whole man
healing helping loving feeding
(please pass the shrimp cocktail).
Render to Him His due acclamation.
    And meanwhile gently ignore the other—
the servant the sufferer the lowly lamb
watching in sorrow from behind
the potted geraniums.

Nancy Thomas
20th century

Frescoes in an Old Church

(STOWELL PARK, GLOUCESTERSHIRE)

Six centuries have gone
Since, one by one,
These stones were laid,
And in air's vacancy
This beauty made.

They who thus reared them
Their long rest have won;
Ours now this heritage—
To guard, preserve, delight in, brood upon;
And in these transitory fragments scan
The immortal longings in the soul of Man.

Walter de la Mare
1873–1956

Celtic Chapel

A rusted grating in the ancient wall
in whose cold squares the child would frame his face;
the roofless gables held their light and space
where monks came singing to the vesper call.

This, they said, used to be the home of God,
this fading whisper of an ancient tale.
A silent chantry without altar rail,
bare ruin reaching for the sailing cloud.

William Neil   20th century

In Canterbury Cathedral

On a day sweet with April showers
the safe tyres of our tour bus
had sung us south from London,

Sightseer pilgrims, cameras slung,
no need or time on patient plodding
horses for long diverting tales.

We stood at last at Beckett's shrine
lost in architecture and dates,
confused by Norman and Gothic.

Our ancient tiny guide seemed shrunk
into his suit, dwarfed by his clothes
as we were all dwarfed by time.

His small precise English voice went on:
pronounced 'Our Lord,' and the words
fell on us like a benediction.

'Our'—incredible assumption of union
offered in passing to American strangers,
mortar for diverse motley stones.

Time and blood and history redeemed
from meaninglessness: two words
turned sightseers into pilgrims.

E.W. Oldenburg
20th century

In Church

Often I try
To analyse the quality
Of its silences. Is this where God hides
From my searching? I have stopped to listen,
After the few people have gone,
To the air recomposing itself
For vigil. It has waited like this
Since the stones grouped themselves about it.
These are the hard ribs
Of a body that our prayers have failed
To animate. Shadows advance
From their corners to take possession
Of places that light held
For an hour. The bats resume
Their business. The uneasiness of the pews
Ceases. There is no other sound
In the darkness but the sound of a man
Breathing, testing his faith
On emptiness, nailing his questions
One by one to an untenanted cross.

R.S.Thomas
20th century

Te Deum Laudamus

High in the steepled church the shining bells
swing tongues unmuted to delight the air
with calls to praise, that anyone awake
might now begin this dawning hour with prayer.

Deep in the wood the hermit thrush,
in spiralled ecstasies to greet the dawn,
loops silver sounds for God's own sake alone,
flings his Te Deum now the night is gone.

If we, bell beckoned, should refuse to sing
Te Deum Laudamus to begin our days,
the very stars would ring, the rocks would shout
as now thrush, lark, and linnet spill his praise.

Marie J. Post
20th century

DAILY LIFE

At Dressing in the Morning

Now I arise, empowered by thee,
    The glorious sun to face;
O clothe me with humility,
    Adorn me with thy grace.

All evil of the day forefend,
    Prevent the Tempter's snare;
Thine angel on my steps attend,
    And give me fruit to prayer.

O make me useful as I go
    My pilgrimage along;
And sweetly soothe this vale of woe
    By charity and song.

Let me from Christ obedience learn,
    To Christ obedience pay;
Each parent duteous love return,
    And consecrate this day.

Christopher Smart
1722–71

Work

Market Women

(CARIBBEAN)

Down from the hills, they come
With swinging hips and steady stride
To feed the hungry Town
They stirred the steep dark land
To place within the growing seed.
And in the rain and sunshine
Tended the young green plants,
They bred, and dug and reaped.
And now, as Heaven has blessed their toil,
They come, bearing the fruits,
These hand-maids of the Soil,
Who bring full baskets down,
To feed the hungry Town.

Daisy Myrie
20th century

Milking Croon

Bless, O God, my little cow,
Bless, O God, my desire;
Bless thou my partnership
And the milking of my hands, O God.

Bless, O God, each teat,
Bless, O God, each finger;
Bless thou each drop
That goes into my pitcher, O God!

Traditional Celtic

Daily Labour

Forth in thy name, O Lord, I go,
　My daily labour to pursue;
Thee, only thee, resolved to know,
　In all I think or speak or do.

The task thy wisdom hath assigned
　O let me cheerfully fulfil,
In all my works thy presence find
　And prove thy acceptable will.

Preserve me from my calling's snare,
　And hide my simple heart above,
Above the thorns of choking care,
　The gilded baits of worldly love.

Thee may I set at my right hand,
　Whose eyes my inmost substance see,
And labour on at thy command,
　And offer all my works to thee.

Give me to bear thy easy yoke,
　And every moment watch and pray,
And still to things eternal look,
　And hasten to thy glorious day;

For thee delightfully employ
　Whate'er thy bounteous grace hath given,
And run my course with even joy
　And closely walk with thee to heaven.

Charles Wesley
1707–88

Glory

Oh, you gotta get a glory
　In the work you do;
A Hallelujah chorus
　In the heart of you.

Paint, or tell a story,
　Sing, or shovel coal,
But you gotta get a glory,
　Or the job lacks soul.

Anonymous

Knitting Woman

In her chosen corner she sits. Rivers of knitting
cascade plaining and purling over her lap
winter and summer together. She has her reasons,
knows that sudden contrary August weather
is worse than blizzards in winter, trusts no seasons.

Her young have escaped. She sees them
at large in the world's cold winds. Her anxious care
follows them all by post, in cumbersome parcels,
cabled and striped and ribbed. She knows no ill
that can't be cured in an Aran jacket, or better
endured in a mohair sweater. God
may temper the wind or not, but never
a lamb of hers will ever be caught shorn.

She sits defying hap and circumstance,
weak chests, ill luck, chaos and old night.

She would like to knit the whole world a pullover.

Evangeline Paterson
20th century

Reflections

An old woman, sitting among petunias
Shelling broad beans.
Delivers one pale green baby after another:
Lumpy forehead, tucked-up legs.
Green placenta below.
She thinks of rice grains, pouring from the jar.
And blow-flies' eggs on meat:
She thinks of water at the plug-hole,
The swirling hearts of daisies,
And far imagined nebulae:
And of herself, a tiny creator
Delighting in all she makes.
An old woman, sitting in the sunshine,
Ponders on the economy of God.

Stephanie Gifford
20th century

Barnyard Miracle

Paulina the heifer would not stand still
while I milked her.
Five times she had kicked
so viciously
that the steel hobbles had sprung
from her legs.
Despite the tender welts where the hobble clamps
had been attached,
she was angry enough to do it again.
The fifth kick had lost me the milk
so I was angry too.
In adolescent temper I took the gutter shovel
and beat the heifer five, eight, eleven strokes
until I heard your voice, Mother.
You were in the barn for some heifer milk
for oyster stew.
Milk from other cows would do,
but heifer milk is better.
'Sietze, Sietze,
God's blessing can never rest on such temper.'
You went to the heifer's head,
served her an extra portion of cornmeal,
and talked to her woman-to-woman:
'You've got to be quiet inside, Paulina,
in order to be quiet outside.'

Paulina stood perfectly still
while I finished milking her.
I wondered guiltily
what manner of woman you were
that even the raging Paulina
obeyed you.
And what's more,
in addition to the pailful spilled,
she still gave enough milk
for oyster stew.

Sietze Buning
20th century

From: The Woman's Labour

When bright Orion glitters in the skies
In winter nights, then early we must rise;
In weather ne'er so bad, wind, rain or snow,
Our work appointed, we must rise and go,
While you on easy beds may lie and sleep,
Till light does through your chamber windows peep.

When to the house we come where we should go,
How to get in, alas! we do not know:
The maid quite tired with work the day before,
O'ercome with sleep; we standing at the door,
Oppressed with cold, and often call in vain,
Ere to our work we can admittance gain.
But when from wind and weather we get in,
Briskly with courage we our work begin;
Heaps of fine linen we before us view,
Where on to lay our strength and patience too;
Cambrics and muslins, which our ladies wear,
Laces and edgings, costly, fine and rare,
Which must be washed with utmost skill and care;
With holland shirts, ruffles and fringes too,
Fashions which our forefathers never knew.
For several hours here we work and slave,
Before we can one glimpse of daylight have;
We labour hard before the morning's past,
Because we fear the time runs on too fast.

At length bright Sol illuminates the skies,
And summons drowsy mortals to arise;
Then comes our mistress to us without fail,
And in her hand, perhaps, a mug of ale
To cheer our hearts, and also to inform
Herself what work is done that very morn;
Lays her commands upon us, that we mind
Her linen well, nor leave the dirt behind.
Not this alone, but also to take care
We don't her cambrics nor her ruffles tear;
And these most strictly does of us require,
To save her soap and sparing be of fire;
Tells us her charge is great, nay furthermore,
Her clothes are fewer than the time before.

Now we drive on, resolved our strength to try,
And what we can, we do most willingly;
Until with heat and work, 'tis often known,
Not only sweat but blood runs trickling down
Our wrists and fingers: still our work demands
The constant action of our labouring hands.

Mary Collier
1690?–1762

The List

Flawlessly typed, and spaced
At the proper intervals,
Serene and lordly, they pace
Along tomorrow's list
Like giftbearers on a frieze.

In tranquil order, arrayed
With the basic human equipment—
A name, a time, a number—
They advance on the future.

Not more harmonious who pace
Holding a hawk, a fish, a jar
(The customary offerings)
Along the valley of the kings.

Tomorrow these names will turn nasty,
Senile, pregnant, late,
Handicapped, handcuffed, unhandy,
Muddled, moribund, mute,

Be stained by living. But here,
Orderly, equal, right,
On the edge of tomorrow, they pause
Like giftbearers on a frieze

With the proper offering,
A time, a number, a home.
I am the artist, the typist;
I did my best for them.

U.A. Fanthorpe
20th century

Hymn and Prayer for Civil Servants

O Thou who seest all things below,
Grant that thy servants may go slow,
That they may study to comply
With regulations till they die.

Teach us, O Lord, to reverence
Committees more than common sense;
To train our minds to make no plan
And pass the baby when we can.

So when the tempter seeks to give
Us feelings of initiative,
Or when alone we go too far,
Chastise us with a circular.

Mid war and tumult, fire and storms,
Give strength, O Lord, to deal out forms.
Thus may thy servants ever be
A flock of perfect sheep for thee.

Published anonymously in the Daily Telegraph

Negotiation with a Higher Power

I will demonstrate
my immediate
obedience
providing you comply
with my demand
for a more satisfying
assignment.

Thomas John Carlisle
20th century

Loom Blessing

Thrums nor odds of thread
My hand never kept, nor shall keep,

Every colour in the bow of the shower
Has gone through my fingers beneath the cross,

White and black, red and madder,
Green, dark grey, and scarlet,

Blue and roan, and colour of the sheep,
And never a particle of cloth was wanting.

I beseech calm Bride the generous,
I beseech mild Mary the loving,
I beseech Christ Jesu the humane,
That I may not die without them,
    That I may not die without them.

Traditional Celtic

Washing Day

Socks and stockings
are strung like crotchets on the line.
White shirts trill a little
beside the trumpeting of
underwear let loose.
Sheets clap, trousers flap,
dishcloths drip in time.
They have come to expect
this ritual of song and dance;
fabric from my world inside.

Rosemary A. Hector
20th century

I Sit and Sew

I sit and sew—a useless task it seems,
My hands grown tired, my head weighed down with dreams—
The panoply of war, the material tread of men,
Grim-faced, stern-eyed, gazing beyond the ken
Of lesser souls, whose eyes have not seen Death,
Nor learned to hold their lives but as a breath—
But—I must sit and sew.

I sit and sew—my heart aches with desire—
That pageant terrible, that fiercely pawing fire
On wasted fields, and writhing grotesque things
Once men. My soul in pity flings
Appealing cries, yearning only to go
There in that holocaust of hell, those fields of woe—
But—I must sit and sew.

The little useless seam, the idle patch;
Why dream I here beneath my homely thatch,
When there they lie in sodden mud and rain,
Pitifully calling me, the quick ones and the slain!
You need me, Christ! It is no roseate dream
That beckons me—this pretty futile seam,
It stifles me—God, must I sit and sew?

Alice Dunbar Nelson
1875–1935

Housekeeper

This is my little town,
My Bethlehem,
And here, if anywhere,
My Christ Child
Will be born.

I must begin
To go about my day—
Sweep out the inn,
Get fresh hay for the manger
And be sure
To leave my heart ajar
In case there may be travellers
From afar.

Elizabeth Rooney
20th century

The Elixir

Teach me, my God and King,
In all things thee to see,
And what I do in any thing,
To do it as for thee:

Not rudely, as a beast,
To run into an action;
But still to make thee prepossessed,
And give it his perfection.

A man that looks on glass,
On it may stay his eye;
Or if he pleaseth, through it pass,
And then the heavens espy.

All may of thee partake:
Nothing can be so mean,
Which with this tincture, 'for thy sake',
Will not grow bright and clean.

A servant with this clause
Makes drudgery divine:
Who sweeps a room, as for thy laws,
Makes that and th'action fine.

This is the famous stone
That turneth all to gold:
For that which God doth touch and own
Cannot for less be told.

George Herbert
1593–1632

Domestic Threat

House-proud housewives, listen to the rumble—
the desert drifting daily closer to your door.
Sand is softly silting the surface like a sea-floor.
You'll snatch a broom like King Canute?
or plant some trees, house-humble?

Grace Westerduin
20th century

Huswifery

Make me, O Lord, thy spinning wheel complete.
  Thy holy word my distaff make for me.
Make mine affections thy swift flyers neat
  And make my soul thy holy spool to be.
  My conversation make to be thy reel
  And reel the yarn thereon spun of thy wheel.

Make me thy loom then; knit therein this twine;
  And make thy Holy Spirit, Lord, wind quills;
Then weave the web thyself. The yarn is fine.
  Thine ordinances make my fulling mills.
  Then dye the same in heavenly colours choice,
  All pinked with varnished flowers of Paradise.

Then clothe therewith mine understanding, will,
  Affections, judgement, conscience, memory,
My words and actions, that their shine may fill
  My ways with glory and thee glorify.
  Then my apparel shall display before ye
  That I am clothed in holy robes for glory.

Edward Taylor
1645–1729

Blessing

The sacred Three be over me
With my working hands this day
With the people on my way
With the labour and the toil
With the land and with the soil
With the tools that I take
With the things that I make
With the thoughts of my mind
With the sharing with mankind
With the love of my heart
With each one who plays a part
The sacred Three be over me
The blessing of the Trinity

David Adam
20th century

By All Means Bless

By all means
bless the cloth
that wiped
the face
of Jesus

By all means
bless the towel
that unfolds
an infant
like miraculous bread

By all means
bless the towel
the boxer returns to
—a brief harbour
after a harassing round

By all means
bless the sacred silk
that garbs
the sumo's
amplitude of loin

But I say this also
bless the towel
that unwraps
your buttocks
(fresh out of the shower)
with such casual ease

we overlook
life's small epiphanies

John Agard
20th century

JESUS THE CARPENTER

Work

Close by the careless worker's side,
  Still patient stands
The Carpenter of Nazareth
  With pierced hands
Outstretched to plead unceasingly,
  His love's demands.

Longing to pick the hammer up
  And strike a blow,
Longing to feel his plane swing out,
  Steady and slow,
The fragrant shavings falling down,
  Silent as snow.

Because this is my work, O Lord,
  It must be thine,
Because it is a human task
  It is divine.
Take me, and brand me with thy cross,
  Thy slave's proud sign.

G.A. Studdert Kennedy
1883–1929

Craftsman

Carpenter's son, carpenter's son,
is the wood fine
and smoothly sanded, or rough-grained,
lying along your back? Was it well-planed?
Did they use
a plumbline
when they set you up? Is the angle true?
Why did they choose
that dark, expensive stain
to gloss the timbers
next to your feet and fingers? You
should know—who
Joseph-trained, judged all trees
for special service.

Carpenter's son, carpenter's son,
were the nails new and cleanly driven
when the dark hammers sang?
Is the earth warped from where you hang,
high enough for a
world view?

Carpenter's son, carpenter's son,
was it a job well done?

Luci Shaw
20th century

A Question of Wood

He who grew up
   with wood around
   ran with infant feet on sawdust ground
   who in childhood played
   with wooden toys made by a caring father
   yet with youthful hand
   learnt to whittle wood
   shaping pieces to his own command.

   What dreadful irony
   decreed that wood should be
   his instrument of death
   and could it be
   that Joseph once embraced
   that traitor tree?

   At the very end
   did wood become his enemy or friend?
   Did splinters stab his arms
   when outstretched
   for the nailing of his palms?
   Or did dear familiarity
   carve comfort even then
   evoking honest kindly men
   ladles or the mother's chair
   and a working carpenter?

Peggy Poole
20th century

Woodworkers' Ballad

All that is moulded of iron
Has lent to destruction and blood;
But the things that are honoured in Zion
Are most of them made from wood.

Stone can be chiselled to Beauty,
And iron shines bright for Defence;
But when Mother Earth pondered her duty
She brought forth the forest, from whence

Come tables, and chairs, and crosses,
Little things that a hot fire warps,
Old ships that the blue wave tosses,
And fiddles for music, and harps;

Oak boards where the carved ferns mingle,
Monks' shrines in the wilderness,
Snug little huts in the dingle,
All things that the sad poets bless.

King Arthur had a wood table;
And our Lord blessed wood; for you see,
He was born in a wooden stable,
And he died on a wooden tree;

And he sailed in a wooden vessel
On the waters of Galilee,
And he worked at a wooden trestle
At his wonderful carpentry.

Oh, all that is moulded of iron
Has lent to destruction and blood;
But the things that are honoured of Zion
Are most of them made from wood.

Herbert Edward Palmer
born 1880

Home

A Thanksgiving to God for his House

Lord, thou hast given me a cell
    Wherein to dwell;
A little house, whose humble roof
    Is weather-proof;
Under the spars of which I lie
    Both soft and dry;
Where thou my chamber for to ward
    Hast set a guard
Of harmless thoughts, to watch and keep
    Me while I sleep.
Low is my porch, as is my fate,
    Both void of state;
And yet the threshold of my door
    Is worn by the poor,
Who thither come and freely get
    Good words, or meat:
Like as my parlour, so my hall
    And kitchen's small:
A little buttery, and therein
    A little bin,
Which keeps my little loaf of bread
    Unchipped, unflead:
Some brittle sticks of thorn or briar
    Make me a fire,
Close by whose living coal I sit,
    And glow like it.
Lord, I confess too, when I dine,
    The pulse is thine,
And all those other bits, that be
    There placed by thee;
The worts, the purslain, and the mess
    Of water-cress,
Which of thy kindness thou hast sent;
    And my content
Makes these and my beloved beet
    To be more sweet.
'Tis thou that crown'st my glittering hearth
    With guiltless mirth,
And giv'st me wassail bowls to drink,
    Spiced to the brink.
Lord, 'tis thy plenty-dropping hand,
    That soils my land;

And gives me, for my bushel sown,
   Twice ten for one:
Thou mak'st my teeming hen to lay
   Her egg each day:
Besides my healthful ewes to bear
   Me twins each year:
The while the conduits of my kine
   Run cream (for wine).
All these, and better thou dost send
   Me, to this end,
That I should render, for my part,
   A thankful heart;
Which, fired with incense, I resign
   As wholly thine;
But the acceptance, that must be,
   My Christ, by thee.

Robert Herrick 1591–1674

The Guardians

May a strong guardian
Stand at the door
With sword and olive branch.

May the keeper of the windows
Be eager-eyed
For dawn and first star,
   snow-light and corn-light.

May the keeper of the fire
See a loaf on the table
And faces of travellers lit with welcome
   and shadow-of-flame, in winter.

May the keeper of the beds be resolute
Against the terror that walks by night,
And herd with gentleness the flocks of sleep.

In a blue-and-silver morning
On the first winter step
Those guardians, and others who hold
   a finger to the lip, smiling
Came about her who holds now the key of the house.

George Mackay Brown 20th century

To the Family Home Awaiting Repair

Oh, long narrow home heavy with living
An age of memories people the walls
Around your naked frame.

Warm shell of love & crowding children
Where the young girls in uniform
Hats worn like horseguards
Speech full of the school diction
Cycle up to ask for who's at home.

And the cool Trade Winds carry echoes
Pavan for A Dead Princess
Played on the Thorens
Until it wore the grooves.

The scent of roses in the slim garden
Growing in the four-hour overhead sun
Smell of bread from the oven
Everything mingling in the wind.

The tales we told around the dining table
Linking the luncheons with their spell
(Sometimes the battlefield for table tennis).

The statue of JT at the desk
Image of the dedicated student.
The stairs are torn away that quivered to the steps
Impatient for games & parties but slow for school.

So many came here—tea-visiting professors,
Exam students, poets, novelists, sculptors,
A Chief Justice—a future Prime Minister
Once talked halfway through the night.

Through a hole in the hooded verandah
The bats spelt six o'clock evening patrol.

And little children to the Kindergarten
Wrestling their way into the hall of learning
Chattering, tormenting the wild cherry-tree
That always yields its fruit.

Oh, crowd your long years of memory
Into a prayer for their future
For all who lived and loved and studied here.

A.J. Seymour
20th century

Poverty

As in the house I sat
Alone and desolate,
No creature but the fire and I,
The chimney and the stool, I lift mine eye
Up to the wall
And in the silent hall
Saw nothing mine
But some few cups and dishes shine:
The table and the wooden stools
Where people used to dine:
A painted cloth there was
Wherein some ancient story wrought
A little entertained my thought
Which light discovered through the glass.

I wondered much to see
That all my wealth should be
Confined in such a little room,
Yet hope for more I scarcely durst presume.
It grieved me sore
That such a scanty store
Should be my all:
For I forgot my ease and health,
Nor did I think of hands or eyes,
Nor soul nor body prize;
I neither thought the sun,
Nor moon, nor stars, nor people, mine,
Though they did round about me shine;
And therefore was I quite undone.

Some greater things I thought
Must needs for me be wrought,
Which till my craving mind could see
I ever should lament my poverty:
I fain would have
Whatever bounty gave;
Nor could there be
Without, or love or deity:

For, should not he be infinite
Whose hand created me?
Ten thousand absent things
Did vex my poor and wanting mind,
Which, till I be no longer blind,
Let me not see the King of kings.

His love must surely be
Rich, infinite, and free;
Nor can he be thought a God
Of grace and power, that fills not his abode,
His holy court,
In kind and liberal sort;
Joys and pleasures,
Plenty of jewels, goods, and treasures,
(To enrich the poor, cheer the forlorn)
His palace must adorn,
And given all to me:
For till his works my wealth became,
No love, or peace, did me enflame:
But now I have a deity.

Thomas Traherne
1636?–74

The Kitchen

I love the sunshine in the kitchen,
The glory of the light awakens
All the familiar textures of pot and china.
This is the home of the house,
The centre of its warmth,
The articulation of its love,
In the rise of bread, the crust of pie,
And the richness of gravy.
It is the place of your caring,
Fleshed out in the daily details,
Too small to be noted one by one,
But each constructing the heart of the house.

Your delight in us is incarnated here,
And this is the place of our true receiving.
Here we come hungry, thirsty and in our need,
To meet the kindness of your hands.
And your friends came,
Finding a warmth they sought and a love they craved.
Not a pretentious place,
A good cause or a moral crusade.
If you will, another Nazareth,
Hidden in the wilderness of the world,
Where kindness feeds a poor Christ and his friends,
And bids them come in from the dark.

Tim Marks
20th century

From: Breakfast

A dinner-party, coffee, tea,
Sandwich, or supper, all may be
In their way pleasant. But to me
Not one of these deserves the praise
That welcomer of new-born days,
A breakfast, merits; ever giving
Cheerful notice we are living
Another day refreshed by sleep,
When its festival we keep.
Now, although I would not slight
Those kindly words we use, 'Good-night',
Yet parting words are words of sorrow,
And may not vie with sweet 'Good-morrow',
With which again our friends we greet,
When in the breakfast-room we meet,
At the social table round,
Listening to the lively sound
Of those notes which never tire,
Of urn, or kettle on the fire.

Mary Lamb
1765–1847

House Communion

Here on this accustomed table
    dull stained by family meals
    and spilled milk of past infancy,
    elbowed in friends' fellowship,

as my own house-guest I break bread,
    hosted by heart's depth,
    charged with mimetic obedience
    offer what is not my own.

May the presence hold on hasty mornings
    and through evenings of weariness
    justifying the repetitions
    of all failures that venture on worthiness.

Raymond Chapman
20th century

Supper Being Ended

In the quiet place
at close of day
he washes the feet of my mind from the dust of its fret.

His infinite eyes
see the staining and wounds of the road, his hands
bring smarting
and cleansing
and balm.

The grace of his health
restores my soul
her place in the circling stars of perpetual praise.

Then, taking again the seamless robe, the Alpha-Omega,
Master and Lord,
we talk together,
friend with friend.

Joan A. Bidwell
20th century

Morning and Night

AT MORNING LIGHT

Morning Hymn

Christ, whose glory fills the skies,
    Christ the true, the only light,
Sun of righteousness, arise,
    Triumph o'er the shades of night!
Day-spring from on high, be near!
Day-star, in my heart appear!

Dark and cheerless is the morn
    Unaccompanied by thee;
Joyless is the day's return,
    Till thy mercy's beams I see;
Till they inward light impart,
    Glad my eyes, and warm my heart.

Visit then this soul of mine,
    Pierce the gloom of sin and grief!
Fill me, radiancy divine,
    Scatter all my unbelief!
More and more thyself display,
Shining to the perfect day.

Charles Wesley
1707–88

Morning Hymn

What's this morn's bright eye to me,
If I see not thine and thee,
Fairer Jesu; in whose face
All my Heaven is spread!—Alas,
Still I grovel in dead night,
Whilst I want thy living light;
Dreaming with wide open eyes
Fond fantastic vanities.

Shine, my only Day-Star, shine:
So mine eyes shall wake by thine;
So the dreams I grope in now
To clear visions all shall grow;
So my day shall measured be
By thy grace's clarity;
So shall I discern the path
Thy sweet law prescribèd hath;
For thy ways cannot be shown
By any light but by thine own.

Joseph Beaumont
1615–99

From: Morning Sacrifice

Awake, my soul, and with the sun,
Thy daily stage of duty run;
Shake off dull sloth, and joyful rise,
To pay thy morning sacrifice.

Thy precious time misspent, redeem;
Each present day thy last esteem;
Improve thy talent with due care,
For the great day thyself prepare...

Wake, and lift up thyself, my heart,
And with the angels bear thy part,
Who all night long unwearied sing
High praise to the eternal King...

Glory to thee, who safe hast kept,
And hast refreshed me while I slept:—
Grant, Lord, when I from death shall wake,
I may of endless light partake.

Thomas Ken
1637–1711

From: Gascoigne's Good-morrow

You that have spent the silent night
In sleep and quiet rest,
And joy to see the cheerful light
That riseth in the east,
Now clear your voice, now cheer your heart,
Come help me now to sing;
Each willing wight come bear a part
To praise the heavenly King.

And you whom care in prison keeps,
Or sickness doth suppress,
Or secret sorrow breaks your sleeps,
Or dolours do distress—
Yet bear a part in doleful wise,
Yea think it good accord
And acceptable sacrifice,
Each sprite to praise the Lord.

The dreadful night with darksomeness
Had overspread the light,
And sluggish sleep with drowsiness
Had overpressed our might:
A glass wherein you may behold
Each storm that holds our breath—
Our bed the grave, our clothes like mould,
And sleep like dreadful death.

Yet as this deadly night did last
But for a little space,
And heavenly day now night is past
Doth show his pleasant face,
So must we hope to see God's face
At last in heaven on high,
When we have changed this mortal place
For immortality ...

Unto which joys for to attain
God grant us all his grace,
And send us after worldly pain
In heaven to have a place,
Where we may still enjoy that light
Which never shall decay.
Lord, for thy mercy lend us might
To see that joyful day.

George Gascoigne 1542–77

GOD, THE SOURCE OF LIGHT

To Christ our Lord

Hail, heavenly beam, brightest of angels thou,
sent unto men upon this middle-earth!
Thou art the true refulgence of the sun,
radiant above the stars, and from thyself
illuminest for ever all the tides of time.
And as thou, God indeed begotten of God,
thou Son of the true Father, wast from aye,
without beginning, in the heaven's glory,
so now thy handiwork in its sore need
prayeth thee boldly that thou send to us
the radiant sun, and that thou comest thyself
to enlighten those who for so long a time
were wrapt around with darkness, and here in gloom
have sat the livelong night, shrouded in sin.

Cynewulf
about 820

Incarnatio est Maximum Dei Donum

Like as the fountain of all light created
Doth pour out streams of brightness undefined
Through all the conduits of transparent kind
That heaven and air are both illuminated,
And yet his light is not thereby abated:
So God's eternal bounty ever shined
The beams of being, moving, life, sense, mind,
And to all things himself communicated.
But see the violent diffusive pleasure
Of goodness, that left not till God had spent
Himself by giving us himself, his treasure,
In making man a God omnipotent.
How might this goodness draw our souls above,
Which drew down God with such attractive love.

William Alabaster
1567–1640

Spectrum

A little window, eastward, low, obscure,
A flask of water on the vestry press,
A ray of sunshine through a fretted door,
And myself kneeling in live quietness:

Heaven's brightness was then gathered in the glass,
Marshalled and analysed, as one by one
In terms of fire I saw the colours pass,
Each in its proper beauty, while the sun

Made his dear daughter Light sing her own praise,
(As Wisdom may, who is a mode of light),
Counting her seven great jewels; then those rays
Remerged in the whole diamond, total sight.

This globe revolved subservient: that just star
Whirled in his place; water and glass obeyed
The laws appointed: with them, yet how far
From their perfection, I still knelt and prayed.

Ruth Pitter
20th century

DARKNESS AND NIGHT

Night-time Prayer

May the Light of lights come
   To my dark heart from thy place;
May the Spirit's wisdom come
   To my heart's tablet from my Saviour.

Celtic traditional

Steadfast Taper

(JOB 28:3)

His candle shines upon my head.
He trims the wick and guards the flame
and though the darkness creeps in close
the steadfast taper shines the same.

The flower of flame sways in the air.
Wind fingers snatch and try to snuff
the stalk his careful hands protect.
The light shines through. It is enough.

His candle shines on me in love,
(protective circle in the gloom)
and through the dreadful night I know
that he is with me in the room.

Throughout the weary waiting-time
the liquid flame shines thin and pure.
When tiredness dims my faith, I look
and see his light, and I am sure.

Luci Shaw
20th century

At Undressing in the Evening

These clothes, of which I now divest
  Myself, All-seeing Eye,
Must be one day (that day be blest)
  Relinquished and laid by.

Thou cordial sleep, to death akin,
  I court thee on my knee;
O let my exit, free from sin,
  Be little more than thee.

But if much agonizing pain
  My dying hour await,
The Lord be with me to sustain,
  To help and to abate.

O let me meet thee undeterred,
  By no foul stains defiled!
According to thy holy word,
  Receive me as a child.

Christopher Smart
1722–71

Evening

She sweeps with many-coloured brooms,
And leaves the shreds behind;
Oh, housewife in the evening west,
Come back, and dust the pond!

You dropped a purple ravelling in,
You dropped an amber thread;
And now you've littered all the East
With duds of emerald!

And still she plies her spotted brooms,
And still the aprons fly,
Till brooms fade softly into stars—
And then I come away.

Emily Dickinson
1830–86

From: Evening Hymn

'ABIDE WITH US: FOR IT IS TOWARD EVENING, AND THE DAY IS FAR SPENT' (LUKE 24:29)

'Tis gone, that bright and orbèd blaze,
Fast fading from our wistful gaze;
Yon mantling cloud has hid from sight
The last faint pulse of quivering light.

In darkness and in weariness
The traveller on his way must press,
No gleam to watch on tree or tower,
Whiling away the lonesome hour.

Sun of my soul! Thou Saviour dear,
It is not night if thou be near:
Oh! may no earth-born cloud arise
To hide thee from thy servant's eyes ...

Abide with me from morn till eve,
For without thee I cannot live:
Abide with me when night is nigh,
For without thee I dare not die ...

Come near and bless us when we wake,
Ere through the world our way we take;
Till in the ocean of thy love
We lose ourselves in Heaven above.

John Keble
1792–1866

The Presence of God

The night is come like to the day,
Depart not thou, great God, away;
Let not my sins, black as the night,
Eclipse the lustre of thy light.
Keep still in my horizon, for to me
The sun makes not the day, but thee.
Thou whose nature cannot sleep,
On my temples sentry keep;
Guard me 'gainst those watchful foes,
Whose eyes are open while mine close.
Let no dreams my head infest,
But such as Jacob's temples blest.
While I do rest, my soul advance,
Make my sleep a holy trance:
That I may, my rest being wrought,
Awake into some holy thought.
And with an active vigour run
My course, as doth the nimble sun.
Sleep is a death, O make me try
By sleeping what it is to die.
And as gently lay my head
On my grave, as now my bed.
Now ere I rest, great God, let me
Awake again at last with thee.
And thus assured, behold I lie
Securely, or to wake or die.
These are my drowsy days, in vain
I do now wake to sleep again.
O come that hour, when I shall never
Sleep again, but wake for ever!

Sir Thomas Browne
1605–82

Night Blessing

Glory to thee, my God, this night
For all the blessings of the light;
Keep me, O keep me, King of kings,
Beneath thy own almighty wings.

Forgive me, Lord, for thy dear Son,
The ills that I this day have done,
That with the world, myself, and thee
I, ere I sleep, at peace may be.

Teach me to live, that I may dread
The grave as little as my bed;
Teach me to die, that so I may
Rise glorious at the awful day.

O may my soul on thee repose,
And with sweet sleep mine eyelids close,
Sleep that may me more vigorous make
To serve my God when I awake.

When in the night I sleepless lie,
My soul with heavenly thoughts supply;
Let no ill dreams disturb my rest,
No powers of darkness me molest.

Praise God, from whom all blessings flow,
Praise him, all creatures here below,
Praise him above, ye heavenly host,
Praise Father, Son, and Holy Ghost.

Thomas Ken
1637–1711

From: Night

Dear night! this world's defeat,
That stop to busy fools, care's check and curb,
The day of spirits; my soul's calm retreat
Which none disturb!
Christ's progress, and his prayer-time,
The hours to which high heaven doth chime.

God's silent, searching flight,
When my Lord's head is filled with dew, and all
His locks are wet with the clear drops of night;
His still, soft call,
His knocking time, the soul's dumb watch,
When spirits their fair kindred catch.

Were all my loud, evil days
Calm and unhaunted as is thy dark tent,
Whose peace but by some angel's wing or voice
Is seldom rent,
Then I in heaven all the long year
Would keep and never wander here.

But living where the sun
Doth all things wake, and where all mix and tire
Themselves and others, I consent and run
To every mire;
And by the world's ill-guiding light
Err more than I can do by might.

There is in God, some say,
A deep, but dazzling darkness: as men here
Say it is late and dusky, because they
See not all clear.
O for that night! when I in him
Might live invisible and dim.

Henry Vaughan
1622–95

The Bright Firmament

When I survey the bright
    Celestial sphere;
So rich with jewels hung, that night
Doth like an Ethiop bride appear:

My soul her wings doth spread
    And heaven-ward flies,
The Almighty's mysteries to read
In the large volumes of the skies.

For the bright firmament
    Shoots forth no flame
So silent, but is eloquent
In speaking the Creator's name.

No unregarded star
    Contracts its light
Into so small a character,
Removed far from our human sight,

But if we steadfast look
    We shall discern
In it, as in some holy book,
How man may heavenly knowledge learn.

It tells the conqueror,
    That far-stretched power,
Which his proud dangers traffic for,
Is but the triumph of an hour:

That from the farthest north,
    Some nation may,
Yet undiscovered, issue forth,
And o'er his new-got conquest sway:

Some nation yet shut in
    With hills of ice
May be let out to scourge his sin,
Till they shall equal him in vice.

And then they likewise shall
    Their ruin have;
For as yourselves your empires fall,
And every kingdom hath a grave.

Thus those celestial fires,
   Though seeming mute,
The fallacy of our desires
And all the pride of life confute:—

For they have watched since first
   The world had birth:
And found sin in itself accurst,
And nothing permanent on earth.

William Habington
1605–54

Evening Praise

Ere I sleep, for every favour
   This day showed
   By my God
I will bless my Saviour.

O my Lord, what shall I render
   To thy name,
   Still the same,
Merciful and tender?

Thou hast ordered all my goings
   In thy way,
   Heard me pray,
Sanctified my doings.

Leave me not, but ever love me:
   Let thy peace
   Be my bliss,
Till thou hence remove me.

Thou my rock, my guard, my tower,
   Safely keep,
   While I sleep,
Me, with all thy power.

So, whene'er in death I slumber,
   Let me rise
   With the wise,
Counted in their number.

John Cennick
1718–55

Evening Prayer

Oh, thou that art unwearying, that dost neither sleep
    Nor slumber, who didst take
All care for Lazarus in the careless tomb, oh keep
    Watch for me till I wake.
If thou think for me what I cannot think, if thou
    Desire for me what I
Cannot desire, my soul's interior Form, though now
    Deep-buried, will not die,
—No more than the insensible dropp'd seed which grows
    Through winter ripe for birth
Because, while it forgets, the heaven remembering throws
    Sweet influence still on earth,
—Because the heaven, moved moth-like by thy beauty, goes
    Still turning round the earth.

C.S. Lewis
1898–1963

Before Sleep

The toil of day is ebbing,
The quiet comes again,
In slumber deep relaxing
The limbs of tired men.

And minds with anguish shaken,
And spirits racked with grief,
The cup of all forgetting
Have drunk and found relief.

The still Lethean waters
Now steal through every vein,
And men no more remember
The meaning of their pain...

Let, let the weary body
Lie sunk in slumber deep.
The heart shall still remember
Christ in its very sleep.

Prudentius
348–about 405
translated from Latin by Helen Waddell

Who Cares?
The Voice of Protest

The Latest Decalogue

Thou shalt have one God only; who
Would be at the expense of two?
No graven images may be
Worshipped, except the currency:
Swear not at all, for, for thy curse
Thine enemy is none the worse:
At church on Sunday to attend
Will serve to keep the world thy friend:
Honour thy parents; that is, all
From whom advancement may befall:
Thou shalt not kill; but needst not strive
Officiously to keep alive:
Do not adultery commit;
Advantage rarely comes of it:
Thou shalt not steal; an empty feat,
When it's so lucrative to cheat:
Bear not false witness; let the lie
Have time on its own wings to fly:
Thou shalt not covet; but tradition
Approves all forms of competition.

The sum of all is, thou shalt love,
If any body, God above:
At any rate shall never labour
More than thyself to love thy neighbour.

Arthur Hugh Clough
1819–61

On Another's Sorrow

Can I see another's woe
And not be in sorrow too.
Can I see another's grief
And not seek for kind relief.

Can I see a falling tear,
And not feel my sorrows share,
Can a father see his child,
Weep, nor be with sorrow filled.

Can a mother sit and hear,
An infant groan an infant fear—
No no never can it be.
Never never can it be.

And can he who smiles on all
Hear the wren with sorrows small,
Hear the small birds grief & care
Hear the woes that infants bear—

And not sit beside the nest
Pouring pity on their breast,
And not sit the cradle near
Weeping tear on infant's tear...

He doth give his joy to all.
He becomes an infant small.
He becomes a man of woe
He doth feel the sorrow too.

Think not, thou canst sigh a sigh,
And thy maker is not by.
Think not, thou canst weep a tear,
And thy maker is not near.

O! he gives to us his joy,
That our grief he may destroy
Till our grief is fled & gone
He doth sit by us and moan.

William Blake
1757–1827

The Poor of London

Almighty God, whose justice like a sun
Shall coruscate along the floors of Heaven,
Raising what's low, perfecting what's undone,
Breaking the proud and making odd things even,
The poor of Jesus Christ along the street
In your rain sodden, in your snows unshod,
They have nor hearth, nor sword, nor human meat,
Nor even the bread of men: Almighty God.

The poor of Jesus Christ whom no man hears
Have waited on your vengeance much too long.
Wipe out not tears but blood: our eyes bleed tears.
Come smite our damnèd sophistries so strong
That thy rude hammer battering this rude wrong
Ring down the abyss of twice ten thousand years.

Hilaire Belloc
1870–1953

Feeding the Poor at Christmas

Every Christmas we feed the poor.
We arrive an hour late. Poor dears,
Like children waiting for a treat.
Bring your plates. Don't move.
Don't try turning up for more.
No. Even if you don't drink
you can't take your share
for your husband. Say thank you
and a rosary for us every evening.
No. Not a towel and a shirt,
even if they're old.
What's that you said?
You're a good man, Robert, yes,
beggars can't be, exactly.

Eunice de Souza
20th century

Ain't I a Woman?

That man over there say
  a woman needs to be helped into carriages
and lifted over ditches
  and to have the best place everywhere.
Nobody ever helped me into carriages
  or over mud puddles
    or gives me a best place...

And ain't I a woman?
  Look at me
Look at my arm!
  I have ploughed and planted
and gathered into barns
  and no man could head me...
And ain't I a woman?
  I could work as much
and eat as much as a man—
  when I could get to it—
and bear the lash as well
  and ain't I a woman?
I have borne thirteen children
  and seen most all sold into slavery
and when I cried out a mother's grief
  none but Jesus heard me...
and ain't I a woman?
  that little man in black there say
a woman can't have as much rights as a man
  cause Christ wasn't a woman
Where did your Christ come from?
  From God and a woman!
Man had nothing to do with him!
  If the first woman God ever made
was strong enough to turn the world
  upside down, all alone
together women ought to be able to turn it
  rightside up again.

Erlene Stetson from a speech by Isabella,
a slave freed in 1827 and known as Sojourner Truth
1797–1883

They Had It Coming

The South East Asians,
they were made to cry,
Look at their eyes all
narrowed up and ready to bawl.
Black Africans:
Obesity wouldn't suit them.
There's a grace about their
slenderness.
Their children would be naked
without a covering of flies.
Indians are perfect for begging
in ragged clothes
and falling dead on the streets
without too much sensation.
There are so many of them
that death is no longer a problem.
Middle Easterners, South Americans,
they were made to look anguished,
the mother crying to God,
the children just crying.
Earthquakes provide opportunity
for this.
While Westerners were made to laugh
in fast cars with beautiful friends.
They were made to drink and spend money.
Do not disturb the balance of nature.

Steve Turner
20th century

Reaction to a Retard

Disgusting, really, the way it disfigures
the face—a lack of intelligence. The retard
on the ferry has nothing going for him
except his mother, who gives him a regard

I struggle to comprehend. I hear a quick
voice cry, Better to kill him before birth!
I look at him and shudder at my own depravity.
How easy it is to deny a person worth—

to limit the human, which is the image
of God, to the beautiful and clever,
and to forget that there is in every person
a spark, a spirit, that abides for ever.

There is a worse disorder than the damaged
brain that disfigures the blameless face.
It is the derangement of the cogent mind
that deforms the heart by a denial of grace.

Andrew Lansdown
20th century

Alcoholic

O all the problems other people face
we have intensified & could not face
until at last we feel completely alone
thick in a quart of company a day.

I knew I had a problem with that stuff
& problems with my wife & child & work;
But all what help I found left me intact
safe with a quart of feral help a day.

DT's, convulsions, hospitals galore.
Projectile vomiting hours, intravenous,
back in the nearest bar the seventh day.
God made a suggestion. I went home

and I am in the 4th week of the third treatment
& I am *hurting*, daily, and when I jerk
a few scales seem to fall away from my eyes
until with perfect clarity enough

seems to be visible to keep me sane
& sober toward the bed where I will die.
I pray that you may grant me a yielding will.

I pray that my will may be attuned to
your will for & with me.

John Berryman
20th century

Caribbean Woman Prayer

Wake up Lord
brush de sunflakes from yuh eye
back de sky a while Lord
and hear dis Mother-woman
on behalf of her pressure-down people

God de Mudder
God de Fadder
God de Sister
God de Brudder
God de Holy fire

Ah don't need to tell yuh
how tings stan
cause right now you know
dat old lizard ah walk
lick land
and you know how de pickney belly laang
an you know how de fork ah hit stone
and tho it rain you know it really drought
an even now de man have start fuh count

de wata he make

God de Fadder
God de Mudder
God de Sister
God de Brudder
God de Holy Fire

Give me faith

O Lord
you know we is ah people
of a proud an generous heart
and how it shame us bad
dat we kyant welcome friend or stranger
when eat time comes around

You know is not we nature
to behave like yard fowl

You know dat is de politics
and de times

and de tricks
dat has reduced we to dis

An talking bout politics Lord
I hope you give de politicians dem
de courage to do what they have to do
and to mek dem see dat tings must grow
from within
an not from without
even as you suffer us not
to walk in de rags of doubt

Mek dem see dat de people
must be at de root of de heart
dat dis place ain't Uncle Sam backyard
Lord, look how Rodney and Bishop get blast

God de Mudder
God de Fadder
God de Sister
God de Brudder
God de Holy Fire

To cut a laang story short
I want to see de children
wake up happy to de sunrise
an food in de pot

I want to see dem stretch limb
and watch dem sleep pon good stomach
I want to see de loss of hope
everywhere replace
wid de win of living

I want to see de man and woman
being in they being

Yes Lord
Halleliuh Lord!

All green tings an hibiscus praises Lord

Grace Nichols
20th century

~ 388 ~

Somewhere in Suburbia

she'd have had her mother's eyes
but she never had her heart
she'd have had her father's smile
but he couldn't spare the time

she could have been a radical
a twice-born evangelical
she could have had her photo
on her grandmother's wall

but the doctors get their money
and the nurses change the bedclothes
and somewhere in suburbia
there'll be one less mouth to feed

King Herod sits in Harley Street
the land of milk and honey
while his bankers in the counting house
are counting out the money

a doctor puts his raincoat on
the nurses hurry home
the Maker gets his image back
a girl drives home alone

now the doctors get their money
and the nurses change the bedclothes
and somewhere in suburbia
there'll be one less mouth to feed

Mike Starkey
20th century

We Were Going to be Twins

What attracted us to one another initially
was we shared the same womb
albeit the unconsidered products of flippant passion
Anyway, we were pre-natal room mates
checking each other's progress
transfixed by the budding of tiny fingernails
and the rhythm of miniscule chests
rising and falling like pale pink bellows
My brother, for that's what he was now becoming,
had a curious almost whimsical shape
his head leaning to one side
as if he were always about to ask a question
He used to poke gentle fun
at my by now rapidly expanding feet
I only had two
but on occasions because of the space they took up
they seemed to number far more
I can't remember exactly when we were terminated
My brother went first
in plunged a knife
ended his life
with a slish and a slash and a silent scream
I proved to be a more unwilling participant
like an irritating piece of dust
in the very corner of a skirting board
a long thin nozzle entered my sanctuary/death cell
and I was sucked into oblivion
along with bits of my brother
all courtesy of the National Health Service
In California some beloved dogs
when they expire
are buried in oak coffins with gold handles
Respectful mourners attend and weep accordingly
We were poured into a black plastic sack
not a hymn nor a prayer was heard
We were going to be twins
my brother and I

Stewart Henderson
20th century

Epitaph

ON A CHILD KILLED
BY PROCURED ABORTION

O thou, whose eyes were closed in death's pale night
Ere fate revealed thee to my aching sight;
Ambiguous something, by no standard fixed,
Frail span, of naught and of existence mixed;
Embryo, imperfect as my torturing thought,
Sad outcast of existence and of naught;
Thou, who to guilty love first ow'st thy frame,
Whom guilty honour kills to hide its shame;
Dire offspring! formed by love's too pleasing power!
Honour's dire victim in a luckless hour!
Soften the pangs that still revenge thy doom:
Nor, from the dark abyss of nature's womb,
Where back I cast thee, let revolving time
Call up past scenes to aggravate my crime.
    Two adverse tyrants ruled thy wayward fate
Thyself a helpless victim to their hate;
Love, spite of honour's dictates, gave thee breath;
Honour, in spite of love, pronounced thy death.

Anonymous
18th century

An Old Andorran Custom Questions the Dead

I spoke to the dead, oiled sea-bird,
questioned the poisoned fish,
saw the finger-sized foetus
asked 'Dead one, who killed you?'
And the dead gave me no answer
but the wind whispered
'You, you, you.'

I looked at the battered baby,
the man blown apart by a bomb,
the suicide pulled from the water
asked: 'Dead one, who killed you?'
And the dead gave me no answer
but the wind whispered
'You, you, you.'

I gazed at a sterile planet
—our erstwhile orbiting earth—
lifeless and pitted with craters
cried: 'Dead one, who killed you?'
And the dead gave me no answer
and there was no wind to whisper
'You, you, you.'

Peggy Poole
20th century

Green

Green.
Green for our fear of what we have spoilt, from the turning
Wave to the grass that rots as we look, the roots
Which break in the ground. What green-sickness there is
In the world we walk on; look up, too, from the edge
    Of a field to the centre of cities where pollution
Stands in the air, blows to the suburbs, then
    Runs through corn and fruit-trees, renders barren
The bushes of blackberries, fields of strawberries, all
    That we ate with relish, bottled once and set
On a high and treasured shelf. We have set ourselves
    Too high too often, thought we ruled the sky,
Owned the arable farmlands, had a say
    In sunlight, starlight, all that atmosphere
Was rich in once. Not any longer. We have
    Watched the foxes run and die, have seen
Pigeon and pheasant fall from sky to our feet,
    And felt exultant. Almost too late we learn
Our lesson. We need a purity, a cleansing
    Ritual for the actual. We must unlearn now,
But all too slowly or else too hectically fast,
    That we must honour the earth and the flying birds,
Not spray chemicals on the delicate buds
    And poison the later fruit. We have been greedy
With land and air but also lecherous;
    We sow our seed too widely and in wrong places
So that we hinder a baby's growth, produce
    A handicapped race. We must be sorry and make
A fertile penitence, look about us, let
    Nature teach us once again. O can
We walk the difficult steps back to Eden garden
    And place the apple back on the poisoned tree?
Is it too late? Not if we deepen our sorrow,
    Give where we used to take, feed orphans, snatch
A million Christ-children back from the three-fold world
    Where the Holy Trinity broods with a lucky number.
So in a green dream of sweet fertility let us
    Kneel in sorrow, carefully plant our seeds
And exhale good air and leave it to others too,
    May the green, unpolluted waves turn over and over
Till green is the colour of safety and survival,
    And may green be our freshness for the last redemption.

Elizabeth Jennings
20th century

Aside

Cold beach, solitary
sea with its monotone
on the shingle; the ring
in the rock prohibiting
the conviction that no one
has been here before.

Man, is there anywhere
you can say this, peering
into the future under
the mushroom cloud? Mixed
with our oldest bones are
disturbing relics, too contemporary
to be there. In pre-history
someone came to this threshold
on which you hesitate
and crossed it, incinerating
the planet, leaving it
to life to lick its wounds
thousands of years. Thought
is as fast as light,
to exceed that brings annihilation
upon us.

      Yet wisdom
is at our elbow, whispering,
as at his once: Progress
is not with the machine;
it is a turning aside,
a bending over a still pool,
where the bubbles arise
from unseen depths, as from truth
breathing, showing us by their roundness
the roundness of our world.

R.S. Thomas
20th century

Still Falls the Rain

(THE RAIDS, 1940. NIGHT AND DAWN)

Still falls the Rain—
Dark as the world of man, black as our loss—
Blind as the nineteen hundred and forty nails
Upon the Cross.

Still falls the Rain
With a sound like the pulse of the heart that is changed to the
    hammer-beat
In the Potter's Field, and the sound of the impious feet

On the Tomb:
                Still falls the Rain
In the Field of Blood where the small hopes breed and the human
    brain
Nurtures its greed, that worm with the brow of Cain.

Still falls the Rain
At the feet of the Starved Man hung upon the Cross.
Christ that each day, each night, nails there,
                  have mercy on us—
On Dives and on Lazarus:
Under the Rain the sore and the gold are as one.

Still falls the Rain—
Still falls the Blood from the Starved Man's wounded Side:
He bears in his Heart all wounds,—those of the light
              that died,
The last faint spark
In the self-murdered heart, the wounds of the sad
                uncomprehending dark,
The wounds of the baited bear,—
The blind and weeping bear whom the keepers beat
On his helpless flesh ... the tears of the hunted hare.

Still falls the Rain—
Then—O Ile leape up to my God: who pulles me doune—
See, see where Christ's blood streames in the firmament:
It flows from the Brow we nailed upon the tree
Deep to the dying, to the thirsting heart
That holds the fires of the world,—dark-smirched with pain
As Caesar's laurel crown.

Then sounds the voice of One who like the heart of man
Was once a child who among beasts has lain—
'Still do I love, still shed my innocent light, my Blood, for thee.'

Edith Sitwell   *1887–1964*

There Have Been Bombs Before

FOR HIROSHIMA DAY

There have been bombs before
As when:
> The serpent slid among the leaves,
> Green and glinting, to the ear,
> Twining gold, as fingers in the hair,
> Sinuous as fingers pressured on the fruit:
> The bite, the bite, so small,
> Puncturing the flesh, bursting juices,
> And crying, crying let there be
> Dark and dark there was, scales
> Dulled, leaves dried up, flesh
> Scragging, the scene cleft only
> By the fiery light arrowing west.
There have been bombs before.

There have been bombs before
As when:
> Abraham pleaded
> In sight
> Of the cities of the Plain
> For the one just man
> In desperate countdown
> For the peace of Zoar
> Should there be fifty
> Forty-five
> Will the judge
> Of the whole earth
> Not administer
> Justice?
> Forty
> Thirty
> As smoke
> From a furnace
> Twenty
> Ten
There have been bombs before.

There have been bombs before
As when:
> Jonah dropped like an anchor
> To the sea, to the whale's teeth,
> White bolts locking him in,
> Into the maw, the gulf, weeds
> About his head and the bones

Of ocean, then, leagues on,
Three days, three nights, the whale
Breeches, upwards to the sun,
And the engulfed repenting prophet,
Ears murmuring with the depths,
Thrusts from his gut, bursting to the air,
Spewed up, on land, headed to Nineveh.
There have been bombs before.

There have been bombs before
As when:
In 1348, at Weymouth,
Along ship's cables, the rats
Nosed ashore, dying and spreading death.
It was the plague. Buboes, like split fruit,
Burst in a million bodies, cousins
Upon cousins, in carts, in pits.
The rotting web of kin, *magna mortalitas*,
Half the kingdom dead. Who knows
Ten thousand faces? Whose is their salvation?
They died of plague, deaths not worked in the cloths
Of war. In the villages, the hand and ink give out,
No one left to write the record, all systems gone.
There have been bombs before.

There have been bombs before
As when:
Gabriel appeared, wings promising
As rainbows, spoke the uncanny words
Of birth, virgin and angel, the twinned
Inclining heads. That time, the lilies
Flowered, and only yes the handmaid
Said and lit the fuse that burned, slow
And gathering, to whips and thorns
And nails, the sunk flesh, the lungs
Sucked in, the caked and stiffening hair.
There have been bombs before.

There have been bombs before
As at:
The resurrection, the rock rolled
Back, the body, perfect in its wounds,
Bursts from the tomb, armour,
Swords spreadeagled, breath misting
The mirror. Life breathes, seed of the fruit,
Not stone but bread, not east, not west,
A great people in white raiment.
By a river-side coming to the Lord,

Pure water raining on pure water.
To God all things come home.

Come those
Who make safe the waters;
Heal sick; make bloods once more
Corpuscular; give back
Eyes to the eyeless fish.

Come those
Who piece the bodies back
Draw faces newly to
The windows of raised-up
Streets; who unpile the stocks.

Come, come those
Shoulders, arms, the hands,
That roll back the rock;
All other bombs annul.

Ronald Tamplin
20th century

Epitaph

They hanged him on a clement morning, swung
between the falling sunlight and women's
breathing, like a black apostrophe to pain.
All morning while the children hushed
their hopscotch joy and the cane kept growing
he hung there sweet and low.
                    At least that's how
they tell it. It was long ago
and what can we recall of a dead slave or two
except that when we punctuate our island tale
they swing like sighs across the brutal
sentences, and anger pauses
till they pass away.

Dennis Scott (Jamaica)
20th century

Jerusalem

And did those feet in ancient time
Walk upon England's mountains green?
And was the holy Lamb of God
On England's pleasant pastures seen?

And did the Countenance Divine
Shine forth upon our clouded hills?
And was Jerusalem builded here
Among these dark Satanic Mills?

Bring me my Bow of burning gold!
Bring me my Arrows of desire!
Bring me my Spear! O clouds, unfold!
Bring me my Chariot of fire!

I will not cease from Mental Fight,
Nor shall my Sword sleep in my hand,
Till we have built Jerusalem
In England's green and pleasant land.

William Blake
1757–1827

PERSON TO PERSON

In a Bath Teashop

'Let us not speak, for the love we bear one another—
    Let us hold hands and look.'
She, such a very ordinary little woman;
    He, such a thumping crook;
But both, for a moment, little lower than the angels
    In the teashop's ingle-nook.

John Betjeman
20th century

Love

The Power of Love

It can alter things;
The stormy scowl can become
Suddenly a smile.

The knuckly bunched fist
May open like a flower,
Tender a caress.

Beneath its bright warmth
Black ice of suspicion melts;
Danger is dazzled.

A plain and dull face
Astounds with its radiance
And sudden beauty.

Ordinary things—
Teacups, spoons and sugar-lumps—
Become magical.

The locked door opens;
Inside are leaves and moonlight;
You are welcomed in.

Its delicate strength
Can lift the heaviest heart
And snap hostile steel.

It gives eloquence
To the dumb tongue, makes plain speech
Blaze like poetry.

Vernon Scannell
20th century

THE LOVE OF FRIENDS

Friendship

When we were idlers with the loitering rills,
    The need of human love we little noted:
Our love was nature; and the peace that floated
On the white mist, and dwelt upon the hills,
To sweet accord subdued our wayward wills:
   One soul was ours, one mind, one heart devoted,
    That, wisely doting, asked not why it doted,
And ours the unknown joy, which knowing kills.
But now I find how dear thou wert to me;
    That man is more than half of nature's treasure,
Of that fair beauty which no eye can see,
    Of that sweet music which no ear can measure;
    And now the streams may sing for others' pleasure,
The hills sleep on in their eternity.

Hartley Coleridge
1796–1849

Wisdom

On a night like this I could wish for wisdom,
To sit outside my kitchen door
In the long twilight hours, draining my glass
And offering my companions more.
What could be better...?
The breeze in our light summer clothing
And blowing the pages of our open Bibles,
Speaking of this world that came from nothing.

Peter Marshall
20th century

To Grimold, Abbot of St Gall

Then live, my strength, anchor of weary ships,
    Safe shore and land at last, thou, for my wreck,
My honour, thou, and my abiding rest,
        My city safe for a bewildered heart.
What though the plains and mountains and the sea
    Between us are, that which no earth can hold
Still follows thee, and love's own singing follows,
        Longing that all things may be well with thee.
Christ who first gave thee for a friend to me,
Christ keep thee well, where'er thou art, for me.
    Earth's self shall go and the swift wheel of heaven
Perish and pass, before our love shall cease.
        Do but remember me, as I do thee,
And God, who brought us on this earth together,
        Bring us together in his house of heaven.

Hrabanus Maurus
776–856
translated from Latin by Helen Waddell

Sheepstor
For Bob Groves, 1946–78

'WE KNOW THAT THE WHOLE CREATION GROANETH
AND TRAVAILETH IN PAIN TOGETHER UNTIL NOW.'

God's intrusion, upthrust granite
offshoulders layers of sediment,
mantle weathered by God's weather.

The grey creature, lichen, adheres
to tor and tower, to raw and tooled
stone, creation or man's good work.

Granite, a crown not won, but worn
by abraded hills; men made out shapes
in the rock's deeps, holy stone or cross.

This was your place, *Dartmoor mountain*;
you trekked roads and mineral tracks,
mapped its toils, endured its terrors.

A piece of mist bleats and stumbles
away. Sometimes in your spirit
we could make out God's shy image.

Your marrow's fire, all that your bones
suffered, weathered your flesh, stripped you
down to something stubborn, exposed,

your igneous love. At Sheepstor,
above the church, by a large stone
plush with lichen, we scatter ash

and our prayers, all that's left of your
physical mess; grains of clinker
speckle the moor, the rain greets them.

But in memory they persist
like grey wethers grazing the air
to be sold to the credulous.

Credulous, I see the granite,
God's intrusion. One flock, lying
in wait for the resurrection.

Paul Hyland
20th century

LOVE BETWEEN MAN AND WOMAN

True Love

Let me not to the marriage of true minds
Admit impediments. Love is not love
Which alters when it alteration finds,
Or bends with the remover to remove:—
O no! it is an ever-fixèd mark
That looks on tempests, and is never shaken;
It is the star to every wandering bark,
Whose worth's unknown, although his height be taken.
Love's not Time's fool, though rosy lips and cheeks
Within his bending sickle's compass come;
Love alters not with his brief hours and weeks,
But bears it out ev'n to the edge of doom.
If this be error, and upon me proved,
I never writ, nor no man ever loved.

William Shakespeare
1564–1616

A Woman's Love

Nothing is to man so dear
As woman's love in good manère.
A good woman is man's bliss
Where her love right and steadfast is.

There is no solace under heaven
Of all that a man may nevene*
That should a man so much glew*
As a good woman that loveth true.
None is dearer in God's herd
Than a chaste woman with lovely word.

Robert Mannying of Brunne
about 1325

* *nevene:* name; *glew:* gladden

Love's Insight

Take me, accept me, love me as I am;
Love me with my disordered wayward past;
Love me with all the lusts that hold me fast
In bonds of sensuality and shame.
Love me as flesh and blood, not the ideal
Which vainly you imagine me to be;
Love me the mixed-up creature that you see;
Love not the man you dream of but the real.
And yet they err who say that love is blind.
Beneath my earthy, sordid self your love
Discerns capacities which rise above
The futile passions of my carnal mind.
Love is creative. Your love brings to birth
God's image in the earthiest of earth.

Robert Winnett
20th century

Contradictions of Love

As fragile as an eggshell bauble
    On a Christmas tree,
But durable as gleaming steel
    Of knife, or sword, or key.

Sweet as the fragrance of the rose
    Or honey from the bee,
But cold and scentless as the snow,
    And salty as the sea.

As gentle as a summer breeze
    Or mother's lullaby,
But burly as a hurricane
    Or thunder in the sky.

As magical as witches' spells
    Or blackbirds in a pie,
But plain and simple as good bread,
    Without which we would die.

Vernon Scannell
20th century

The Way They Live Now

You make love and you live together now
Where we were shy and made love by degrees.
By kiss and invitation we learnt how
Our love was growing. You know few of these

Tokens and little gifts, the gaze of eye
To eye, the hand shared with another hand.
You know of few frustrations, seldom cry
With passion's stress, yet do you understand

The little gestures that would mean so much,
The surging hope to be asked to a dance?
You take the whole of love. We lived by touch

And doubt and by the purposes of chance
And yet I think our slow ways carried much
That you have missed—the guess, the wish, the glance.

Elizabeth Jennings
20th century

Love Song

I see the pattern of stars and sun
And while they remain
You are fixed in my mind

And the course of the fox and the rabbit
A lad and his lady
The way of a woman with child.

While the waves run onto the beach
And the whale ploughs his road through the ocean
My love reaches out.

As long as the deer runs his race;
Until you can measure the edges of space
I will keep you.

Cathy Anderson
20th century

Winter Song

Ask me no more, my truth to prove,
What I would suffer for my love.
With thee I would in exile go
To regions of eternal snow,
O'er floods by solid ice confined,
Through forest bare with northern wind:
While all around my eyes I cast,
Where all is wild and all is waste.
If there the tim'rous stag you chase,
Or rouse to fight a fiercer race,
Undaunted I thy arms would bear,
And give thy hand the hunter's spear.
When the low sun withdraws his light,
And menaces an half-year's night,
The conscious moon and stars above
Shall guide me with my wandering love.
Beneath the mountain's hollow brow,
Or in its rocky cells below,
Thy rural feast I would provide,
Nor envy palaces their pride.
The softest moss should dress thy bed,
With savage spoils about thee spread:
While faithful love the watch should keep,
To banish danger from thy sleep.

Elizabeth Tollett
1694–1754

A Marriage Ring

The ring, so worn as you behold,
So thin, so pale, is yet of gold:
The passion such it was to prove—
Worn with life's care, love yet was love.

George Crabbe
1754–1832

A Wife to a Husband

(SONNETS FROM THE PORTUGUESE)

How do I love thee? Let me count the ways.
I love thee to the depth and breadth and height
My soul can reach, when feeling out of sight
For the end of Being and ideal Grace.
I love thee to the level of everyday's
Most quiet need, by sun and candlelight.
I love thee freely, as men strive for right;
I love thee purely, as they turn from praise.
I love thee with the passion put to use
In my old griefs, and with my childhood's faith.
I love thee with a love I seemed to lose
With my lost saints,—I love thee with the breath,
Smiles, tears, of all my life!—and, if God choose,
I shall but love thee better after death.

Elizabeth Barrett Browning
1806–61

Prothalamion

FOR JIM AND SUE

How like an arch your marriage! Framed
in living stone, its gothic arrow aimed
at heaven, with Christ (its Capstone and
its Arrowhead) locking your coupled
weakness into one, the leaning
of two lives into a strength.
Thus he defines your joining's length
and width, its archetypal shape. Its meaning
is another thing: a letting in of light,
an opening to a varied landscape, planned
but yet to be explored. A paradox, for you
who doubly frame his arch may now step through
its entrance into his promised land!

Luci Shaw
20th century

Epithalamion

All our love is deeply (as a folk
tale in the memory of once upon
a time the golden-haired princess awoke
from spellbound slumbers to a carillon
of kisses) grounded in the depth of his
own dying. For the risk of love we dare
(the peasant boy with rustic pleasantries
courted the princess of the golden hair)
because the tale is told (how she was brought
a virgin victim to the dragon's lair,
a bride self-bartered for her people's weal)
of love as strong as death (our hero fought
with death's dark reptile) that our hearts may bear
his true love as an everlasting seal.

Richard Bauckham
20th century

The Gate

When they moved into the house he said
'I'll fix that creaking gate one day.'
In later years he changed his tune—
'Creaking gates hang longest—look at me!'
She came to love the gate, it told her things,
told her when he was coming home.

　　After the funeral her son said
　　'I'll get that gate replaced, Dad
　　never got round to it.'

The new gate is silent, swings smooth
on oiled hinges, closes
with a well-ordered click,
but the music has gone out of her life
and she is left with a feeling of betrayal.

R.P. Fenwick
20th century

Civilisation

Saturday afternoon. Professor Paterson
walks in his garden, bends on his daffodils
looks fond yet stern. His brain, unoccupied, idles.
He hums. Half-heartedly, the watery sun
attempts to gild him, like a saint. He moves
away, deeply ponders a hole in the fence,
reproves a dangling creeper.

   His wife, in the kitchen,
scours the pans. The radio chatters calamity.
Civilisation is teetering to a fall.
Music erupts, with thud and boom and crash
—the mangonels* of the last assault? She sluices
water around the sink. She drops a cup.
It shatters.

   Professor Paterson
sits in his usual chair, and reads. Daffodils
stand in a vase behind him. He looks kindly
over his spectacles. The world settles
back on its base.
   Civilisation, it seems,
is with us yet. She goes to make him tea.

Evangeline Paterson
20th century

* *mangonel:* a military engine for casting stones

To my Dear and Loving Husband

If ever two were one, then surely we.
If ever man were loved by wife, then thee;
If ever wife was happy in a man,
Compare me with ye women if you can.
I prize thy love more than whole mines of gold,
Or all the riches that the East doth hold.
My love is such that rivers cannot quench,
Nor aught but love from thee, give recompense.
Thy love is such I can no way repay,
The heavens reward thee manifold, I pray.
Then while we live, in love let's so persever
That when we live no more, we may live ever.

Anne Bradstreet
1612–72

A Marriage

We met
   under a shower
of bird-notes.
   Fifty years passed,
love's moment
   in a world in
servitude to time.
   She was young;
I kissed with my eyes
   closed and opened
them on her wrinkles.
   'Come' said death,
choosing her as his
   partner for
the last dance. And she,
   who in life
had done everything
   with a bird's grace,
opened her bill now
   for the shedding
of one sigh no
   heavier than a feather.

R.S. Thomas
20th century

An Epitaph upon Husband and Wife

WHO DIED AND WERE BURIED TOGETHER

To those whom death again did wed
This grave's the second marriage-bed.
For though the hand of Fate could force
'Twixt soul and body a divorce,
It could not sever man and wife,
Because they both lived but one life.
Peace, good reader, do not weep;
Peace; the lovers are asleep.
They, sweet turtles, folded lie
In the last knot that love could tie.
Let them sleep, let them sleep on,
Till the stormy night be gone,
And the eternal morrow dawn;
Then the curtains will be drawn,
And they wake into a light
Whose day shall never die in night.

Richard Crashaw
1613–49

On the Death of Sir Albert Morton's Wife

He first deceased—she, for a little tried
To live without him, liked it not and died.

Sir Henry Wotton
1568–1639

Introspective

Alone

'*When I'm alone*'—the words tripped off his tongue
As though to be alone were nothing strange.
'*When I was young,*' he said; '*when I was young...*'

I thought of age, and loneliness, and change.
I thought how strange we grow when we're alone,
And how unlike the selves that meet and talk,
And blow the candle out, and say good night.
Alone... The word is life endured and known.
It is the stillness where our spirits walk
And all but inmost faith is overthrown.

Siegfried Sassoon
1886–1967

Gold Leaves

Lo! I am come to autumn,
   When all the leaves are gold;
Grey hairs and golden leaves cry out
   The year and I are old.

In youth I sought the prince of men,
   Captain in cosmic wars,
Our Titan, even the weeds would show
   Defiant, to the stars.

But now a great thing in the street
   Seems any human nod,
Where shift in strange democracy
   The million masks of God.

In youth I sought the golden flower
   Hidden in wood or wold,
But I am come to autumn,
   When all the leaves are gold.

G.K. Chesterton
1874–1936

Middle Age

When I was a child, I thought as a child,
And when I saw an elder sitting
Hands clasped, legs crossed, head tilted,
Immobile on a chair,
I thought he must be doing nothing.
There before me, at that time, I thought would be
The incarnation of vacuity:
An adult shell, a hoary crust
Enveloping a void.

But now I am become a man I put away such childish things.
Now I sit
Hands clasped, legs crossed, head tilted,
Immobile in a chair,
Quite still within this empty room
While bloodless sunshine breaks the clouds
And till the next autumnal shower
Projects a pallid spotlight on this hour.

Oh could this child who was the Father to this man
Have seen me now!
What lacerating adjectives would crown
The epithets by which he'd make me known
Unto himself.

So, crown, sit velvet barbed upon my brow,
For I know what has forever been
The content of such stillness.

Now as I sit thus unemployed
The stockpiled libraries of the mind
Unship their heavy burdens
On the shores of meditation,
Divulge their hidden riches, disgorge their great processions
The unrelated treasures of the years.

As pallid sunshine probes this empty room
A bloodless omen of storms past and storms to come,
The mind deploys its plunder with delight:
All gold and crimson,
Blazing blues, encyclopaedic greens and musky
Purples, sucked
From a million memories and sensations
Shift slowly to great pressures from the depths
Move marvellously to that resolution of the soul
Which is some small Amen

To that great Word
By which the worlds were made.

The heart is full, the mind is charged, the spirit climbs,
And in this quintessential life
The body rests.
Amen.

Dick Williams 20th century

The Retreat

Happy those early days, when I
Shined in my Angel-infancy!
Before I understood this place
Appointed for my second race,
Or taught my soul to fancy aught
But a white celestial thought:
When yet I had not walked above
A mile or two from my first Love,
And looking back—at that short space—
Could see a glimpse of his bright face:
When on some gilded cloud or flower,
My gazing soul would dwell an hour,
And in those weaker glories spy
Some shadows of eternity:
Before I taught my tongue to wound
My Conscience with a sinful sound,
Or had the black art to dispense
A several sin to every sense,
But felt through all this fleshly dress
Bright shoots of everlastingness.

O how I long to travel back,
And tread again that ancient track!
That I might once more reach that plain
Where first I left my glorious train;
From whence th'enlightened spirit sees
That shady City of Palm-trees.
But ah! my soul with too much stay
Is drunk, and staggers in the way!
Some men a forward motion love,
But I by backward steps would move;
And when this dust falls to the urn,
In that state I came, return.

Henry Vaughan 1621–95

The Salutation

These little limbs,
These eyes and hands which here I find,
This panting heart wherewith my life begins,
Where have ye been? Behind
What curtain were ye from me hid so long?
Where was, in what abyss, my new-made tongue?

When silent I
So many thousand thousand years
Beneath the dust did in a *chaos* lie,
How could I *smiles*, or *tears*,
Or *lips*, or *hands*, or *eyes*, or *ears* perceive?
Welcome ye treasures which I now receive.

I that so long
Was *nothing* from eternity
Did little think such joys as ear and tongue
To celebrate or see;
Such sounds to hear, such hands to feel, such feet,
Such eyes and objects, on the ground to meet.

New burnished joys!
Which finest gold and pearl excel!
Such sacred treasures are the limbs of boys
In which a soul doth dwell;
Their organized joints and azure veins
More wealth include than the dead world contains.

From dust I rise
And out of Nothing now awake.
These brighter regions which salute mine eyes
A gift from God I take.
The earth, the seas, the light, the lofty skies,
The sun and stars are mine; if these I prize.

A stranger here
Strange things doth meet, strange glory see,
Strange treasures lodged in this fair world appear,
Strange all and new to me;
But that they *mine* should be who Nothing was,
That strangest is of all; yet brought to pass.

Thomas Traherne
1637?–74

To the Body

Thou inmost, ultimate
Council of judgment, palace of decrees,
Where the high senses hold their spiritual state,
Sued by earth's embassies,
And sign, approve, accept, conceive, create;

Create—thy senses close
With the world's pleas. The random odours reach
Their sweetness in the place of thy repose,
Upon thy tongue the peach,
And in thy nostrils breathes the breathing rose.

To thee, secluded one,
The dark vibrations of the sightless skies,
The lovely inexplicit colours run;
The light gropes for those eyes.
O thou august! thou dost command the sun.

Music, all dumb, hath trod
Into thine ear her one effectual way;
And fire and cold approach to gain thy nod,
Where thou call'st up the day,
Where thou awaitest the appeal of God.

Alice Meynell
1847–1922

Who Shall Deliver Me?

God strengthen me to bear myself;
That heaviest weight of all to bear,
Inalienable weight of care.

All others are outside myself;
I lock my door and bar them out,
The turmoil, tedium, gad-about.

I lock my door upon myself,
And start self-purged upon the race
That all must run! Death runs apace.

If I could set aside myself,
And start with lightened heart upon
The road by all men overgone!

God harden me against myself,
This coward with pathetic voice
Who craves for ease, and rest, and joys:

Myself, arch-traitor to myself;
My hollowest friend, my deadliest foe,
My clog whatever road I go.

Yet one there is can curb myself,
Can roll the strangling load from me,
Break off the yoke and set me free.

Christina Rossetti
1830–94

Self Ease

My own heart let me more have pity on; let
Me live to my sad self hereafter kind,
Charitable; not live this tormented mind
With this tormented mind tormenting yet.

I cast for comfort I can no more get
By groping round my comfortless, than blind
Eyes in their dark can day or thirst can find
Thirst's all-in-all in all a world of wet.

Soul, self; come, poor Jackself, I do advise
You, jaded, let be; call off thoughts awhile
Elsewhere; leave comfort root-room; let joy size

At God knows when to God knows what; whose smile
's not wrung, see you; unforeseen times rather—as skies
Betweenpie mountains—lights a lovely mile.

Gerard Manley Hopkins   1844–89

Thou Shalt Not Kill

I had grown weary of him; of his breath
And hands and features I was sick to death.
Each day I heard the same dull voice and tread;
I did not hate him: but I wished him dead.
And he must with his blank face fill my life—
Then my brain blackened, and I snatched a knife.

But ere I struck, my soul's grey deserts through
A voice cried, 'Know at least what thing you do.
This is a common man: knowest thou, O soul,
What this thing is? somewhere where seasons roll
There is some living thing for whom this man
Is as seven heavens girt into a span,
For some one soul you take the world away—
Now know you well your deed and purpose. Slay!'
Then I cast down the knife upon the ground
And saw that mean man for one moment crowned.
I turned and laughed: for there was no one by—
The man that I had sought to slay was I.

G.K. Chesterton   1874–1936

Cock Crow

Wanting to be myself, alone,
Between the lit house and the town
I took the road, and at the bridge
Turned back and walked the way I'd come.

Three times I took that lonely stretch,
Three times the dark trees closed me round,
The night absolved me of my bonds
Only my footsteps held the ground.

My mother and my daughter slept,
One life behind and one before,
And I that stood between denied
Their needs in shutting-to the door.

And walking up and down the road
Knew myself, separate and alone,
Cut off from human cries, from pain,
And love that grows about the bone.

Too brief illusion! Thrice for me
I heard the cock crow on the hill,
And turned the handle of the door
Thinking I knew his meaning well.

Rosemary Dobson
20th century

Sonnet CXLVI

Poor soul, the centre of my sinful earth,
Fooled by these rebel powers that thee array,
Why dost thou pine within and suffer dearth,
Painting thy outward walls so costly gay?
Why so large cost, having so short a lease,
Dost thou upon thy fading mansion spend?
Shall worms, inheritors of this excess,
Eat up thy charge? Is this thy body's end?
Then, soul, live thou upon thy servant's loss,
And let that pine to aggravate thy store;
Buy terms divine in selling hours of dross;
Within be fed, without be rich no more:
   So shalt thou feed on Death, that feeds on men,
   And Death once dead, there's no more dying then.

William Shakespeare
1564–1616

Epitaph

Don't give the children
my ash,
to turn them to dust
when I'm dead.
I lie in
the grain of a star,
safe in earth's crust;
God's bread.

Isobel Thrilling
20th century

Epitaph

Even such is Time, which takes in trust
Our youth, our joys, and all we have,
And pays us but with age and dust;
Who in the dark and silent grave,
When we have wandered all our ways,
Shuts up the story of our days:
And from which earth, and grave, and dust,
The Lord shall raise me up, I trust.

Sir Walter Ralegh
about 1552–1618

Radbod's Epitaph

Hunger and thirst, O Christ, for sight of thee
Came between me and all the feasts of earth.
Give thou thyself the bread, thyself the wine,
Thou, sole provision for the unknown way.
Long hunger wasted the world wanderer,
With sight of thee may he be satisfied.

Radbod
died 917
translated by Helen Waddell

Samuel Taylor Coleridge

EPITAPH ON HIMSELF

Stop, Christian passer-by!—Stop, child of God,
And read with gentle breast. Beneath this sod
A poet lies, or that which once seem'd he.
O lift one thought in prayer for S.T.C.;
That he who many a year with toil of breath
Found death in life, may here find life in death!
Mercy for praise—to be forgiven for fame
He asked, and hoped, through Christ. Do thou the same!

Samuel Taylor Coleridge
1772–1834

Parents and Children

ABOUT PARENTS

First Friday Bell

... IN MEMORY OF MAMA WHO DIED SUFFERING

The first Friday bell shatters the morning
and shuffling feet respond to the call

your dim, grey shape joins the procession
again pulling a dozen wagons which

are the churches you used to hurry to
filled with plaster saints and incantations,

you treasured them and kept bright shiny
beads while at death's door you lay pain wracked

and tortured, eaten away by some greedy
demon, your flesh falling off and melting

into air; and I could only watch you
mumble, eating your pain to spare me

no church no god seemed to help you and I
watched you with dread and admiration and

love and hate. Yes, hate! I hated your
suffering like Job or some dumb animal

there with nerves aquiver and sunken eyes
and painful submission to your loving

Maker. How I wished to relieve you but
you were content to bite your teeth and hold

back the bitter tears while I looked helplessly
and admired you, pitied you, and loved you

and as the first Friday bell rings, I hear
your footsteps join the band of faithful and

your lips fluttering as you pass the beads
and drag your wagon-churches and I weep

Anson Gonzalez   20th century

Obedience

Were my parents right or wrong
not to mow the ripe oats that Sunday morning
with the rainstorm threatening?

I reminded them that the Sabbath was made for man
and of the ox fallen into the pit.
Without an oats crop, I argued,
the cattle would need to survive on town-bought oats
and then it wouldn't pay to keep them.
Isn't selling cattle at a loss like an ox in a pit?

My parents did not argue.
We went to church.
We sang the psalms louder than usual—
we, and the others whose harvests were at stake:

> Jerusalem, where blessing waits,
> Our feet are standing in thy gates.

> God, be merciful to me;
> On thy grace I rest my plea.

Dominie's spur-of-the-moment concession:
'He rides on the clouds, the wings of the storm;
The lightnings and wind his missions perform.'

Dominie made no concessions on sermon length:
'Five Good Reasons for Infant Baptism,'
though we heard little of it,

for more floods came and more winds blew and beat upon the
House than we had figured on, even,
more lightning and thunder
and hail the size of pullet eggs.
Falling branches snapped the electric wires.
We sang the closing psalm without the organ and in the dark

> Ye seed from Abraham descended,
> God's covenant love is never ended.

Afterward we rode by our oat field,
flattened.

'We still will mow it,' Dad said.
'Ten bushels to the acre, maybe, what would have been fifty
if I had mowed right after milking
and if the whole family had shocked.
We could have had it weatherproof before the storm.'

Later at dinner Dad said,
'God was testing us. I'm glad we went.'
'Those psalms never gave me such a lift as this morning.'
Mother said, 'I wouldn't have missed it.' And even I
    thought but did not say,
How guilty we would feel if we had saved the harvest!

My father once asked why I live in a black neighbourhood,
and I reminded him of that Sunday morning thirty years ago.
If my sons ever ask me why we live in a black neighbourhood,
I shall sing my favourite psalm in answer:

  The Moor, with the Philistine and the Tyrian,
  Shall soon, O Zion, throng thy holy gates.

And I hope my sons will forgive me
(who knows exactly what for?)
as they will hope their sons will forgive them
(who knows exactly what for?)
as I have long ago forgiven my father
(who knows exactly what for?)

Fathers inevitably fail to pass on to sons
their harvest customs
for harvesting grain or real estate or any crop.
But Christian fathers pass on to sons
another more important pattern
defined as absolutely as muddlers like us can manage:
obedience.

                    Sietze Buning
                    20th century

For my Mother

V

SUDDEN REMEMBRANCE

Orphaned and elderly and yet a child,
For so I am when thoughts of you return,
Return and batter me and I'm not mild
But close to tears and scarred for these tears burn.
You tamed me when most wild,

You comforted my nightmares, came and sat
Beside my bed when sleep was far away.
You were a healing presence. More than that,
You were a joy, a treasure, could display
High spirits when the flat

Dull mood took charge of me. You always were
Busy and quick and swift to suffer too,
But only now and then did I know fear
When I could see a troubled look on you.
Tonight you feel so dear.

It is a cold wet June, the flowers are blown
In tangled throngs, the charcoal clouds hang near
The tousled tree-tops. Had we ever known
So dull a June? I doubt it. How I care
For you. Where have you gone?

My faith speaks of another life and I
Find your nature a right proof of that.
A child, I'd have you crowned up in the sky,
And growing old I see your star well set.
O your death will not die.

Elizabeth Jennings
20th century

PARENTS AND CHILDREN

Having Our Tea

There's something religious in the way we sit
At the tea table, a tidy family of three.
You, my love, slicing the bread and butter, and she,
The red-cheeked tot a smear of blackberry jam, and me . . .
A new creation is established, a true presence.
And talking to each other, breaking words over food
Is somehow different from customary chatting.

Bobi Jones (originally in Welsh)
20th century

Woman to Man

The eyeless labourer in the night,
the selfless, shapeless seed I hold,
builds for its resurrection day—
silent and swift and deep from sight
foresees the unimagined light.

This is no child with a child's face;
this has no name to name it by:
yet you and I have known it well.
This is our hunter and our chase
the third who lay in our embrace.

This is the strength that your arm knows,
the arch of flesh that is my breast,
the precise crystals of our eyes.
This is the blood's wild tree that grows
the intricate and folded rose.

This is the maker and the made;
this is the question and reply;
the blind head butting at the dark,
the blaze of light along the blade.
Oh hold me, for I am afraid.

Judith Wright
20th century

The Catalyst

Long after the birth,
she held up the X-ray
of her second-born son
in the womb.

There he hung
against the light,
head-down to the lintel,
translucent
as wax in a glass.

What she saw
was not simply
the curve of the spine,
the seal at the cervix,

but sacrament brightly stilled;
an angelical stone
that cannot be weighed;

the catalyst
of sun through wax—
the ghostly body—
at the casual supper
Christ eating the honeycomb.

Pauline Stainer   20th century

Three a.m.—A Mother Waits

Nuns keep vigil with psalm and measured voice;
nurses manoeuvre amidst groans and snores.
Rocked against the long-drawn ticking night,
dry-mouthed, driven from sleep, I wait,
imagine in each bang and engine noise
the overdue return, the rasping key.
Get up, grope for his empty bed and pray
no less devoutly than the devoted soeurs,
as anxiously as nurses watch for day.
Morning is now four short hours away.
The wind blows litter over silent streets.
Dossers and drunks find huddled brief respite
and junkies dream gaunt nightmares. My fears
fuse with relief and fury—the boy appears.

Jenny Robertson
20th century

Enigma

O Lord support
all the day long
him whom you have
builded wrong.
Squirrel of the children he
hoarding to himself the map
of his singularity.

Through his half eyes
in thrust back head
what he sees
he has not said.
His squirrel fingers do not well
clutch the things he loves and still
unsprung his tongue his loves to tell.

O Lord a lark
trapped in his breast
that beats
and will not give him rest.
Inside his mouth it beats its wings
And stops his lips and makes him cry
and quivering in him it sings.

Lord, loose the lark
that here is trapped
and trace the maze
that you have mapped.
Squirrel light yet lead with weight
what you mismade do not desert
speak to the inarticulate.

Patience Tuckwell
20th century

Two Women

Two women meet each morning to pray
One is a mother, the other her daughter
They belong to different religions
Only blood binds them together

Stephen is the object of their prayer
He is the grandson of one, the son of the other
He lives abroad
He does not want to come home
He wants to be left alone

So the women pray silently—each in her own way
Their words do not cross
They rise and converge
Stephen will be safe for another day.

Neville Braybrooke
20th century

A Wish for my Children

On this doorstep I stand
year after year
and watch you leaving

and think: May you not
skin your knees. May you
not catch your fingers
in car doors. May
your hearts not break.

May tide and weather
wait for your coming

and may you grow strong
to break
all webs of my weaving.

Evangeline Paterson
20th century

CRADLE SONGS

From: A Cradle Song

Hush! my dear, lie still and slumber,
   Holy Angels guard thy bed!
Heavenly blessings without number
   Gently falling on thy head.

Sleep, my babe; thy food and raiment,
   House and home, thy friends provide;
All without thy care or payment,
   All thy wants are well supplied.

How much better thou'rt attended
   Than the Son of God could be,
When from heaven he descended,
   And became a child like thee!

Soft and easy is thy cradle:
   Coarse and hard thy Saviour lay:
When his birthplace was a stable,
   And his softest bed was hay . . .

Lo, he slumbers in his manger,
   Where the hornèd oxen fed;
—Peace, my darling, here's no danger;
   Here's no ox a-near thy bed!

May'st thou live to know and fear him,
   Trust and love him all thy days;
Then go dwell for ever near him,
   See his face, and sing his praise!

Isaac Watts
1674–1748

A Lullaby

Sweet baby sleep! what ails my dear,
    What ails my darling thus to cry?
Be still, my child, and lend thine ear,
    To hear me sing thy lullaby:
My pretty lamb, forbear to weep;
Be still, my dear; sweet baby, sleep.

Thou blessed soul, what canst thou fear
    What thing to thee can mischief do?
Thy God is now thy Father dear,
    His holy spouse, thy mother too.
Sweet baby, then forbear to weep;
Be still, my babe; sweet baby, sleep.

Sweet baby, sleep, and nothing fear;
    For whatsoever thee offends
By thy protector threatened are,
    And God and angels are thy friends.
Sweet baby, then forbear to weep;
Be still, my babe; sweet baby, sleep . . .

The King of kings, when he was born,
    Had not so much for outward ease;
By him such dressings were not worn,
    Nor such-like swaddling-clothes as these;
Sweet baby, then forbear to weep;
Be still, my babe; sweet baby, sleep.

Within a manger lodged thy Lord,
    Where oxen lay, and asses fed:
Warm rooms we do to thee afford,
    An easy cradle or a bed.
Sweet baby, then forbear to weep;
Be still, my babe; sweet baby, sleep.

Thou hast, yet more, to perfect this,
    A promise and an earnest got
Of gaining everlasting bliss,
    Though thou, my babe, perceiv'st it not;
Sweet baby, then forbear to weep;
Be still, my babe; sweet baby, sleep.

William Austin
1587–1634

Born to Sorrow

Lullay, lullay, little child, why weepest thou so sore?
Needs must thou weep—it was ordained thee yore
Ever to live in sorrow, and sigh and mourn alway
As thine elders did before thee in their day.
Lullay, lullay, little child, child, lullay, lullow,
In a strange world a stranger art thou.

Beast and birds, the fish in the flood,
And every living creature, made of bone and blood,
When they come to the world, do themselves some good,
All but the wretched child that is of Adam's brood.
Lullay, lullay, little child, to care thou art born
Thou knowest not this world's waste before thee lies forlorn.

Child, if it betide that thou shalt wealthy be,
Think thou wert fostered on thy mother's knee;
Ever have in mind and heart these things three:
Whence thou comest, what thou art, and what shall come of thee.
Lullay, lullay, little child, lullay, lullay,
With sorrow thou camest into the world, with sorrow shalt wend away.

Trust not to this world: it is thy great foe,
The rich it makes poor, the poor rich also,
It turneth woe to weal, and also weal to woe;
Let no man trust this world while it turneth so.
Lullay, lullay, little child, thy foot is in the wheel:
Thou knowest not where it turns, to woe or to weal.

Child, thou art a pilgrim, in sin thy mother bore thee;
Thou wanderest in this false world—look well before thee!
Death shall come with a blast, out of his dark door,
Adam's kin down to cast, as he hath done before.
Lullay, lullay, little child, so Adam wove thy woe
In the land of Paradise, through Satan our foe.

Child, thou art no pilgrim, but a foreign guest:
Thy days are told, thy journey's die is cast.
Whither thou shalt wend, to north or to east,
Death shall come to thee with sore grief in thy breast.
Lullay, lullay, little child, this sorrow Adam wrought
When he of the apple ate that Eve to him brought.

Anonymous
14th century
translated by Veronica Zundel

A Lullaby

Lullee, lullay,
I could not love thee more
If thou wast Christ the King.
Now tell me, how did Mary know
That in her womb should sleep and grow
The Lord of everything?

Lullee, lullay,
An angel stood with her
Who said, 'That which doth stir
Like summer in thy side
Shall save the world from sin.
Then stable, hall and inn
Shall cherish Christmas-tide.'

Lullee, lullay,
And so it was that day.
And did she love him more
Because an angel came
To prophesy his name?
Ah no, not so,
She could not love him more,
But loved him just the same.
Lullee, lullee, lullay.

Janet Lewis
born 1899

Youth and Age

The Old Woman

As a white candle in a holy place
So is the beauty of an agèd face.

As the spent radiance of the winter sun
So is a woman with her travail done.

Her brood gone from her and her thoughts as still
As the waters under a ruined mill.

Joseph Campbell
1879–1944

Old Woman to Cat

Cat, smoother soother than a velvet glove,
How can you thus reply to my caress?
In giving, I receive the touch of love
Yet the gnarled knuckle and the brown age-blotch
Are there for those mysterious eyes to watch
And I thought beauty shrank from ugliness.

Queen Cat, to whom I kneel with joints that creak,
There is no grace in my antiquity
But only movements difficult and weak,
Whereas you move with pure fluidity.
Bear with me, lovely one, and though I grow
Unlovelier still, pretend you do not know.

M. Bond
20th century

New Every Day

I'd never wish my childhood back to me.
But there at least we knew the laws
that ruled the universe of every day, when we, being tied, were
free.
Poverty, dependency, best friends, go side by side;
we were only children and, for children, someone can decide.

I hope that they still
give this great freedom of the will
to kids who only need to concentrate
upon what's on the plate.
You cannot fight the dragons of tomorrow
till tomorrow comes,
because you don't know what they are . . .
today is sums.

My early schooling is a parable
of something given before we knew the need.
The blackboard cleaned in chalky clouds,
erasing name and deed;
forgotten was forgiven.

And chairs
stacked on top of little desks,
and prayers . . .
hands together, eyes not quite closed
and then a chanted spell,
our sing-song farewell.
And then . . . The Bell.

It burst like dams the classrooms
and corridors, rivers, flowed with us.
Cloakrooms and the clang
of buckets said the rule of school
cleaners had begun.
They swept us out towards the gate,
where our mothers, outlaws,
waited.
Then, long after, very late,
Night, like a caretaker
locked all the doors.

Piecemeal we lived, new every day
and kept no scores.
All our fights were silly little ones.
Battles, not wars.

Patience Tuckwell 20th century

'You Don't Know What to Do When You Get Old'

In the shuffling melancholy
of life's grey haired rituals
where the misplaced pension book
routine becomes habitual
a nation of confused dissenters
huddles in the aftermath
of governmental legislation
video shops and sauna baths

Left to doze in plastic armchairs
nodding in and out of woe
hearts prepared for termination
by a babbling TV show
dignity of fading people
thin anxiety in their walk
some will freeze whilst some will fall
into repetitious talk
Soon the functional undertaker
watches yet one more last kiss
the coffin's sealed as grief consumes
there must be more to death than this.

Stewart Henderson
20th century

Old Woman

See where she sits now,
The green-fern twilight
Green-staining her bones
Almost,
The dust motes dancing
Round her who to dust
Is returned,
Almost.
Inside the fragile
Domed head that is
Skull, almost,
And in and out the eyes
Dart fishtail shadows
Of noonday passions
And midnight terrors
That cause no flicker now
In her moonstone stare.
Sunk fathoms deep now
To where lies only
In the green-fern gloom
The enduring bone.

Evangeline Paterson   20th century

Four-Square Gospel

Old Uncle Fred could squint along forty-foot beams
And catch the gentlest wayward drift toward a curve
That no one else saw. His calloused, pitch-stained hands
Would tenderly stroke the flush seams of a perfect joint.
We used to see him astride his unwavering rafters,
Tall as the echoing blows of his worshipping arms,
Looking with pride on the loving work of his mitred,
Four-square world. He always looked sharply to see
If some sinning board in somebody's house were off square,
And longed to redeem it with the righteous tongue of his plane.

And then he slumped into arches and curves of age,
Propped up in a bed, looking out at the slanted east
While unseen termites encircled his squared-off house.
Puzzled, he eyed the long, sad arc of the geese,
The easy bend of a tree-limb heavy with fruit,
And then—we knew by the softening line of his mouth—
Saw the curve of a neck swinging free from the beams of a cross.

Roderick Jellema   20th century

From: Life Begins at Forty and Closes Early

VI
SHOWING

From his chair
by a window
he showed me
the maps on his face.
He showed me
where the lines
would form, how
my flesh would hang
in years to come.
He'd been around
the corner of the
last ambition
this side of breathing.
He was hoping that
God believed in him
in a deeper way
than he had believed
in God.

Then he went on
living in his chair
and growing fat on the past.

Steve Turner
20th century

From: Rabbi Ben Ezra

Grow old along with me!
The best is yet to be,
The last of life, for which the first was made:
Our times are in his hand
Who saith 'A whole I planned,
Youth shows but half; trust God: see all nor be afraid!'...

Not on the vulgar mass
Called 'work' must sentence pass,
Things done, that took the eye and had the price:
O'er which, from level stand,
The low world laid its hand,
Found straightway to its mind, could value in a trice:

But all, the world's coarse thumb
And finger failed to plumb,
So passed in making up the main account:
All instincts immature,
All purposes unsure,
That weighed not as his work, yet swelled the man's amount:

Thoughts hardly to be packed
Into a narrow act,
Fancies that broke through language and escaped;
All I could never be,
All, men ignored in me,
This, I was worth to God, whose wheel the pitcher shaped...

But I need, now as then,
Thee, God, who mouldest men;
And since, not even while the whirl was worst,
Did I,—to the wheel of life
With shapes and colours rife,
Bound dizzily,—mistake my end, to slake thy thirst:

So, take and use thy work:
Amend what flaws may lurk,
What strains o' the stuff, what warpings past the aim!
My times be in thy hand!
Perfect the cup as planned!
Let age approve of youth, and death complete the same!

Robert Browning
1812–89

Communion for the Aged

Hands that steered the tractor,
arranging properly the day's soil,
ploughed autumn toward sundown,
grateful to hear darkness fall,
harvested wheat that read
forty bushels an acre,
talked to cows with milk pails,
filling with a steady swish
the empty bottom, then adding
three gallons more,
sweat tears as they knocked
against locked doors of life,
hungered and held silent communion
with chicken and fried potatoes;
knuckles now gnarled like the old oak
trunks they watered to green the prairies,
useless now except to dream of plough or udder
or of dying, bow and tremble as they take
bread and wine, body and blood
passed from one veined hand to another.

Elmer F. Suderman 20th century

Unacceptables

Aged, infirm and incontinent,
They come to Sunday and to prayers
From ward behind recessed ward;
Buttoned to beds and chairs,
Buttoned to stiff upright clothes,
They come, not to see
Not to hear, not to respond;
Yet who knows what offering
Their ills make upon the altars?
Eroded out of the world's way,
They have been folded, closeted
Like old linens, old faces like embroidered linen
Folded in upon themselves, unacceptable
Longer to kin and to community;
Yet who knows in this communion
How they may be adequate
In the sight of one likewise unacceptable
To those he lived among, the outcast
Buttoned to crossed hoists and spat upon?

Nancy Westerfield 20th century

~ 443 ~

Old Age

The maples are burning,
Kindled with a silent flame,
Like russet torches in the forest depths.
I hear no splutter or crackle of resin,
yet they burn and burn.

Does he see them,
Offering this last sacrifice of summer?
Does he see them in a different time,
Flower in fire,
And suddenly put on winter?

For us in exquisite slowness,
They turn in the cool embrace of Autumn.
In silent dance,
The leaves curl, blush, flame out,
In appalling submission,
To bring him this yearly gift of colour,
amid the Autumn drab.

Lord, in my old age grant me
One last passionate flowering—
Let love burn off my summer green,
In sudden, splendid fire.

Tim Marks
20th century

Grandparents

Grannie

I stayed with her when I was six then went
To live elsewhere when I was eight years old.
For ages I remembered her faint scent
Of lavender, the way she'd never scold
No matter what I'd done, and most of all
The way her smile seemed, somehow, to enfold
My whole world like a warm, protective shawl.

I knew that I was safe when she was near,
She was so tall, so wide, so large, she would
Stand mountainous between me and my fear,
Yet oh, so gentle, and she understood
Every hope and dream I ever had.
She praised me lavishly when I was good,
But never punished me when I was bad.

Years later war broke out and I became
A soldier and was wounded while in France.
Back home in hospital, still very lame,
I realized suddenly that circumstance
Had brought me close to that small town where she
Was living still. And so I seized the chance
To write and ask if she could visit me.

She came. And I still vividly recall
The shock that I received when she appeared
That dark cold day. Huge grannie was so small!
A tiny, frail, old lady. It was weird.
She hobbled through the ward to where I lay
And drew quite close and, hesitating, peered.
And then she smiled: and love lit up the day.

Vernon Scannell
20th century

Grandmother's Arthritis

after all
her house is
full of useful legs
(chairs tables
beds) that
can't walk
and arms stiff
as boards

Luci Shaw   20th century

Grandmother: Dying

Aged in one stroke
the old woman lies
in silence,
her lips caved in
in unaccustomed severity
around her toothless gums.

Yet she is not without
dignity. The lines
of her life betray
no hidden gall,
no secret sin for years
eating at her conscience.

Others shout and scream,
abuse their nurses, and
their long-dead husbands.
The grace she learned
in childhood
still wears new.

And when she speaks to us
and says, 'I've been
talking with an angel,'
we know that if our eyes
were opened we would see
a company of angels
standing at her wounded side.

John Leax   20th century

The Way of All Flesh

You were, till now
When I stepped in, unexpected,
To ask you to do mending,
Never old, just—Grandma.
But today, your hair down,
Flying about your face in aged frizzes,
As you sat facing an evening alone
And talked of the pain returning
(For the first time with a shade of 'Why?')
You suddenly seemed all your eighty years.

I came home to tell you, 'Mother,
Grandma is suddenly old.'
You were on the couch,
Collapsed after another day's work
Slightly harder than yesterday's,
Your second chin appearing
And more new crow's feet,
Facing an evening of ironing.
I choked the words back,
Not sure why.

And you, self in the mirror,
First crow's feet just appearing
(But only when I'm tired),
Frizzes not from age but choice,
Your freshness slightly faded,
Why so wooden?
Had you forgotten
The way of all fall flesh?

Carol Addink
20th century

Grandfather

Grandfather sits and begins breakfast,
staring into his coffee cup...

'Grandfather, here, your slippers...'

but little moves him mornings: his glasses
slide slowly down his nose & threaten
to fall. He always frowns, & catches them
in time. He cocks his head, favouring
his good ear, as always, to listen
upstairs: what the snow is doing
to the roof: shushes to silence
grandma & his radio. Winters

always slow him down a bit. Arthritis.
& he, contrary, tests it, moving
out to the uninsulated porch, freezing
in his flannel shirt and baggy pants
reading the paper. Ask him,

'Grandpa, come in, it's warmer here.'
'Only good chair's this one.'
'Bring it in, why don't you.'
'No room for it.' & he turns
the page, & shoves his glasses back
with his thumb without slowing
the movement of his hand & eyes.

An explanation is in order. Grandpa
was an orphan immigrant at twelve; knew
only Dutch; worked hard, & went to school;
taught himself English, finished
college at seventeen, taught algebra,
geometry & catechism sixty years;
believes predestination; decries depravity;
is quick to find evidences
of gradual (but constant) degeneration.

His reading finds him sin: murder, rape.
He grunts. It hurts. But comes as no surprise.
Drunkenness. Divorce. Debauchery.
He has grown, now, almost to expect it.
He misses his dog, loves
his children, prays
humbly & unceasingly for them & their children.

He is a Calvinist, to be sure, sound & wise
if settled in his ways. He believes
in hell, & firmly in damnation, but
will not call it down. He sees himself
growing out of this world: trying hard
not to grow bitter. He folds
his glasses into his pocket, his paper,
& sets it aside. Rises. Stands
very still at the window, hands
on the ledge, looking out across the snow.

& when you see him, you remember
Christ in the weakness of his power
weeping over Jerusalem. & from the cross
praying a final forgiveness. Now,
seeing him, you have to believe
that this is not futile, what he does.
That here, at least, prayer is valid.
This once, & for this little while
you have to believe.

Robert D. Swets
20th century

TIME AND ETERNITY

Last Aid

Time's running out,
(as life-blood seeps
out of a mortal wound).
Nothing now,
short of eternity,
shall ever serve to staunch it!

Grace Westerduin
20th century

The Passing Beat of Time

Cool Siloam

By cool Siloam's shady rill
  How sweet the lily grows!
How sweet the breath beneath the hill
  Of Sharon's dewy rose!

Lo, such the child whose early feet
  The paths of peace have trod;
Whose secret heart, with influence sweet,
  Is upward drawn to God.

By cool Siloam's shady rill
  The lily must decay;
The rose that blooms beneath the hill
  Must shortly fade away.

And soon, too soon, the wintry hour
  Of man's maturer age
Will shake the soul with sorrow's power,
  And stormy passion's rage...

Dependent on thy bounteous breath,
  We seek thy grace alone,
In childhood, manhood, age and death,
  To keep us still thine own!

Reginald Heber
1783–1826

Give T'anks

Anodda year of love.
Give t'anks. An' pray
dat God-Above
will seh to time, No way,
No way:
de word is love.

Mervyn Morris
20th century

Knole

The white hill-side is prickled with antlers
And the deer wade to me through the snow.
From John Donne's church the muffled and galoshed
Patiently to their holy dinners go.

And never do those antlered heads reflect
On the gentle flanks where in autumn they put their seed
Nor Christians on the word which, that very hour,
Their upturned faces or their hearts received.

But spring will bring the heavy doe to bed;
The fawn will wobble and soon after leap.
Those others will die at this or the next year's turn
And find the resurrection encased in sleep.

C.H. Sisson
20th century

Change Should Breed Change

New doth the sun appear,
The mountains' snows decay,
Crowned with frail flowers forth comes the baby year.
My soul, time posts away,
And thou yet in that frost
Which flower and fruit hath lost,
As if all here immortal were, dost stay:
For shame! thy powers awake,
Look to that heaven which never night makes black,
And there, at that immortal sun's bright rays,
Deck thee with flowers which fear not rage of days.

William Drummond of Hawthornden
1585–1649

From: A Prayer for the Past

All sights and sounds of day and year,
All groups and forms, each leaf and gem,
Are thine, O God, nor will I fear
To talk to thee of them.

Too great thy heart is to despise,
Whose day girds centuries about;
From things which we name small, thine eyes
See great things looking out.

Therefore the prayerful song I sing
May come to thee in ordered words:
Though lowly born, it needs not cling
In terror to its chords.

I think that nothing made is lost;
That not a moon has ever shone,
That not a cloud my eyes hath crossed
But to my soul is gone.

That all the lost years garnered lie
In this thy casket, my dim soul;
And thou wilt, once, the key apply,
And show the shining whole.

George MacDonald 1824–1905

To my Watch

Little monitor, by thee
Let me learn what I should be;
Learn the round of life to fill,
Useful and progressive still.
Thou can'st gentle hints impart
How to regulate the heart;
When I wind thee up at night,
Mark each fault and set thee right,
Let me search my bosom too,
And my daily thoughts review;
Mark the movements of my mind,
Nor be easy till I find
Latent errors brought to view,
Till all be regular and true.

Anne Steele died 1779?

Stanzas

SUBJOINED TO THE YEARLY BILL OF MORTALITY
OF THE PARISH OF ALL SAINTS, NORTHAMPTON:
FOR THE YEAR 1790

He who sits from day to day,
   Where the prisoned lark is hung,
Heedless of his loudest lay,
   Hardly knows that he has sung.

Where the watchmen in his round
   Nightly lifts his voice on high,
None, accustomed to the sound,
   Wakes the sooner for his cry.

So your verse-man I, and clerk,
   Yearly in my song proclaim
Death at hand—yourselves his mark—
   And the foe's unerring aim.

Duly at my time I come,
   Publishing to all aloud—
'Soon the grave must be your home
   And your only suit a shroud.'

But the monitory strain,
   Oft repeated in your ears,
Seems to sound too much in vain,
   Wins no notice, wakes no fears.

Can a truth, by all confessed
   Of such magnitude and weight,
Grow, by being oft expressed,
   Trivial as a parrot's prate?

Pleasure's call attention wins,
   Hear it often as we may;
New as ever seem our sins,
   Though committed every day.

Death and Judgement, Heaven and Hell—
   These alone, so often heard,
No more move us than the bell
   When some stranger is interred.

Oh then, ere the turf or tomb
   Cover us from every eye,
Spirit of instruction, come;
   Make us learn that we must die.

William Cowper
1731–1800

Sonnet VII

How soon hath Time, the subtle thief of youth,
  Stol'n on his wing my three and twentieth year!
  My hasting days fly on with full career,
  But my late spring no bud or blossom shew'th.
Perhaps my semblance might deceive the truth,
  That I to manhood am arrived so near,
And inward ripeness doth much less appear,
  Than some more timely-happy spirits endu'th.
Yet be it less or more, or soon or slow,
  It shall be still in strictest measure ev'n
  To that same lot, however mean or high,
Towards which Time leads me, and the will of Heav'n;
  All is, if I have grace to use it so,
As ever in my great Task-Master's eye.

John Milton
1608–74

On Time

Fly envious Time, till thou run out thy race,
Call on the lazy leaden-stepping hours,
Whose speed is but the heavy plummets pace;
And glut thy self with what thy womb devours,
Which is no more than what is false and vain,
And merely mortal dross;
So little is our loss,
So little is thy gain.
For when as each thing bad thou hast entombed,
And last of all, thy greedy self consumed,
Then long eternity shall greet our bliss
With an individual kiss;
And joy shall overtake us as a flood
When everything that is sincerely good
And perfectly divine,
With truth, and peace, and love shall ever shine
About the supreme throne
Of him, t'whose happy-making sight alone,
When once our heavenly-guided soul shall climb,
Then all this earthy grossness quit,
Attired with stars, we shall for ever sit,
Triumphing over death, and chance, and thee, O Time.

John Milton
1608–74

From: Hurrying Time

My glass is half unspent; forbear to arrest
My thriftless day too soon: my poor request
Is, that my glass may run but out the rest.

My time-devourèd minutes will be done
Without thy help; see, see how swift they run:
Cut not my thread before my thread be spun.

The gain's not great I purchase by this stay;
What loss sustain'st thou by so small delay,
To whom ten thousand years are but a day?

My following eye can hardly make a shift
To count my wingèd hours; they fly so swift,
They scarce deserve the bounteous name of gift.

The secret wheels of hurrying time do give
So short a warning, and so fast they drive,
That I am dead before I seem to live.

And what's a life? a weary pilgrimage,
Whose glory in one day doth fill thy stage
With childhood, manhood, and decrepit age...

Read on this dial, how the shades devour
My short-lived winter's day; hour eats up hour;
Alas! the total's but from eight to four...

Shade not that dial, night will blind too soon;
My non-aged day already points to noon;
How simple is my suit! how small my boon!...

I have a world of sins to be lamented;
I have a sea of tears that must be vented:
O spare till then; and then I die contented.

Francis Quarles
1592–1644

O Fly My Soul

O fly my soul, what hangs upon
  thy drooping wings,
    and weighs them down,
With love of gaudy mortal things?
The Sun is now in the East, each shade
  as he doth rise,
    is shorter made,
That Earth may lessen to our eyes:
O be not careless then, and play
  until the Star of peace
Hide all his beams in dark recess;
Poor Pilgrims needs must lose their way,
When all the shadows do increase.

James Shirley   1596–1666

Now

The *Past* can be no more—
Whose misemploying I deplore:
    The *Future* is to me
An absolute uncertainty:
The *Now*, which will not with me stay,
Within a second flies away.

  I heard God often say,
Now, of salvation is the day,—
    But turned from heaven my view,
I still had something else to do;
Till God a dream instructive sent,
To warn me timely to repent.

  Methought Death, with his dart,
Had mortally transfixed my heart;
    And devils round about,
To seize my spirit flying out,
Cried—'Now, of which you took no care,
Is turned to *Never* and despair!'

  I gave a sudden start,
And waked with *Never* in my heart:
    Still I that *Never* felt,
Never upon my spirit dwelt;—
A thousand thanks to God I paid,
That my sad *Never* was delayed.

Thomas Ken   1637–1711

From: Times Go by Turns

The lopped tree in time may grow again,
   Most naked plants renew both fruit and flower;
The sorriest wight may find release of pain,
   The driest soil suck in some moistening shower.
      Times go by turns, and chances change by course,
      From foul to fair, from better hap to worse.

The sea of fortune doth not ever flow,
   She draws her favours to the lowest ebb;
Her tides hath equal times to come and go,
   Her loom doth weave the fine and coarsest web.
      No joy so great but runneth to an end,
      No hap so hard but may in fine amend.

Not always fall of leaf, nor ever spring,
   No endless night, yet not eternal day;
The saddest birds a season find to sing,
   The roughest storm a calm may soon allay.
      Thus with succeeding turns, God tempereth all,
      That man may hope to rise, yet fear to fall.

A chance may win that by mischance was lost;
The net, that holds no great, takes little fish;
In some things all, in all things none are crossed;
Few all they need, but none have all they wish.
Unmeddled joys here to no man befall;
Who least, hath some; who most, hath never all.

Robert Southwell
1561–95

From: Contemplations

O Time the fatal wrack of mortal things,
That draws oblivious curtains over kings,
Their sumptuous monuments, men know them not,
Their names without a record are forgot,
Their parts, their ports, their pomp's all laid in th' dust
Nor wit nor gold, nor buildings scape times rust;
But he whose name is graved in the white stone
Shall last and shine when all of these are gone.

Anne Bradstreet
1612–72

Death and Beyond

Wait

These are
the good
old days.

Just wait
and see.

Steve Turner *20th century*

Eternity

Because I could not stop for Death
He kindly stopped for me,
The carriage held but just ourselves—
And immortality.

We slowly drove, he knew no haste,
And I had put away
My labour and my leisure too,
For his civility.

We passed the school, where children strove
At recess, in the ring,
We passed the fields of gazing grain,
We passed the setting sun—

Or rather, he passed us;
The dews drew quivering and chill;
For only gossamer, my gown,
My tippet only tulle.

We paused before a house that seemed
A swelling of the ground,
The roof was scarcely visible,
The cornice in the ground.

Since then 'tis centuries, and yet
Feels shorter than the day
I first surmised the horses' heads
Were towards eternity.

Emily Dickinson *1830–86*

Eternity

He who bends to himself a joy
Does the wingèd life destroy;
But he who kisses the joy as it flies
Lives in eternity's sunrise.

William Blake
1757–1827

Christ in the Universe

With this ambiguous earth
His dealings have been told us. These abide:
The signal to a maid, the human birth,
The lesson, and the young Man crucified.

But not a star of all
The innumerable host of stars has heard
How he administered this terrestrial ball.
Our race have kept their Lord's entrusted Word...

No planet knows that this
Our wayside planet, carrying land and wave,
Love and life multipled, and pain and bliss,
Bears, as chief treasure, one forsaken grave.

Nor, in our little day,
May his devices with the heavens be guessed,
His pilgrimage to thread the Milky Way,
Or his bestowals there be manifest.

But, in the eternities,
Doubtless we shall compare together, hear
A million alien Gospels, in what guise
He trod the Pleiades, the Lyre, the Bear.

O be prepared, my soul!
To tread the inconceivable, to scan
The million forms of God those stars unroll
When, in our turn, we show to them a Man.

Alice Meynell
1847–1922

Death

Death Blessing

May the Father take you
    In his fragrant clasp of love,
When you go across the flooding streams
    And the black river of death

Traditional Celtic
Collected by Alexander Carmichael
19th century

Crossing the Bar

Sunset and evening star,
    And one clear call for me!
And may there be no moaning of the bar,
    When I put out to sea,

But such a tide as moving seems asleep,
    Too full for sound and foam,
When that which drew from out the boundless deep
        Turns again home.

Twilight and evening bell,
    And after that the dark!
And may there be no sadness of farewell,
    When I embark;

For though from out our bourne of Time and Place
    The flood may bear me far,
I hope to see my Pilot face to face
    When I have crossed the bar.

Alfred Lord Tennyson
1809–92

The Dying Christian to his Soul

Vital spark of heavenly flame!
Quit, O quit this mortal frame:
Trembling, hoping, lingering, flying,
O the pain, the bliss of dying!
Cease, fond Nature, cease thy strife,
And let me languish into life.

Hark! they whisper; angels say,
Sister Spirit, come away!
What is this absorbs me quite?
Steals my senses, shuts my sight,
Drowns my spirits, draws my breath?
Tell me, my soul, can this be death?

The world recedes; it disappears!
Heaven opens on my eyes! my ears
With sounds seraphic ring!
Lend, lend your wings! I mount! I fly!
O Grave! where is thy victory?
O Death! where is thy sting?

Alexander Pope
1688–1744

To Death

Thou bidst me come away,
And I'll no longer stay,
Than for to shed some tears
For faults of former years;
And to repent some crimes,
Done in the present times:
And next, to take a bit
Of bread, and wine with it:
To don my robes of love,
Fit for the place above;
To gird my loins about
With charity throughout;
And so to travail hence
With feet of innocence:
These done, I'll only cry
God Mercy! and so die.

Robert Herrick
1591–1674

Miserere

Miserere, my Maker,
O have mercy on me, wretch, strangely distressèd,
Cast down with sin oppressèd;
Mightily vexed to the soul's bitter anguish,
E'en to the death I languish.
Yet let it please thee
To hear my ceaseless crying:
Miserere, miserere, I am dying.

Miserere, my Saviour,
I, alas, am for my sins fearfully grievèd,
And cannot be relievèd
But by thy death, which thou didst suffer for me,
Wherefore I adore thee.
And do beseech thee
To hear my ceaseless crying:
Miserere, miserere, I am dying.

Holy Spirit, miserere,
Comfort my distressèd soul, grieved for youth's folly,
Purge, cleanse and make it holy;
With thy sweet due of grace and peace inspire me,
How I desire thee.
And strengthen me now
In this, my ceaseless crying:
Miserere, miserere, I am dying.

Anonymous
about 1615

Deathbed

Now, when the frail and fine-spun
Web of mortality
Gapes, and lets slip
What we have loved so long
From out our lighted present
Into the trackless dark

We turn, blinded,
Not to the Christ in Glory,
Stars about his feet,

But to the Son of Man,
Back from the tomb,
Who built fires, ate fish,
Spoke with friends, and walked
A dusty road at evening.

Here, in this room, in
This stark and timeless moment,
We hear those footsteps

And
With suddenly lifted hearts
Acknowledge
The irrelevance of death.

Evangeline Paterson
20th century

Prospice

Fear death?—to feel the fog in my throat,
    The mist in my face,
When the snows begin, and the blasts denote
    I am nearing the place,
The power of the night, the press of the storm,
    The post of the foe;
Where he stands, the Arch Fear in a visible form,
    Yet the strong man must go:
For the journey is done and the summit attained,
    And the barriers fall,
Though a battle's to fight ere the guerdon be gained,
    The reward of it all.
I was ever a fighter, so—one fight more,
    The best and the last!
I would hate that death bandaged my eyes, and forebore,
    And bade me creep past.
No! let me taste the whole of it, fare like my peers
    The heroes of old,
Bear the brunt, in a minute pay glad life's arrears
    Of pain, darkness and cold.
For sudden the worst turns the best to the brave,
    The black minute's at end,
And the element's rage, the fiend-voices that rave,
    Shall dwindle, shall blend,
Shall change, shall become first a peace out of pain,
    Then a light, then thy breast,
O thou soul of my soul! I shall clasp thee again,
    And with God be the rest!

Robert Browning
1812–89

Bede's Death Song

Before he leaves on his fated journey
No man will be so wise that he need not
Reflect while time still remains
Whether his soul will win delight
Or darkness after his death-day.

From Cuthbert's account of Bede's death
about 735

From: Upon the Image of Death

Before my face the picture hangs,
   That daily should put me in mind
Of those cold qualms and bitter pangs,
   That shortly I am like to find:
     But yet, alas, full little I
     Do think hereon, that I must die.

I often look upon a face
   Most ugly, grisly, bare and thin;
I often view the hollow place,
   Where eyes and nose had sometimes been;
     I see the bones across that lie,
     Yet little think that I must die.

I read the label underneath,
   That telleth me whereto I must;
I see the sentence eke that saith
   'Remember, man, that thou art dust!'
     But yet, alas, but seldom I
     Do think indeed that I must die.

Continually at my bed's head
   A hearse doth hang, which doth me tell,
That I ere morning may be dead,
   Though now I feel myself full well:
     But yet, alas, for all this, I
     Have little mind that I must die.

The gown which I do use to wear,
   The knife wherewith I cut my meat,
And eke that old and ancient chair
   Which is my only usual seat;
     All these do tell me I must die,
     And yet my life amend not I.

My ancestors are turned to clay,
   And many of my mates are gone,
My youngers daily drop away,
   And can I think to 'scape alone?
     No, no, I know that I must die,
     And yet my life amend not I . . .

If none can 'scape death's dreadful dart,
  If rich and poor his beck obey,
If strong, if wise, if all do smart,
  Then I to 'scape shall have no way.
    Oh! grant me grace, O God, that I
    My life may mend, sith I must die.

Robert Southwell?
1561–95

The Border

What shall avail me
When I reach the border?
This staff will fail me,
This pass all in order.

These words I have learned
Will not help me then,
These honours hard earned,
And applause of men.

My harp truly set
Will break string by string;
I shall quite forget
That once I could sing.

Absence pure and cold
Of sense and memory
Lightly will hold
All that is me.

All, all will fail me,
Tongue, foot and hand.
Strange I shall hale me
To that strange land.

Edwin Muir
1887–1959

Extreme Unction

Upon the eyes, the lips, the feet,
   On all the passages of sense,
The atoning oil is spread with sweet
   Renewal of lost innocence.

The feet, that lately ran so fast
   To meet desire, are soothly sealed;
The eyes, that were so often cast
   On vanity, are touched and healed.

From troublous sights and sounds set free;
   In such a twilight hour of breath,
Shall one retrace his life, or see,
   Through shadows, the true face of death?

Vials of mercy! Sacring oils!
   I know not where nor when I come,
Nor through what wanderings and toils,
   To crave of you Viaticum.

Yet, when the walls of flesh grow weak,
   In such an hour, it may be,
Through mist and darkness, light will break,
   And each anointed sense will see.

Ernest Dowson
1867–1900

Last Verses

The seas are quiet when the winds give o'er;
So calm are we when passions are no more.
For then we know how vain it was to boast
Of fleeting things, so certain to be lost.
Clouds of affection from our younger eyes
Conceal that emptiness which age descries.

The soul's dark cottage, battered and decayed,
Lets in new light through chinks that Time hath made:
Stronger by weakness, wiser, men become
As they draw near to their eternal home.
Leaving the old, both worlds at once they view
That stand upon the threshold of the new.

Edmund Waller
1606–87

Death, be not Proud

Death, be not proud, though some have called thee
Mighty and dreadful, for thou art not so;
For those whom thou thinkst thou dost overthrow
Die not, poor Death, nor yet canst thou kill me.
From rest and sleep, which but thy pictures be,
Much pleasure—then, from thee much more must flow;
And soonest our best men with thee do go,
Rest of their bones and soul's delivery.
Thou'rt slave to fate, chance, kings, and desperate men,
And dost with poison, war, and sickness dwell;
And poppy or charms can make us sleep as well,
And better than thy stroke. Why swellst thou then?
One short sleep past, we wake eternally,
And death shall be no more. Death, thou shalt die.

John Donne
1572–1631

A Contemplation Upon Flowers

Brave flowers—that I could gallant it like you,
    And be as little vain!
You come abroad, and make a harmless show,
    And to your beds of earth again.
You are not proud: you know your birth:
For your embroidered garments are from earth.

You do obey your months and times, but I
    Would have it ever Spring:
My fate would know no Winter, never die,
    Nor think of such a thing.
O that I could my bed of earth but view
And smile, and look as cheerfully as you!

O teach me to see Death and not to fear,
    But rather to take truce!
How often have I seen you at a bier,
    And there look fresh and spruce!
You fragrant flowers! then teach me, that my breath
Like yours may sweeten and perfume my death.

Henry King
1592–1669

Before the Beginning

Before the beginning thou hast foreknown the end,
Before the birthday the death-bed was seen of thee:
Cleanse what I cannot cleanse, mend what I cannot mend,
O Lord, All-Merciful, be merciful to me.

While the end is drawing near I know not mine end;
Birth I recall not, my death I cannot foresee:
O God, arise to defend, arise to befriend,
O Lord All-Merciful, be merciful to me.

Christina Rossetti
1830–94

Eternity, I'm Coming

A wife at daybreak I shall be,
Sunrise, thou hast a flag for me?
At midnight I am yet a maid—
How short it takes to make it bride!
Then, Midnight, I have passed from thee
Unto the East and Victory.

Midnight, 'Good night'
I hear thee call.
The angels bustle in the hall,
Softly my Future climbs the stair,
I fumble at my childhood's prayer—
So soon to be a child no more!
Eternity, I'm coming, sir—
Master, I've seen that face before.

Emily Dickinson
1830–86

Death Lib.

The liberating thing about death
is in its fairness to women,
its acceptance of blacks,
its special consideration
for the sick.

And I like the way
that children aren't excluded,
homosexuals are welcomed,
and militants aren't banned.

The really wondering thing
about death
is that all major religions
agree on it, all beliefs
take you there, all philosophy
bows before it, all arguments
end there.

Con men can't con it
Thieves can't nick it
Bullies can't share it
Magicians can't trick it.

Boxers can't punch it
Nor critics dismiss it
Don't knows can't not know
The lazy can't miss it.

Governments can't ban it
Or the army defuse it
Judges can't jail it
Lawyers can't sue it.

Capitalists can't bribe it
Socialists can't share it
Terrorists can't jump it
The Third World aren't spared it.

Scientists can't quell it
Nor can they disprove it
Doctors can't cure it
Surgeons can't move it.

Einstein can't halve it
Guevara can't free it
The thing about dead
Is we're all gonna be it.

Steve Turner
20th century

Dark Verge of Life

Be near me when my light is low,
   When the blood creeps, and the nerves prick
   And tingle; and the heart is sick
And all the wheels of Being slow.

Be near me when the sensuous frame
   Is racked with pangs that conquer trust;
   And Time, a maniac scattering dust,
And Life, a Fury slinging flame.

Be near me when my faith is dry,
   And men the flies of latter spring,
   That lay their eggs, and sting and sing
And weave their petty cells and die.

Be near me when I fade away,
   To point the term of human strife,
   And on the low dark verge of life
The twilight of eternal day.

Alfred Lord Tennyson
1809–92

Come Quickly, Lord, and Take Me

Never weather-beaten sail more willing bent to shore,
   Never tired pilgrim's limbs affected slumber more,
Than my weary spirit now longs to fly out of my troubled breast,
O come quickly, sweetest Lord, and take my soul to rest!

Ever blooming are the joys of heaven's high paradise,
Cold age deafs not there our ears nor vapour dims our eyes:
Glory there the sun outshines; whose beams the blessed only see,
O come quickly, glorious Lord, and raise my sprite to thee!

Thomas Campion
1567–1620

Memento Mori

When as man's life, the light of human lust,
In socket of his earthly lantern burns,
That all this glory unto ashes must,
And generation to corruption turns;
   Then fond desires that only fear their end
   Do vainly wish for life but to amend.

But when this life is from the body fled,
To see itself in that eternal glass
Where time doth end, and thoughts accuse the dead,
Where all to come is one with all that was;
   Then living men ask how he left his breath
   That while he livèd never thought of death.

Fulke Greville, Lord Brooke
1554–1628

The Soul's Garment

Great Nature clothes the soul, which is but thin,
With fleshly garments, which the Fates do spin;
And when these garments are grown old and bare,
With sickness torn, Death takes them off with care,
And folds them up in peace and quiet rest,
And lays them safe within an earthly chest:
Then scours them well and makes them sweet and clean,
Fit for the soul to wear those clothes again.

Margaret Cavendish, Duchess of Newcastle
1625–73

A Prayer Before Death

FROM: THE BATTLE OF MALDON
(FOUGHT IN AD 991)

I give you thanks, Lord God of nations,
For all the worldly joys that I have known.
But now, gracious Maker, I have the greatest need
That you grant my spirit to God,
That my soul may set out to you,
Prince of Angels, going in peace
Into your power. I pray
That the hell-fiends may not humiliate me.

Anonymous
written soon after 991

Mercy in our Time

Let not mistaken mercy
blind my fading sight,
no false euphoria lull me.
I would not unprepared
take this last journey.
Give me a light to guide me
through dark valleys,
a staff to lean upon,
bread to sustain me,
a blessing in my ear
that fear may not assail me.
Then leaving do not hold my hand,
I go to meet a friend—
    that same who traced
    compassion in the sand.

Nancy Hopkins
20th century

Dominus Illuminatio Mea

In the hour of death, after this life's whim,
When the heart beats low, and the eyes grow dim,
And pain has exhausted every limb—
    The lover of the Lord shall trust in him.

When the will has forgotten the lifelong aim,
And the mind can only disgrace its fame,
And a man is uncertain of his own name—
    The power of the Lord shall fill this frame.

When the last sigh is heaved, and the last tear shed,
And the coffin is waiting beside the bed,
And the widow and child forsake the dead—
    The angel of the Lord shall lift this head.

For even the purest delight may pall,
And power must fail, and the pride must fall,
And the love of the dearest friends grow small—
    But the glory of the Lord is all in all.

Richard Doddridge Blackmore
1825–1900

The Progress of the Soul

Think then, my soul, that Death is but a groom
Which brings a taper to the outward room,
Whence thou spiest first a little glimmering light
And after brings it nearer to thy sight;
For such approaches doth heaven make in death.
Think thyself labouring now with broken breath,
And think those broken and soft notes to be
Division and thy happiest harmony.
Think thee laid on thy deathbed, loose and slack,
And think that but unbinding of a pack
To take one precious thing, thy soul, from thence.
Think thyself parched with fever's violence;
Anger thine ague more by calling it
Thy physic; chide the slackness of the fit.
Think that thou hear'st thy knell, and think no more
But as bells callèd thee to church before,
So this to the Triumphant Church calls thee.

John Donne
1572–1631

Death Prayer

O God, give me of thy wisdom,
O God, give me of thy mercy,
O God, give me of thy fulness,
And of thy guidance in face of every strait.

O God, give me of thy holiness,
O God, give me of thy shielding,
O God, give me of thy surrounding,
And of thy peace in the knot of my death.

O give me of thy surrounding,
    And of thy peace at the hour of my death!

Traditional Celtic
Collected by Alexander Carmichael
19th century

On the Death of Others

For a Friend Dying

(1 JOHN 4: 7–10)

When light broadens behind the curtains, and I wake
　　　to my peaceful morning,
my thoughts go at once to you, setting out on your slow
　　　day's business of dying.

In the midst of my life I am living your death, seeing
　　　with your eyes the shining
of sun on the leaf. All day I am keeping pace
　　　with your slow journey

and wishing that those you love may be there to send you
　　　—from love into Love going—
and may you launch out gently into the dark
　　　like keel into water moving.

Evangeline Paterson
20th century

In Memory of my Dear Grandchild

WHO DECEASED JUNE 20 1669, BEING THREE YEARS AND SEVEN MONTHS OLD.

With troubled heart and trembling hand I write,
The heavens have changed to sorrow my delight.
How oft with disappointment have I met,
When I on fading things my hopes have set.
Experience might 'fore this have made me wise,
To value things according to their price.
Was ever stable joy yet found below?
Or perfect bliss without mixture of woe?
I knew she was but as a withering flower,
That's here today, perhaps gone in an hour;
Like as a bubble, or the brittle glass,
Or like a shadow turning as it was.
More fool then I to look on that was lent
As if mine own, when thus impermanent.
Farewell dear child, thou ne'er shall come to me,
But yet a while, and I shall go to thee;
Meanwhile my throbbing heart's cheered up with this:
Thou with thy Saviour art in endless bliss.

Anne Bradstreet 1612–72

On the Death of Mr William Hervey

It was a dismal, and a fearful night,
Scarce could the Morn drive on the unwilling light,
When Sleep, Death's image, left my troubled breast
    By something like Death possessed.
My eyes with tears did uncommanded flow,
    And on my soul hung the dull weight
    Of some intolerable fate.
What bell was that? Ah me! too much I know!

My sweet companion, and my gentle peer,
Why hast thou left me thus unkindly here,
Thy end for ever, and my life to moan?
    O thou hast left me all alone!
Thy soul and body, when death's agony
    Besieged around thy noble heart,
    Did not with more reluctance part
Than I, my dearest Friend, do part from thee.

My dearest Friend, would I had died for thee!
Life and this world henceforth will tedious be:
Nor shall I know hereafter what to do
    If once my griefs prove tedious too.
Silent and sad I walk about all day,
    As sullen ghosts stalk speechless by
    Where their hid treasures lie;
Alas! my treasure's gone; why do I stay? ...

With as much zeal, devotion, piety,
He always lived, as other saints do die.
Still with his soul severe accounts he kept,
    Weeping all debts out ere he slept.
Then down in peace and innocence he lay,
    Like the sun's laborious light,
    Which still in water sets at night,
Unsullied with his journey of the day.

But happy Thou, ta'en from this frantic age,
Where ignorance and hypocrisy does rage!
A fitter time for Heaven no soul e'er chose—
    The place now only free from those.
There 'mong the blest thou dost for ever shine;
    And whereso'er thou casts thy view
    Upon that white and radiant crew,
See'st not a soul clothed with more light than thine.

Abraham Cowley
1618–67

The Blessed Dead

They lie at rest, our blessed dead;
The dews drop cool above their head,
They knew not when fleet summer fled.

Together all, yet each alone;
Each laid at rest beneath his own
Smooth turf or white allotted stone.

When shall our slumber sink so deep,
And eyes that wept and eyes that weep
Weep not in the sufficient sleep?

God be with you, our great and small,
Our loves, our best-beloved of all,
Our own beyond the salt sea-wall.

Christina Rossetti
1830–94

After the Funeral

It is no time for tears now.
The time for tears is over.
It is the time, now,
To bar the gates.

See how the mind now
Prowls its beleaguered city,
Testing its defences, trying
Its strength, counting
Its treasure
(For there will be no more
Now the harvest is gathered)
It looks not to the plain
Where the ranked battalions of grief
Wait for the coming of night
But it knows
That the siege will be a long one
And the winter

Cold.

Evangeline Paterson
20th century

Pine Forest

(IN MEMORIAM—K.A.M.W.)

Among the towering pines
of perennial pride,
falling but not fallen,
the mossy path astride,
adding a new dimension,
one leans across the ride.

Caught at sixty degrees,
it makes a special mark
with shafts of angled light
in the criss-cross dark,
dead among the living,
lying bark to bark.

When will it fall completely,
all support withdrawn
by neighbour pines,
their roots outworn,
on a brushwood couch
to be stripped and sawn?

We stand together now,
silent among the trees,
wondering at the limit
of life's harmonies,
as the wind passing over,
another death decrees.

Randle Manwaring
20th century

Dirge

Calm on the bosom of thy God,
   Fair spirit, rest thee now!
E'en while with ours thy footsteps trod,
   His seal was on thy brow.

Dust, to its narrow house beneath!
   Soul, to its place on high!
They that have seen thy look in death
   No more may fear to die.

Felicia Dorothea Hemans
1793–1835

Friends Departed

They are all gone into the world of light!
   And I alone sit lingering here;
Their very memory is fair and bright,
     And my sad thoughts doth clear.

It glows and glitters in my cloudy breast,
   Like stars upon some gloomy grove,
Or those faint beams in which this hill is dressed
     After the sun's remove.

I see them walking in an air of glory,
   Whose light doth trample on my days:
My days, which are at best both dull and hoary,
     Mere glimmering and decays.

O holy Hope! and high Humility!
   High as the heavens above!
These are your walks, and you have showed them me,
     To kindle my cold love.

Dear, beauteous Death! the jewel of the just,
   Shining nowhere, but in the dark;
What mysteries do lie beyond thy dust,
     Could man outlook that mark! . . .

O Father of eternal life, and all
   Created glories under thee!
Resume thy spirit from this world of thrall
     Into true liberty.

Either disperse these mists, which blot and fill
   My perspective still as they pass:
Or else remove me hence unto that hill,
     Where I shall need no glass.

Henry Vaughan
1621–95

Early Death

She passed away like morning dew
    Before the sun was high;
So brief her time, she scarcely knew
    The meaning of a sigh.

As round the rose its soft perfume,
    Sweet love around her floated;
Admired she grew—while mortal doom
    Crept on, unfeared, unnoted.

Love was her guardian angel here,
    But Love to Death resigned her;
Though Love is kind, why should we fear
    But holy Death is kinder?

Hartley Coleridge   1796–1849

Safe

Safe where I cannot lie yet,
    Safe where I hope to lie too,
Safe from the fume and fret;
    You, and you,
Whom I never forget.

Safe from the frost and snow,
    Safe from the storm and the sun,
Safe where the seeds wait to grow
    One by one
And to come back in blow.

Christina Rossetti   1830–94

Requiem for the Abbess of Gandesheim Who Died Young

Thou hast come safe to port
    I still at sea,
The light is on thy head,
    Darkness in me.

Pluck thou in heaven's field
    Violet and rose,
While I strew flowers that will thy vigil keep
Where thou dost sleep,
    Love, in thy last repose.

Taken from 'Poetry in the Dark Ages', a lecture delivered by Helen Waddell

Hereafter

From: The Task

He is the happy man, whose life ev'n now
Shows somewhat of the happier life to come;
Who doomed to an obscure but tranquil state,
Is pleased with it, and, were he free to choose,
Would make his fate his choice; whom peace, the fruit
Of virtue, and whom virtue, fruit of faith,
Prepare for happiness; bespeak him one
Content indeed to sojourn while he must
Below the skies, but having there his home.

William Cowper
1731–1800

Fidele's Dirge

Fear no more the heat o' the sun
   Nor the furious winter's rages;
Thou thy worldly task hast done,
   Home art gone, and ta'en thy wages.
Golden lads and girls all must,
As chimney sweepers, come to dust.

Fear no more the frown o' the great,
   Thou art past the tyrant's stroke;
Care no more to clothe and eat,
   To thee the reed is as the oak.
The sceptre, learning, physic must
All follow this and come to dust.

Fear no more the lightning-flash,
   Nor the all-dreaded thunder-stone;
Fear not slander, censure rash;
   Thou hast finished joy and moan.
All lovers young, all lovers must
Consign to thee, and come to dust.

William Shakespeare
1564–1616

The Last Enemy

And he who each day
reveals a new masterpiece of sky
and whose joy
can be seen in the eyelash of a child
who when he hears of our smug indifference
can whisper an ocean into lashing fury
and talk tigers into padding roars
This my God
whose breath is in the wings of eagles
whose power is etched in the crags of mountains
It is he whom I will meet
And in whose Presence I will find tulips and clouds
kneeling martyrs and trees
the whole vast praising of his endless creation
and he will grant the uniqueness
that eluded me
in my earthly bartering with Satan
That day when he will erase the painful gasps of my ego
and I will sink my face into the wonder of his glorylove
and I will watch as planets converse with sparrows
On that day
when death is finally dead.

Stewart Henderson
20th century

The Grave Grows Firm with Grasses

(REVELATION 2:17)

The grave grows firm with grasses;
the fevered leaves lie down.
Then even summer withers,
and we are left alone

in that insensate winter
which whitens all the mind
and drives us deep for moments
in hallways underground

to wait the many mansions
where avenues are full
of all the shining people
who loved and wished us well.

Till then, each gravestone naming
each name stands high and glad
and gleams—an April angel
that smiles and shakes his head.

James E. Warren Jr.
20th century

Eternity

O years! and age! farewell:
    Behold I go
    Where I do know
Infinity to dwell.

And these mine eyes shall see
    All times, how they
    Are lost i' th' sea
Of vast eternity.

Where never moon shall sway
    The stars; but she,
    And night, shall be
Drowned in one endless day.

Robert Herrick
1591–1674

Meditations on the Sepulchre in the Garden

(JOHN 19:41)

The sepulchres, how thick they stand
Through all the road on either hand!
And burst upon the startling sight
In every garden of delight!

Thither the winding alleys tend;
There all the flowery borders end;
And forms, that charmed the eyes before,
Fragrance, and music are no more.

Deep in that damp and silent cell
My fathers and my brethren dwell;
Beneath its broad and gloomy shade
My kindred and my friends are laid.

But while I tread the solemn way,
My faith that Saviour would survey
Who deigned to sojourn in the tomb,
And left behind a rich perfume.

My thoughts with ecstasy unknown,
While from his grave they view his throne,
Through mine own sepulchre can see
A paradise reserved for me.

Philip Doddridge
1702–51

Resurrection

The wintry winds have ceased to blow,
   And trembling leaves appear;
The fairest flowers succeed the snow,
   And hail the infant year.

So, when the world and all its woes
   Are vanished far away,
Fair scenes and wonderful repose
   Shall bless the new-born day,—

When, from the confines of the grave,
   The body too shall rise;
No more precarious passion's slave,
   Nor error's sacrifice.

'Tis but a sleep—and Sion's king
   Will call the many dead:
'Tis but a sleep—and then we sing,
   O'er dreams of sorrow fled.

Yes!—wintry winds have ceased to blow,
   And trembling leaves appear,
And nature has her types to show
   Throughout the varying year.

George Crabbe
1754–1832

Presences Unseen

The Visionary

Silent is the house: all are laid asleep:
One alone looks out o'er the snow-wreaths deep,
Watching every cloud, dreading every breeze
That whirls the wildering drift, and bends the groaning trees.

Cheerful is the hearth, soft the matted floor;
Not one shivering gust creeps through pane or door;
The little lamp burns straight, its rays shoot strong and far:
I trim it well, to be the wanderer's guiding-star.

Frown, my haughty sire! chide, my angry dame;
Set your slaves to spy; threaten me with shame:
But neither sire nor dame, nor prying serf shall know,
What angel nightly tracks that waste of frozen snow.

What I love shall come like visitant of air,
Safe in secret power from lurking human snare;
Who loves me, no word of mine shall e'er betray,
Though for faith unstained my life must forfeit pay.

Burn, then, little lamp; glimmer straight and clear—
Hush! a rustling wing stirs, methinks, the air:
He for whom I wait, thus ever comes to me;
Strange Power! I trust thy might; trust thou my constancy.

Emily Brontë
1818–48

Presence

Your solid bodies fill a little of the room,
two of you, lightly weaving words
on the loom of your time and space.

A blind-cord taps, the face of the younger
turns towards the window, smiling slightly:
Charlie again, she says. Charlie, the name
you use when inexplicable things happen—
a tap spurts, an untouched door clicks open.

It is not my name, but it is my self.

How, how to make you know that we are here?
uncountable millions of us, in a little space
that three of you would crowd:
not the space that is full of you and your existence—
but this you have no image for, not yet...

There—the other of you looks up startled:
I coincided somehow with your sense,
made you aware (or was it someone else?) of us here:

the presence and presentness of Eternity
crowding the vast emptiness of your air.

Freda Cave
20th century

Kinship

I am aware,
As I go commonly sweeping the stair,
Doing my part of the everyday care—
Human and simple my lot and share—
    I am aware of a marvellous thing:
    Voices that murmur and ethers that ring
    In the far stellar spaces where cherubim sing;
I am aware of the passion that pours
Down the channels of fire through Infinity's doors;
    Forces terrific, with melody shod,
    Music that mates with the pulses of God.
I am aware of the glory that runs
From the core of myself to the core of the suns,
    Bound to the stars by invisible chains,
    Blaze of eternity now in my veins,
    Seeing the rush of ethereal rains,
Here in the midst of the everyday air—
    I am aware.

I am aware,
As I sit quietly here in my chair,
Sewing or reading or braiding my hair—
Human and simple my lot and my share—
    I am aware of the systems that swing
Through the aisles of creation on heavenly wing,
    I am aware of a marvellous thing,
Trail of the comets in furious flight,
Thunders of beauty that shatter the night,
    Terrible triumph of pageants that march
To the trumpets of time through eternity's arch.
I am aware of the splendour that ties
All the things of the earth to the things of the skies,
    Here in my body the heavenly heat,
    Here in my flesh the melodious beat
    Of the planets that circle Divinity's feet.
As I silently sit here in my chair,
    I am aware.

Angela Morgan
20th century

The Barranong Angel Case

You see that bench in front of Meagher's store?
That's where the angel landed.
What? An angel?
Yes. It was just near smoko* time on a sale day.
Town was quite full. He called us all together.
And was he obeyed?
Oh yes. He got a hearing.
Made his announcement, blessed us and took off
Again, straight up.
He had most glorious wings . . .
What happened then?
There were some tasks he'd set us
Or rather that sort of followed from his message.
And were they carried out?
At first we meant to,
But after a while, when there had been some talk
Most came to think he'd been a bit, well, haughty,
A bit overdone, with those flourishes of wings
And that plummy accent.
Lot of the women liked that.
But the men who'd knelt, off their own bat, mind you,
They were specially crook* on him, as I remember.

Did he come again?
Oh yes. The message was important.
The second time he hired the church hall,
Spoke most politely, called us all by name.
Any result?
Not much. At first we liked him.
But, after all, he'd singled out the Catholics.
It was their hall. And another thing resented
By different ones, he hadn't charged admission.
We weren't all paupers, and any man or angel
With so little regard for local pride, or money,
Ends up distrusted.

Did he give up then?
Oh no. The third time round
He thought he had our measure. Came by car,
Took a room at Morgan's, didn't say a word
About his message for the first two days
And after that dropped hints. Quite clever ones.
He made sure, too, that he spoke to all the Baptists.
I'll bet that worked.
You reckon? Not that I saw.

We didn't like him pandering to our ways
For a start. Some called it mockery, straight out.
He was an angel, after all. And then
There was the way he kept on coming back
Hustling the people.
And when all's said and done
He was a stranger. And he talked religion.

Did he keep on trying?
No. Gave us away.
Would it have helped if he'd settled in the district?
Don't think so, mate. If you follow me, he was
Too keen altogether. He'd have harped on that damn message
All the time—or if he'd stopped, well then
He'd have been despised because he'd given in, like.
He'd just got off on the wrong foot from the start
And you can't fix that up.

But what—Oh Hell!—what if he'd been, say, born here?
Well, that sort of thing's a bit above an angel,
Or a bit below. And he'd grow up too well known.
Who'd pay any heed to a neighbour's boy, I ask you,
Specially if he came out with messages?
Besides, what he told us had to do with love
And people here don't think that's quite—manly.

Les A. Murray
20th century

* *smoko:* a work-break
crook on: hostile to; abusive

Heaven

Heaven is not Far

Heaven is not far, tho' far the sky
Overarching earth and main.
It takes not long to love and die,
   Die, revive and rise again.
Not long: how long? Oh long re-echoing song!
O Lord, how long?

Christina Rossetti
1830–94

Care in Heaven

And is there care in heaven? and is there love?
In heavenly spirits to these creatures base,
That may compassion of their evils move?
There is: else much more wretched were the case
Of men than beasts. But O th'exceeding grace
Of highest God that loves his creatures so,
And all his works with mercy doth embrace,
That blessed angels he sends to and fro,
To serve to wicked man, to serve his wicked foe.

How oft do they their silver bowers leave,
To come to succour us that succour want!
How oft do they with golden pinions cleave
The flitting skies, like flying Pursuivant,
Against foul fiends to aid us militant!
They for us fight, they watch and duly ward,
And their bright squadrons round about us plant,
And all for love, and nothing for reward:
O why should heavenly God to men have such regard?

Edmund Spenser
1552–99

Peace

My soul, there is a country
　Far beyond the stars,
Where stands a winged sentry
　All skilful in the wars:
There, above noise and danger,
　Sweet Peace sits crowned with smiles,
And one born in a manger
　Commands the beauteous files.
He is thy gracious Friend,
　And—O my soul, awake!—
Did in pure love descend
　To die here for thy sake.
If thou canst get but thither,
　There grows the flower of Peace,
The Rose that cannot wither,
　Thy fortress and thy ease.
Leave then thy foolish ranges;
　For none can thee secure
But one who never changes—
　Thy God, thy life, thy cure.

Henry Vaughan
1622–95

'And That Will be Heaven'

and that will be heaven

and that will be heaven
at last　　the first unclouded
seeing

　　　　to stand like the sunflower
turned full face to the sun　　drenched
with light　　in the still centre
held　　while the circling planets
hum with an utter joy

　　　　seeing and knowing
at last　　in every particle
seen and known　　and not turning
away

　　never turning away
again

Evangeline Paterson　20th century

St Agnes' Eve

Deep on the convent-roof the snows
Are sparkling to the moon:
My breath to heaven like vapour goes:
   May my soul follow soon!
The shadows of the convent-towers
   Slant down the snowy sward,
Still creeping with the creeping hours
   That lead me to my Lord:
Make thou my spirit pure and clear
   As are the frosty skies,
Or this first snowdrop of the year
   That in my bosom lies.

As these white robes are soiled and dark,
   To yonder shining ground;
As this pale taper's earthly spark,
   To yonder argent round;
So shows my soul before the Lamb,
   My spirit before thee;
So in mine earthly house I am,
   To that I hope to be.
Break up the heavens, O Lord! and far,
   Thro' all yon starlight keen,
Draw me, thy bride, a glittering star,
   In raiment white and clean.

He lifts me to the golden doors;
   The flashes come and go;
All heaven bursts her starry floors,
   And strows her lights below,
And deepens on and up! the gates
   Roll back, and far within
For me the heavenly Bridegroom waits,
   To make me pure of sin.
The sabbaths of eternity,
   One sabbath deep and wide—
A light upon the shining sea—
   The Bridegroom with his bride!

Alfred, Lord Tennyson
1809–92

A Land of Pure Delight

There is a land of pure delight
   Where saints immortal reign;
Infinite day excludes the night,
   And pleasures banish pain.

There everlasting spring abides,
   And never-withering flowers:
Death like a narrow sea divides
   This heavenly land from ours.

Sweet fields beyond the swelling flood
   Stand dressed in living green:
So to the Jews old Canaan stood,
   While Jordan rolled between.

But timorous mortals start and shrink
   To cross this narrow sea,
And linger shivering on the brink
   And fear to launch away.

O could we make our doubts remove,
   These gloomy doubts that rise,
And see the Canaan that we love,
   With unbeclouded eyes.

Could we but climb where Moses stood,
   And view the landscape o'er,
Not Jordan's stream, nor Death's cold flood,
   Should fright us from the shore.

Isaac Watts
1674–1748

From: Hierusalem, My Happy Home

Hierusalem, my happy home,
    When shall I come to thee?
When shall my sorrows have an end,
    Thy joys when shall I see?

O happy harbour of the saints,
    O sweet and pleasant soil,
In thee no sorrow may be found
    No grief, no care, no toil...

No dampish mist is seen in thee,
    Nor cold nor darksome night;
There every soul shines as the sun,
    There God himself gives light.

There lust and lucre cannot dwell,
    There envy bears no sway;
There is no hunger, heat, nor cold,
    But pleasure every way.

Hierusalem, Hierusalem,
    God grant I once may see
Thy endless joys, and of the same
    Partaker aye to be.

Thy walls are made of precious stones,
    Thy bulwarks diamonds square;
Thy gates are of right orient pearl,
    Exceeding rich and rare.

Thy turrets and thy pinnacles
    With carbuncles do shine;
The very streets are paved with gold
    Surpassing clear and fine.

The houses are of ivory,
    The windows crystal clear,
Thy tiles are made of beaten gold,
    O God, that I were there.

Within thy gates nothing doth come
    That is not passing clean;
No spider's web, no dirt, no dust,
    No filth may there be seen...

There trees for evermore bear fruit
   And evermore do spring;
There evermore the angels sit
   And evermore do sing...

Our Lady sings *Magnificat*
   With tune surpassing sweet;
And all the virgins bear their parts
   Sitting about her feet...

Hierusalem, my happy home,
   Would God I were in thee!
Would God my woes were at an end,
   Thy joys that I might see!

Anonymous
This version from a Catholic Commonplace Book
dated 1616

There

There, in that other world, what waits for me?
What shall I find after that other birth?
No stormy, tossing, foaming, smiling sea,
   But a new earth.

No sun to mark the changing of the days,
No slow, soft falling of the alternate night,
No moon, no star, no light upon my ways,
   Only the Light.

No grey cathedral, wide and wondrous fair,
That I may tread, where all my fathers trod.
Nay, nay, my soul, no house of God is there,
   But only God.

Mary Coleridge
1861–1907

Exile

Yes, it is beautiful country,
the streams in the winding valley,
the knowes and the birches,
and beautiful the mountain's bare shoulder
and the calm brows of the hills,
but it is not my country,
and in my heart there is a hollow place always.

And there is no way to go back—
maybe the miles indeed, but the years never.

Winding are the roads that we choose,
and inexorable is life,
driving us, it seems, like cattle
farther and farther away from what we remember.

But when we shall come at last
to God, who is our home and country,
there will be no more road stretching before us
and no more need to go back.

Evangeline Paterson
20th century

I Never Saw a Moor

I never saw a moor
I never saw the sea;
Yet know I how the heather looks
And what a wave must be.

I never spoke with God,
Nor visited in Heaven;
Yet certain am I of the spot
As if the chart were given.

Emily Dickinson
1830–86

The Return of Christ and the Last Judgment

The Heavenly Aeroplane

One of these nights about twelve o'clock
The old world's going to reel and rock,
The sinner's going to tremble and cry for pain
And the Lord will come in his aeroplane.

   O ye thirsty of every tribe
   Get your ticket for an aeroplane ride,
   Jesus our Saviour is a-coming to reign
   And take you up to glory in his aeroplane.

Talk about your joy-rides in automobiles,
Talk about your fast time on motor wheels,
We'll break all records as we upwards fly
For an aeroplane joy-ride through the sky.

There will be no punctures or muddy roads,
No broken axles from overloads,
No shocks to give trouble or cause delay
As we soon will rapture up the narrow way.

You will have to get ready if you take this ride,
Quit all your sins and humble your pride,
You must furnish a lamp both bright and clean
And a vessel of oil to run the machine.

When our journey is over and we'll all sit down
At the marriage supper with a robe and a crown
We'll blend our voices with the heavenly throng
And praise our Saviour as the years roll on.

Anonymous
about 1935

From: A Song for St Cecilia's Day 1687

GRAND CHORUS

As from the power of sacred lays
   The spheres began to move,
And sung the great Creator's praise
   To all the blest above;
So when the last and dreadful hour
This crumbling pageant shall devour,
The trumpet shall be heard on high,
The dead shall live, the living die,
And music shall untune the sky!

John Dryden
1631–1700

Hymn for Advent

Lord, come away!
   Why dost thou stay?
Thy road is ready; and thy paths made straight
   With longing expectations wait
The consecration of thy beauteous feet.
   Ride on triumphantly; behold we lay
   Our lusts and proud will in thy way!

Hosanna! Welcome to our hearts! Lord, here
Thou hast a temple too; and full as dear
As that of Sion, and as full of sin:
Nothing but thieves and robbers dwell therein:
Enter, and chase them forth, and cleanse the floor:
Crucify them, that they may never more
      Profane that holy place
   Where thou hast chose to set thy face!
   And then if our stiff tongues shall be
      Mute in the praises of thy deity,
      The stones out of the temple wall
         Shall cry aloud and call
   Hosanna! And thy glorious footsteps greet!

Jeremy Taylor
1613–67

Travail Hymn

Make speed, you tidal waves,
   Your God commands.
Explode your vitals, earth,
   Your Lord descends.
Skies shall be torn away,
The stars shall blaze like hay
That cataclysmic day
   When Christ returns.

Sin warped the perfect world
   With wrenching groans.
Slick horrors scummed the ground;
   Man, abject, moans
Again earth's frame disjoints
As God's just wrath appoints
Wild waters from his founts
   Of cloud and stone.

Old Egypt felt his rage;
   The Nile turned blood.
Cities dissolved in ash—
   Flame flowed from God.
But when Christ's cross touched heaven,
With joy we saw him risen,
Then worked the Gospel leaven:
   God's ways are good.

         Merle Meeter
         20th century

The Last Judgement

When rising from the bed of death,
　O'erwhelmed with guilt and fear,
I see my Maker face to face,
　O how shall I appear?

If yet, while pardon may be found,
　And mercy may be sought,
My heart with inward horror shrinks,
　And trembles at the thought;

When thou, O Lord, shalt stand disclosed
　In majesty severe,
And sit in judgement on my soul
　O how shall I appear?

But thou hast told the troubled mind,
　Who does her sins lament,
The timely tribute of her tears
　Shall endless woe prevent.

Then see the sorrows of my heart
　Ere yet it be too late;
And hear my Saviour's dying groans,
　To give those sorrows weight.

For never shall my soul despair
　Her pardon to procure,
Who knows thine only Son has died
　To make her pardon sure.

Joseph Addison
1672–1719

Chaff

Chaff.
Sorted and sifted,
good from bad when God brings Judgement.
Sordid and twisted, victims from villains,
when we try to do it for him.

Driving the supposed chaff from us
with our own hot air,
instead of the appointed four winds
of the Revelation,
we often trample the elect-yet-unconfessed
as pearls before swine,
forgetting what pearls look like
from the outside of the oyster.

The silo barn is
filled with fat-bellied wheat,
layer upon layer,
prouder upon proud stacked in pews.
We reach the vantage of the silo top,
yet from greatest to least
we are carpeted wall to wall,
suspended by the chaff that is
pressed into the damp dirt reality ...
in every crack chaff fills.

Settled wheat
ground under so much pressure
looks (to us) like any chaff hogs walk on.

E. Neil Culbertson
20th century

Dies Irae

That day of wrath, that dreadful day,
When heaven and earth shall pass away,
What power shall be the sinner's stay?
How shall he meet that dreadul day?

When, shrivelling like a parched scroll,
The flaming heavens together roll;
When louder yet, and yet more dread,
Swells the high trump that wakes the dead;

Oh! on that day, that wrathful day,
When man to judgement wakes from clay,
Be THOU the trembling sinner's stay,
Though heaven and earth shall pass away!

Sir Walter Scott
1771–1832

Telephone

I am a telephone
I have heard
Many voices in confidence
I ring and they jump,
And pick up
My hand set.
Then they get set
For a talk.
'Hullo, who's speaking?'
'It's me' and they continue
In topics legal and illegal
They indulge in conversation
They think is all secret
But I listen
And wait like a computer
For the day I will be summoned
As witness
To all the dialogues
That transpired
That will be, the day of judgement.

Mamman J. Vatsa
20th century

A Hope

And oh! there lives within my heart
  A hope long nursed by me;
(And should its cheering ray depart
  How dark my soul would be!)

That as in Adam all have died,
  In Christ shall all men live;
And ever round his throne abide,
  Eternal praise to give.

That even the wicked shall at last
  Be fitted for the skies;
And when their dreadful doom is past
  To light and life arise.

I ask not how remote the day,
  Nor what the sinner's woe,
Before their dross is purged away;
  Enough for me to know—

That when the cup of wrath is drained,
  The metal purified,
They'll cling to what they once disdained,
  And live by him that died.

Anne Brontë
1820–49

The Last Word

Be still and know . . .

But they walked and they ran,
And they marched and they rode,
And they flew and they drove,
And they bused and they commuted.

Be still and know that . . .

But they gathered and they met,
And they communed and they congregated,
And they assembled in circles,
And lined up in rows and they organized.

Be still and know that I . . .

But they conversed and they spoke,
And they shouted and they shook,
And they cried and they laughed,
And they murmured and complained.

Be still and know that I am . . .

But the marchers went forward,
The buses rolled on,
The circles went round,
The lines kept moving,
And the shouts and the cries,
And the laughter and the sighs,
And the murmurings and the complaints,
Grew louder and stronger
Whirling and swirling
Faster and faster
Until suddenly—it stopped.

And everybody fell off.

Be still and know that I am God.

Sandra Duguid
20th century

Pen Portraits

To a Lady Saying Grace in a Station Buffet

Step nearer to my canvas gracious traveller
That I may paint a portrait of you
Sitting tranquilly against a backcloth
Of trains and timetables,
As, mindful of Cana, you offer thanks
For lukewarm coffee
And the veiled hostility of slab cake.

Sheila Nottage
20th century

Bible Characters

OLD TESTAMENT

Forbidden Fruit

They wondered why the fruit had been forbidden;
It taught them nothing new. They hid their pride,
But did not listen much when they were chidden;
They knew exactly what to do outside.

They left: immediately the memory faded
Of all they'd learnt; they could not understand
The dogs now who, before, had always aided;
The stream was dumb with whom they'd always planned.

They wept and quarrelled: freedom was so wild.
In front, maturity, as he ascended,
Retired like a horizon from the child;

The dangers and the punishments grew greater;
And the way back by angels was defended
Against the poet and the legislator.

W.H. Auden
20th century

From: Eve

'While I sit at the door
Sick to gaze within
Mine eye weepeth sore
For sorrow and sin:
As a tree my sin stands
To darken all lands;
Death is the fruit it bore . . .

'I, Eve, sad mother
Of all who must live,
I, not another
Plucked bitterest fruit to give
My friend, husband, lover—
O wanton eyes run over;
Who but I should grieve?—
Cain hath slain his brother:
Of all who must die mother,
Miserable Eve!'

Thus she sat weeping,
Thus Eve our mother,
Where one lay sleeping
Slain by his brother.
Greatest and least
Each piteous beast
To hear her voice
Forgot his joys
And set aside his feast.

The mouse paused in his walk
And dropped his wheaten stalk;
Grave cattle wagged their heads
In rumination;
The eagle gave a cry
From his cloud station;
Larks on thyme beds
Forbore to mount or sing;
Bees dropped upon the wing;...

Huge camels knelt as if
In deprecation;
The kind hart's tears were falling;
Chattered the wistful stork;
Dove-voices with a dying fall
Cooed desolation
Answering grief by grief.
Only the serpent in the dust
Wriggling and crawling
Grinned an evil grin and thrust
His tongue out with its fork.

Christina Rossetti
1830–94

Abraham

The rivulet-loving wanderer Abraham
Through waterless wastes tracing his fields of pasture
Led his Chaldean herds and fattening flocks
With the meandering art of wavering water
That seeks and finds, yet does not know its way.
He came, rested and prospered, and went on,
Scattering behind him little pastoral kingdoms,
And over each one its own particular sky,
Not the great rounded sky through which he journeyed,
That went with him but when he rested changed.
His mind was full of names
Learned from strange peoples speaking alien tongues,
And all that was theirs one day he would inherit.
He died content and full of years, though still
The Promise had not come, and left his bones,
Far from his father's house, in alien Canaan.

Edwin Muir
1887–1959

He Passed the Test

Long before
most of the world's
recorded happenings happened,
Abraham
underwent
his Ordeal by Hope.

He believed God
to be faithful who promised
a seed (concept not viable)
a son (less
    than knife-edge survival potential)
a land (one burial lot—
    a life-time's total investment)
and descendants in such profusion
    that
    their number would rival
    the stars!

Mixed up, yet
fiercely battling
circumstantial contradiction,
awesomely, Abram/Abraham
became the friend of God.

His trusting tortured endurance,
his strong argumentative prowess,
and his finely-honed obedience
crashed through ancient harsh blood-rites
staking all on God keeping his word.

His never-swerving conviction:
THE ALMIGHTY IS, AND HE ANSWERS
prefigured to men's understanding
the God
who raises
the dead.

Abraham's faith has earned him
a posthumous decoration:
'Reckoned by God as righteous.'

With inheritance rights for the children.

Grace Westerduin
20th century

Lot's Wife

1

My home, my lovely home, she wept
while God was sharpening his shafts
against the cities of the plain.
My mother too was called at dawn
and for me Lot's wife has her face,
the same companionable hands
touch what they shall not hold again;
it was because it meant her life
that she was loath to leave that place.
And while her daughters were already running
she stayed to look at a familiar sight:
flowers responding to the early sun
—the valley emulated Paradise;
sweet view, she sighed, if I could leave my eyes...
no one will love you after I have gone

2

What was she doing, waiting there
with darkness spattering the air;
don't hang your hearts on things, she'd said:
a nomad used to moving on
with only a shabby, a makeshift home
and daughters who still needed her
hurrying ahead?

3

I'd be content with yesterday, she thought,
her memories like clothing in her hands:
her daughters small, herself reckless and young,
and Lot her shelter, and their wanderings.
If God must take, she thought, let him take all...
and shivered as the ground began to shake.

Karen Gershon
20th century

The Burning Bush

When Moses, musing in the desert, found
The thorn bush spiking up from the hot ground,
And saw the branches, on a sudden, bear
The crackling yellow barberries of fire,

He searched his learning and imagination
For any logical, neat explanation,
And turned to go, but turned again and stayed,
And faced the fire and knew it for his God.

I too have seen the briar alight like coal,
The love that burns, the flesh that's ever whole,
And many times have turned and left it there,
Saying: 'It's prophecy—but metaphor'.

But stinging tongues like John the Baptist shout:
'That this is metaphor is no way out.
It's dogma too, or you make God a liar;
The bush is still a bush, and fire is fire'.

Norman Nicholson
20th century

Coming and Going

The word came
and he went
in the other
direction.
    God said: Cry
tears of compassion
tears of repentance;
cry against
the reek
of unrighteousness;
cry for
the right turn
the contrite spirit.
    And Jonah rose
and fled
in tearless
silence.

Thomas John Carlisle
20th century

NEW TESTAMENT

Saint John Baptist

The last and greatest herald of heaven's King,
Girt with rough skins, hies to the deserts wild,
Among that savage brood the woods forth bring,
Which he than man more harmless found and mild.
His food was locusts, and what young doth spring
With honey that from virgin hives distilled;
Parched body, hollow eyes, some uncouth thing
Made him appear, long since from earth exiled.
There burst he forth: 'All ye, whose hopes rely
On God, with me amidst these deserts mourn;
Repent, repent, and from old errors turn!'
    —Who listened to his voice, obeyed his cry?
        Only the echoes, which he made relent,
        Rung from their marble caves 'Repent! Repent!'

William Drummond of Hawthornden
1585–1649

John the Baptist

As the brittle water dripped
from the young man standing
upright again to the waist
I heard, we all felt we heard
I saw, we all thought we saw
a visionary presence, a voice;
but where are they gone?

I staked almost everything
on the truth of that moment.
This is the lamb (I blurted out)
the very lamb (or some such phrase)
this is the lamb of God ... but
that was some years ago.

Now in danger of life, I know
that tyranny will take its course,
and neither the lamb of God nor
anyone else will intervene
to save me.

Where is the hope of his coming?
Was not this the one?
Is the kingdom not after all
at hand?

I waited to see the whole
country rising to his name.
I am waiting

The time is ripe, the world ready
to be reborn, but now

What am I is it the end is he

Simon Baynes
20th century

Joseph

He wrestles straining flesh
To free the stubborn child
From clutching womb
While whispered grumblings slip
With sweat from trembling lips,
An awful fit
Compared to angled boards
With just right joints
On firm wood bench.
How far from steady here,
Away from home and youth's
Clear questions, answers cleaned
And ready.

These knots once came with looks
Of age, their smiles and frowns
Among wood grains—
Like hill-side grass in fact
Where wheat and barley browns
Joined pasture greens,
Where rough met smooth
And flat reached round
And sun out far kissed stone in close
Quite warmly. There he soared
In pictured thoughts and deeds,
Or slipped between the blades
Quite nimbly.

To frame those thoughts and deeds
He worked with wood from day
To ordered day.
But here the blood-strewn straw
Brought all the gnarls of Mary back
Again. Her screams
Were caught in slimy folds
On babe's dark head from womb
Now pushing through
But how? And how or what
Began these months of mess
And sexless tomb?
Just how then?

But most of all he wished
A simple peace
With her whose life seemed strange
And far from his own skill
To please. Her fears and joys
She had apart.
Elizabeth alone
Might know those dream desires
Of womb, apart from him,
A man of faith but not
Much hope, belief without
Clear vision, ready though
For waiting.

He shared some good times too,
And once her angel came.
But all in all didn't fit
At all since Mary—
There! And Mary smiled.
Joseph looked around
At dumbly staring cows
Then back again
To see the baby out
Against the breast that he
Loved too, a picture good
Enough to frame,

He dried his hands and heard
New sounds. The baby cooed,
Or was it cried?
Joseph smiled, then Mary smiled
Again. 'And didn't I do
Quite well? And didn't I tell
You God was here?
What was it like for *you?*—
It didn't *feel* like God!'
Joseph kissed the child
With Mary's hope and smoothed
Her knotted string-wet hair
Just now then.

Paul Borgman
20th century

O Sapientia

It was from Joseph first I learned
Of love. Like me he was dismayed.
How easily he could have turned
Me from his house; but, unafraid,
He put me not away from him
(O God-sent angel, pray for him).
Thus through his love was Love obeyed.

The Child's first cry came like a bell:
God's word aloud, God's word in deed.
The angel spoke: so it befell,
And Joseph with me in my need.
O Child whose father came from heaven,
To you another gift was given,
Your earthly father chosen well.

With Joseph I was always warmed
And cherished. Even in the stable
I knew that I would not be harmed.
And, though above the angels swarmed,
Man's love it was that made me able
To bear God's love, wild, formidable,
To bear God's will, through me performed.

Madeleine L'Engle
20th century

The Widow's Mites

Two mites, two drops (yet all her house and land).
Falls from a steady heart, though trembling hand.
The other's wanton wealth foams high, and brave,
The other cast away, she only gave.

Richard Crashaw 1613?–49

Tithes

(MATTHEW 23:23)

All in bunches the furred leaves
are hung—narrow and stiff and
greyer than they grew
under the wall—
starred with a few
dry seeds. I've crushed and weighed
a small part of them into God's pot,
spikes, stalks and all.
The sun drained all the green
they'd got.
All they can give now is a tithe of death,
a thin spice in the air. But has God seen?
Has he the nose to savour
the last fine fragrance of their breath?
Will caraway mask my justice—
make it seem fair? Can mint
sweeten a meagre mercy, or a hint
of dill improve the flavour
of my faith? Why ask? It's his affair—
and his prerogative to bless or not to bless.
The love he wants is too wide for my inches;
his righteousness
too heavy. And like the sun, not just a tenth
but 'all,' he says. 'With all your heart,'
and that's nine-tenths too much!
(Such burdens and my good intention fails.)
I'll stick to weighing herbs on garden scales,
and my white-painted wall is thick enough,
I think, to keep out conscience, questions,
critics, seekers, friends, rough
beggars and itinerant carpenters,
though I suppose
God could leap it if I asked him to
or if he chose.

Luci Shaw 20th century

Lazarus

While Mary wept within her darkened room,
While Martha served the guests and broke her heart,
Where were you, Lazarus, those four days?

Not in the garden-tomb, cool from the sun,
But in a world of light, glory beyond
The toys of sense, the friend of Time.

'The undiscover'd country from whose bourn
No traveller returns'—
But you, bewildered Lazarus, came back,
Answering his mighty word of power:
'Lazarus, come forth!'
You stood, bound in your grave-clothes, in the sun,
While awe fell on the shaking crowd,
Your amazed soul caged dumbly in your eye.

How could you, Lazarus, speak to them of that?
Words would fall baffled back
Beating against the doors of sense,
The myth of Time.

How make the deaf to hear?
The blind to see?
So your soul kept a secret: unguessed Heaven.
Dazed, you walked softly all your length of hours,
A silent man, a quiet man, remote,
A man who guards a dream.

Joseph Braddock
20th century

Lazarus

Sister, you placed my heart in its stone room
where no flowers curiously come, and sun's voice
rebuffed, hangs on the stones dumb. What I could not bear
I still must hear. Why do your tears fall?

why does their falling move him, the friend, the
unsuspected lightning: that he walk our garden
with no flowers upon his friend, but a voice splitting
my stone to a dream gone, my sleep

to day? what, what do tears say to him?

what did he say in tears, that his grief fall
scalding my hands, that cold hands sprung
sleep like a manacle, and drew my eyes a space
that had seen God, back to his human face?

Daniel Berrigan
20th century

John in Gethsemane

The grass is pleasant here
rains have given the earth a chance to soften
I wonder we have not come to Gethsemane
        more often.

We are worn out from the Temple crowds
I can hardly stay awake
I wish he would join us and get some rest
        for his own sake.

But ever since supper he has seemed strange—
something on his mind—
I expect it will all work out tomorrow
        and we can all unwind.

How drowsy it all seems this evening
        and the earth
            how kind.

Shirwood E. Wirt
20th century

From: On Holy Week

PILATE'S WIFE

I dreamt us strolling, arm in loving arm,
along the avenue that skirts the border;
our tender courting days wheeled back.
Just then we heard a yapping,
loud, a pack in full pursuit!

Into our lives he crashed,
a lamb, bleeding and bruised,
and weary with the chase.
I picked him up and cuddled him
in my warm arms, my newest baby boy.

The hounds were yelping louder,
nuzzling the hedge. And then
(but why? but why?) you snatched
the poor thing from my arms,
and with 'We must not interfere,
my love, the dogs demand their prey,'
you tossed their quarry over
the prickly hedge. The ravenous pack
were through him in an instant,
ravaging the body.

That moment, in my dream,
our sweet love died; that afternoon
I sat alone, playing with thorns.
At length I turned to you
to plead forgiveness.
You offered that, and love;
but, broken in simple grief,
I could not take your proffered
bread and wine.

Mervyn Morris
20th century

The Thief

'Say bold but blessed thief,
That in a trice
Slipped into paradise,
And in plain day
Stol'st heaven away,
What trick couldst thou invent
To compass thy intent?
What arms?
What charms?'
'Love and belief.'

'Say bold but blessed thief,
How couldst thou read
A crown upon that head?
What text, what gloss,
A kingdom on a cross?
How couldst thou come to spy
God in a man to die?
What light?
What sight?'
'The sight of grief—

'I sight to God his pain;
And by that sight
I saw the light;
Thus did my grief
Beget relief.
And take this rule from me,
Pity thou him, he'll pity thee.
Use this,
Ne'er miss,
Heaven may be stol'n again.'

Anonymous
17th century

St Stephen's Day

Yesterday the gentle
Story: the summoning star,
Shepherd and beast and King
In their enchanted ring,
The moment still with awe.

Shepherd and beast and King
Wince at a cry:
It is no new born cry
For he is asleep,
But a cry alerting night.

Who saw the hanging star
Shudder and fall?
I, Stephen, saw
Fragments of hot stone
Whistle down, smite the earth.

Stones thud on flesh,
The bestial mob howls,
No Kings are here to witness.
Yesterday birth blood,
Today pulped flesh and death blood

Streaming from broken eyes:
Yet the triumphant cry,
I see my God.
So was the first day
After the gentle birth.

Patric Dickinson
20th century

Saints Official –
and Saints in the Making

Soeur Marie Emilie

Soeur Marie Emilie
is little and very old:
her eyes are onyx,
and her cheeks vermilion,
her apron wide and kind
and cobalt blue.

She comforts
generations and generations
of children,
who are 'new'
at the convent school.
When they are eight,
they are already up to her shoulder,
they grow up and go into the world,
she remains,
for ever,
always incredibly old,
but incredibly, never older.

Generations of children
sit in turn by her side,
and help her to shell the peas,
her dry and twisted fingers crackle,
snapping the green pods,
generations of children
sit in turn by her side,
helping to stone the plums,
that will be made into jam,
for the greater glory of God.

She has affinity with the hens,
when a hen dies,
she sits down on a bench and cries,
she is the only grown-up, whose tears
are not frightening tears.
Children can weep without shame,
at her side.
She is simple as flax.
She collects the eggs,

they are warm and smooth,
and softly coloured,
ivory, ochre,
and brown and rose.
They fit the palm of her hand.
Her eyes kindle upon them,
the children, watching gravely,
understand
her dumb, untroubled love.

We have grown up,
and gone away,
'into the world'
and grown cold
in the service of God,
but we would love him
even less than we do,
if we had never known
Soeur Marie Emilie,
with the green peas and the plums,
and the hens and the beautiful eggs,
and her apron as wide and kind
as skies on a summer day,
and as clean and blue.

Caryll Houselander 20th century

Sister Bertha

Who would guess that thin-breasted body
has wheezed Christ into three languages?
She walks down aisles to pews, an oddity
of God's redeeming grace; her sober thighs
are shut against all time and place and cause.
Who would guess her brambled hands held skies
matter-of-factly down to earth, spliced lengths
of heathen centuries to ours with their strength.

And who would guess that at night somewhere off in
a room where the loveliest thing is a fly that drones,
lying, her untouched body on a mattressed coffin,
she stares in the nervous dark, mad or blind,
a lover who primps her soul, and thinks whole poems
into a time and place out of mind.

Jeanne Murray Walker 20th century

St Teresa

O thou undaunted daughter of desires!
By all thy dower of lights and fires;
By all the eagle in thee, all the dove;
By thy large draughts of intellectual day,
And by thy thirsts of love more large than they;
By all thy brim-filled bowls of fierce desire,
By thy last morning's draught of liquid fire;
By the full kingdom of that final kiss
That seized thy parting soul, and sealed thee his;
By all the heaven thou hast in him
(Fair sister of the seraphim!);
By all of him we have in thee;
Leave nothing of myself in me.
Let me so read thy life that I
Unto all life of mine may die!

Richard Crashaw
1613–49

Monica's Last Prayer

'Oh could thy grave at home, at Carthage, be!'—
Care not for that, and lay me where I fall.
Everywhere heard will be the judgement-call.
But at God's altar, oh! remember me.

Thus Monica, and died in Italy,
Yet fervent had her longing been, through all
Her course, for home at last, and burial
With her own husband, by the Libyan sea.

Had been; but at the end, to her pure soul
All tie with all beside seemed vain and cheap,
And union before God the only care.

Creeds pass, rites change, no altar standeth whole;
Yet we her memory, as she prayed, will keep,
Keep by this: *Life in God, and union there!*

Matthew Arnold
1822–88

Mould of Castile

(TO ST TERESA)

A streak of Sappho, it is said,
Inflamed you, the painted and imperious
Charmer in velvet robes at Avila;
But soon your withered young bones rattled
On convent stones: gaunt postulant,
You had fled, still dead to God, from a goblin-flare.

No mist or dream had softened
The bold Castilian flint: there was sun-glare
On bull-fights and flashing lizards
And the hot black stems of olives, pungent cistus,
Awaiting the shift and shock, an El Greco storm.

Did you waste thirty years
In fighting the sun, flashing out
With a gay jest between swoons and fears
Of those winged visions? Did election dare
Molest your Spanish pride
To that length, fan a fury of love
That soared, bled in the trap,
Lapped a wilful ease, lastly, in brisk reform?

You were ageing, an enigma still,
When your mules arrived at San Jose,
And a thunder that thrills my flint
In Cornwall now, spread from the wooden waggons,
Filled with your nuns, lurching over calcined plains,
Up primitive mountain tracks, drifting aground
On river ferries. You and they were bound
For new cells in Elisha's shadow:
Traditional rock like that which my poet-soul,
As wasted and adamant,
Split and gay as yours, descried
Beyond sly bramble, misted kiln
And the dried voluptuary veins.

Jack Clemo
20th century

Mother Teresa

No revolution will come in time
  to alter this man's life
  except the one
  surprise of being loved.

It is too late to talk of Civil Rights,
  neo-Marxism
  psychiatry
  or any kind of sex.

He has only twelve more hours to live.
  Forget about
  a cure for cancer, smoking, leprosy
  or osteo-arthritis.

Over this dead loss to society
  you pour your precious ointment,
  wash the feet
  that will not walk tomorrow.

Mother Teresa, Mary Magdalene,
  your love is dangerous, your levity
  would contradict
  our local gravity.

But if love cannot do it, then I see
  no future for this dying man or me.
  So blow the world to glory,
  crack the clock. Let love be dangerous.

Sydney Carter   20th century

Christmas Trees

Bonhoeffer in his skylit cell
bleached by the flares' candescent fall,
pacing out his own citadel,

restores the broken themes of praise,
encourages our borrowed days,
by logic of his sacrifice.

Against wild reasons of the state
his words are quiet but not too quiet.
We hear too late or not too late.

Geoffrey Hill   20th century

Miss Pettigrew and Tree

In her small single room
   Miss Pettigrew
      —bird bones and parchment skin—
      lives in a leaf world
         made by her pavement tree.

When the wind blows,
   the moving patterns dance
      across her walls
         and lift her heart like music

and when the wind is still
   leaf shadows touch her face
      with Love that never reached her
         through humankind.

In stark-branched winter
   she feels companioned in
      adversity
and buds in April
   bring her a sign
      from that Far Country
         where she will flower, beyond
            this alien world.

Daily Miss Pettigrew
   —shrunk from life's jostling,
      frail essence in
         a birdcage skeleton—
            wonders why she should be
               so recompensed

and lives, content, in shelter
   of Love enough for her
      beneath her tree.

Evangeline Paterson
20th century

The Misses Norman

The Misses Norman lived on Marine Square
just as you turn from Broadway at the corner
where now a granite bank shines like new coins;
two short white matrons that I remember
like Lord's Prayers on a rosary that joins
a knotted childhood to their acts of care.

To my young mind it seemed a threatening place.
You pierced the wooden gate through its small door
and stepped into a dimness armed with plants,
cringed up the half-gloom to the upper floor
and called good morning nervous in your pants.
But there you spoke with goodness face to face.

With thanks now rising in me like a lake
an image flashes fresh as yesterday:
a slippered sister in Edwardian dress
shuffling to hear each stanza of distress,
bribing the waiting teeth of reefs away.
It is a bonding that time cannot break.

The lifeguards of this heaving world are rare,
the sinking swimmers thick as August rain.
But one whose feet touched safety when that pair
of spinsters anchored themselves to pain
that was not theirs attempts a line of praise
in words like them, as faithful and as plain.

Cecil Gray
20th century

On a Portrait of a Deaf Man

The kind old face, the egg-shaped head
    The tie, discreetly loud,
The loosely fitting shooting clothes,
    A closely fitting shroud.

He liked old City dining-rooms,
    Potatoes in their skin,
But now his mouth is wide to let
    The London clay come in.

He took me on long silent walks
    In country lanes when young,
He knew the name of ev'ry bird
    But not the song it sung.

And when he could not hear me speak
    He smiled and looked so wise
That now I do not like to think
    Of maggots in his eyes.

He liked the rain-washed Cornish air
    And smell of ploughed-up soil,
He liked a landscape big and bare
    And painted it in oil.

But least of all he liked that place
    Which hangs on Highgate Hill
Of soaked Carrara-covered earth
    For Londoners to fill.

He would have liked to say goodbye,
    Shake hands with many friends,
In Highgate now his finger-bones
    Stick through his finger-ends.

You, God, who treat him thus and thus,
    Say 'Save his soul and pray.'
You ask me to believe you and
    I only see decay.

John Betjeman
20th century

Johannes Milton, Senex

Since I believe in God the Father Almighty,
Man's Maker and Judge, Overruler of Fortune,
'Twere strange should I praise anything and refuse him praise,
Should love the creature forgetting the Creator,
Nor unto him in suffering and sorrow turn me:
Nay how could I withdraw me from his embracing?

But since that I have seen not, and cannot know him,
Nor in my earthly temple apprehend rightly
His wisdom and the heavenly purpose eternal;
Therefore will I be bound to no studied system
Nor argument, nor with delusion enslave me,
Nor seek to please him in any foolish invention,
Which my spirit within me, that loveth beauty
And hateth evil, hath reproved as unworthy:

But I cherish my freedom in loving service,
Gratefully adoring for delight beyond asking
Or thinking, and in hours of anguish and darkness
Confiding always on his excellent greatness.

Robert Bridges
1844–1930

The Country Clergy

I see them working in old rectories
By the sun's light, by candlelight,
Venerable men, their black cloth
A little dusty, a little green
With holy mildew. And yet their skulls,
Ripening over so many prayers,
Toppled into the same grave
With oafs and yokels. They left no books,
Memorial to their lonely thought
In grey parishes; rather they wrote
On men's hearts and in the minds
Of young children sublime words
Too soon forgotten. God in his time
Or out of time will correct this.

R.S. Thomas
20th century

From: The Prologue to The Canterbury Tales

THE PARSON

A holy-minded man of good renown
There was, and poor, the Parson to a town,
Yet he was rich in holy thought and work.
He also was a learned man, a clerk,
Who truly knew Christ's gospel and would preach it
Devoutly to parishioners, and teach it.
Benign and wonderfully diligent,
And patient when adversity was sent
(For so he proved in great adversity)
He much disliked extorting tithe or fee,
Nay rather he preferred beyond a doubt
Giving to poor parishioners round about
From his own goods and Easter offerings.
He found sufficiency in little things.
Wide was his parish, with houses far asunder,
Yet he neglected not in rain or thunder,
In sickness or in grief, to pay a call
On the remotest whether great or small
Upon his feet, and in his hand a stave.
This noble example to his sheep he gave,
First following the word before he taught it,
And it was from the gospel he had caught it ...

His business was to show a fair behaviour
And draw men thus to Heaven and their Saviour,
Unless indeed a man were obstinate;
And such, whether of high or low estate,
He put to sharp rebuke to say the least.
I think there never was a better priest.
He sought no pomp or glory in his dealings,
No scrupulosity had spiced his feelings.
Christ and his Twelve Apostles and their lore
He taught, but followed it himself before.

THE PLOWMAN

There was a Plowman with him there, his brother.
Many a load of dung one time or other
He must have carted through the morning dew.
He was an honest worker, good and true,
Living in peace and perfect charity,
And, as the gospel bade him, so did he,
Loving God best with all his heart and mind
And then his neighbour as himself, repined

At no misfortune, slacked for no content,
For steadily about his work he went
To thrash his corn, to dig or to manure
Or make a ditch; and he would help the poor
For love of Christ and never take a penny
If he could help it, and, as prompt as any,
He paid his tithes in full when they were due
On what he owned, and on his earnings too.
He wore a tabard smock and rode a mare.

Geoffrey Chaucer
1340?–1400
translated by Nevill Coghill

From: The Deserted Village

THE VILLAGE PREACHER

Near yonder copse, where once the garden smiled,
And still where many a garden flower grows wild;
There, where a few torn shrubs the place disclose,
The village preacher's modest mansion rose.
A man he was to all the country dear,
And passing rich with forty pounds a year;
Remote from towns he ran his godly race,
Nor e'er had changed, nor wished to change his place;

. . . .

At church, with meek and unaffected grace,
His looks adorned the venerable place;
Truth from his lips prevailed with double sway,
And fools, who came to scoff, remained to pray.
The service passed, around the pious man,
With steady zeal, each honest rustic ran;
Even children followed with endearing wile,
And plucked his gown, to share the good man's smile.
His ready smile a parent's warmth expressed,
Their welfare pleased him, and their cares distressed;
To them his heart, his love, his griefs were given,
But all his serious thoughts had rest in Heaven.
As some tall cliff, that lifts its awful form,
Swells from the vale, and midway leaves the storm,
Though round its breast the rolling clouds are spread,
Eternal sunshine settles on its head.

Oliver Goldsmith
1728–74

A Conversion (1741)

Nathan Cole quit his plow
& hurry'd to hear Whitefield preach
& found his religion useless ash
before the stern words
'election' 'grace'

'Hellfire hellfire
ran Swift in my mind

'And while these thoughts
were in my mind
God appeared unto me
and made me Skringe: …
and I was Shrinked away
into nothing'

And in that nothing
Nathan Cole burst
with light, found
Farmington, Connecticut
ablaze with matter for praise:

all walls & common fences;
weeds, trees,
    and vines in special;
stones he'd earlier envy'd
for lack of soul—
now were new tongues to hymn
Election's glory,
Jehovah's sure salvation.
Selah.

Eugene Warren
20th century

A Letter to John Donne

ON 27 JULY 1617, DONNE PREACHED AT THE PARISH CHURCH AT SEVENOAKS,
OF WHICH HE WAS RECTOR, AND WAS ENTERTAINED AT KNOLE,
THEN THE COUNTRY RESIDENCE OF RICHARD SACKVILLE, THIRD EARL OF DORSET.

I understand you well enough, John Donne
First, that you were a man of ability
Eaten by lust and by the love of God

Then, that you crossed the Sevenoaks High Street
As rector of Saint Nicholas:
I am of that parish.

To be a man of ability is not much
You may see them on the Sevenoaks platform any day
Eager men with despatch cases
Whom ambition drives as they drive the machine
Whom the certainty of meticulous operation
Pleasures as a morbid sex a heart of stone.

That you could have spent your time in the corruption of courts
As these in that of cities, gives you no place among us:
Ability is not even the game of a fool
But the click of a computer operating in a waste
Your cleverness is dismissed from this suit
Bring out your genitals and your theology.

What makes you familiar is this dual obsession;
Lust is not what the rutting stag knows
It is to take Eve's apple and to lose
The stag's paradisal look:
The love of God comes readily
To those who have most need.

You brought body and soul to this church
Walking there through the park alive with deer
But now what animal has climbed into your pulpit?
One whose pretension is that the fear
Of God has heated him into a spirit
An evaporated man no physical ill can hurt.

Well might you hesitate at the Latin gate
Seeing such apes denying the church of God:
I am grateful particularly that you were not a saint
But extravagant whether in bed or in your shroud.
You would understand that in the presence of folly
I am not sanctified but angry.

Come down and speak to the men of ability
On the Sevenoaks platform and tell them
That at your Saint Nicholas the faith
Is not exclusive in the fools it chooses
That the vain, the ambitious and the highly sexed
Are the natural prey of the incarnate Christ.

C.H. Sisson
20th century

BIOGRAPHIES OF AUTHORS

ABELARD, Peter 1079–1142
French philosopher and scholar best remembered for his love for Heloise.
He wrote a collection of hymns.

ADAM, David 20th century
Vicar of Holy Island, Northumberland, England, has a deep interest
in the Celtic Christian tradition. His poems and prayers are
in Celtic style.

ADDINK, Carol (now Von Klompenburg) 20th century
American poet, graduate of Dordt College with an MA in drama.

ADDISON, Joseph 1672–1719
Essayist and politician, co-founder of the *Spectator* magazine.

AGARD, John 20th century
Guyanan poet, performer and children's author. He has lived in the
United Kingdom since 1977.

ALABASTER, William 1567–1640
Chaplain to Earl of Essex on the Cadiz expedition of 1596.
He ended life as a country parson.

ANDERSON, Cathy 20th century
Housewife, living in South Wales.

ARNOLD, Matthew 1822–88
Literary critic and leading 19th-century poet, son of Dr Thomas Arnold,
headmaster of Rugby School.

ASHWORTH, Anne 20th century
Librarian who also teaches poetry at a sixth-form college.

AUDEN, Wystan Hugh 20th century
English poet who later lived in the United States and became an American citizen.
He was Professor of Poetry at the University of Oxford.

AUDLEY, (AUDELAY) John 1426?
Priest. In the manuscript of his verses he describes himself as 'deaf, sick, blind'.

AUSTIN, John 1613–69
Forced to leave University and Law because he became a Roman Catholic, wrote under the
pseudonym of William Birchley. He travelled widely and was a good linguist.

AUSTIN, William 1587–1634
Writer and barrister, his religious writings were published after his death.

AVISON, Margaret 20th century
Leading Canadian poet, also involved in Christian work in downtown Toronto.

BABBAGE, Humphrey 20th century
Leading Australian poet. He taught in Papua New Guinea for four years.
Later involved in Christian work in New South Wales.

BALDWIN, William 1547?

A 'corrector of the press' for a printer, later a schoolmaster, provided theatrical exhibitions for Queen Mary's court. He wrote metrical translations of scripture.

BARENDRECHT, Cor W. 20th century

American poet, literary editor of *Calvinist–Contact*.

BAUCKHAM, Richard 20th century

Poet and university lecturer in theology.

BAXTER, Richard 1615–91

Nonconformist clergyman, chaplain to the Puritan army. Wrote *The Saint's Everlasting Rest*.

BAYLY, Joseph 20th century

American poet and writer, on the editorial staff of the David C. Cook publishing company.

BAYNES, Simon 20th century

Vicar of Winkfield, Windsor. He has lived and worked in Japan.

BEAUMONT, Joseph 1615–99

Born in Suffolk. From 1663 he was Master of Peterhouse College, Cambridge.

BEDE, the Venerable 673?–735

Anglo-Saxon scholar, theologian and historian. He studied and taught at the monastery in Jarrow, Northumberland. Canonized in 1899.

BELLERBY, Frances 1899–1975

Poet, novelist and short story writer, deeply influenced by the First World War.

BELLOC, Hilaire 1870–1953

French-born British writer and Roman Catholic apologist; close friend of G.K. Chesterton.

BENNETT, John 20th century

American poet, was Professor of English at St Norbert College, Wisconsin.

BERRIGAN, Daniel 20th century

American poet, teacher, priest and apologist, has taught theology at Fordham University.

BERRY, Wendell 20th century

American poet and academic, taught at Stanford and New York Universities and has won poetry prizes.

BERRYMAN, John 1914–72

American poet, biographer, novelist and academic, won the Pulitzer prize in 1965. An alcoholic who finally took his own life.

BETJEMAN, John 1906–84

Poet, broadcaster and writer on architecture. Poet Laureate in 1972, knighted in 1969.

BIDWELL, Joan 20th century

Poet, born in Devon. She was a design artist before retirement.

BINNEY, Thomas 1798–1874

Born at Newcastle-on-Tyne, England, a nonconformist minister. He wrote some fifty books and several hymns.

BINYON, Laurence 1869–1943

Poet and art critic, for 20 years in charge of Oriental prints and paintings at the British Museum. Professor of Poetry at Harvard University.

BLACKMORE, Richard 1825–1900
Poet and novelist. His best-known book is *Lorna Doone.*

BLAKE, William 1757–1827
Poet, artist and mystic. Worked as an engraver. Created his own beliefs from Christianity and various philosophies.

BONAR, Horatius 1809–89
Scottish hymn-writer, minister of Chalmers Memorial Church in Edinburgh.

BORGMAN, Paul 20th century
American Christian poet and academic.

BRADSTREET, Anne 1612–72
English-born American Puritan poet. She emigrated to New England and her husband became governor of Massachusetts. She brought up eight children in conditions of hardship.

BRAYBROOKE, Neville 20th century
He has published poems in the *New Statesman*, the *Spectator* and the *Tablet*.

BRIDGES, Robert 1844–1930
Medical doctor then poet and amateur musician. He became Poet Laureate in 1913 and received the Order of Merit in 1929.

BRONTË, Anne 1820–49
Wrote as Acton Bell for the three Brontë sisters' volume *Poems*. She worked as a governess and wrote two novels.

BRONTË, Emily 1818–48
Wrote as Ellis Bell in *Poems* published by the three sisters. Best known for her only novel, *Wuthering Heights*.

BROWN, George Mackay 20th century
Leading Scottish poet and writer who lives in Orkney, background to much of his verse and prose.

BROWN, T.E. 1830–97
Brilliant scholar, teacher and curate from the Isle of Man. Much of his poetry in Manx. 'Full of Celtic fire and sensitiveness to beauty'.

BROWNE, Simon 1680–1732
Minister of an Independent Chapel. Tragedy brought on mental illness. He wrote theological treatises and hymns.

BROWNE, Sir Thomas 1605–82
Writer and physician, born in London. His best-known work is his confession of faith, *Religio Medici.*

BROWNING, Elizabeth Barrett 1806–61
Poet and author. Her marriage to Robert Browning freed her from her sickroom and a possessive father. They settled in Italy.

BROWNING, Robert 1812–89
Leading Victorian poet. His innovative poetry showed great psychological and spiritual insight.

BRYANT, William 1794–1878
American poet, born in New England, studied and practised law. He campaigned against slavery and for free speech.

BUNING, Sietze 20th century
American poet and academic, born to Reformed Protestant parents in Middleburg, Iowa.

BUNYAN, John 1622–88
Puritan preacher and writer, imprisoned for preaching as a nonconformist.
The first part of his great allegory, *Pilgrim's Progress*, was written in Bedford gaol.

BURNS, Robert 1759–96
National poet of Scotland. Early influenced by ballads and songs,
he rescued and renewed the Scottish folk tradition.

BYROM, John 1692–1763
Poet and stenographer, studied medicine but invented and patented a new system of shorthand.

BYRON, Catherine 20th century
Grew up in Belfast and studied at Oxford. She has had several collections of poetry published.

CAEDMON 7th century
The earliest Christian English poet known by name. According to Bede, he received a divine call to
compose when he was a herdsman and became a monk at Whitby, under the abbess Hilda.

CAMPION, Thomas 1567–1620
Poet, musician and physician. His aim: 'to couple words and notes lovingly together'.

CARLISLE, Thomas 20th century
American Presbyterian pastor and poet.

CARMICHAEL, Alexander 19th century
Scottish Celtic scholar, who spent a lifetime collecting prayers, songs and poetry of the Scottish
Hebridean islands.

CARMICHAEL, Amy 1867–1951
Writer and missionary in India who founded the Dohnavur Fellowship,
a rescue home for children. Housebound after an accident in 1932.

CARPENTER, Edward 1844–1929
Priest, social reformer and writer, who left the church and turned to socialism
and the craft movement of William Morris.

CARTER, Sidney 20th century
Folk singer, performing poet, teacher, hymnwriter and satirist.

CAUSLEY, Charles 20th century
Prize-winning poet, educator and anthologist, who has also compiled poetry collections for children.

CAVE, Freda 20th century
Lives in Wiltshire and has published in poetry magazines.

CAVENDISH, Margaret, Duchess of Newcastle 1625–73
Exiled during the Civil War when she married William Cavendish.
She wrote philosophy, poetry and drama.

CENNICK, John 1718–55
Prolific hymn-writer, from a Quaker family, brought up in the Church of England,
and became a Moravian minister.

CHAPMAN, Raymond 20th century
Professor of English at the London School of Economics and Priest in Auxiliary Ministry.

CHAUCER, Geoffrey 1343?–1400
Founding English poet, best known for the *Canterbury Tales*.
He travelled abroad widely and later received various crown offices.

CHESTERTON, Gilbert Keith 1874–1936
Critic, novelist, poet, studied art at the Slade School. He became a Roman Catholic in 1922.
Popular for his Father Brown detective stories.

CLARE, John 1793–1864
Worked on his father's farm and had little schooling; He became successful as 'the peasant poet'.
Sadly, ended his days in an asylum.

CLEMO, Jack 1916–94
Lived many years among the Cornish clay-pits, which inspired his writing. Deaf for forty years and
blind for twenty-five, late marriage brought him much happiness.

CLOUGH, Arthur Hugh 1819–61
Resigned his fellowship at the University of Oxford when he rejected the dogmas of the Church of
England. Commemorated in Matthew Arnold's poem *Thyrsis*.

COGHILL, Nevill 20th century
Irish-born medievalist and university professor, friend of Tolkien and C.S. Lewis.
He translated Chaucer's *Canterbury Tales* into idiomatic modern English verse.

COLERIDGE, Hartley 1796–1849
Man of letters, eldest son of Samuel Taylor Coleridge. He was brought up by the poet Southey,
and had a very chequered career.

COLERIDGE, Mary 1861–1907
Novelist, essayist and poet, a great-great niece of Samuel Coleridge.
She taught at the Working Women's College.

COLERIDGE, Samuel Taylor 1772–1834
Published *Lyrical Ballads* with Wordsworth in 1798. Once a revolutionary,
he moved to orthodox Christianity.

COLLIER, Mary 1690?–1762
Her parents taught her to read, but could not afford schooling. She worked hard at 'washing,
brewing and such labour', devoting all her spare time to books.

CONSTABLE, Henry 1562–1613
Friend of Sir Philip Sidney, became a Roman Catholic and went to Paris where he was probably
employed on secret missions to England and Scotland.

COSIN, John 1594–1672
Doctor of Divinity, Vice-Chancellor of Cambridge University. A friend of Archbishop Laud,
he contributed to the final revision of the Prayer Book.

COWLEY, Abraham 1618–67
Went with Queen Henrietta Maria to Paris on the defeat of Charles I by Cromwell
and was sent on Royalist missions. He returned to England at the Restoration.

COWPER, William 1731–1800
A great poet dogged by bouts of madness. A friend of John Newton, he contributed to his *Olney Hymns*.
Two women—Mrs Unwin and Lady Austen—helped and encouraged him.

CRABBE, George 1754–1832
Son of a violent father and pious mother, he became a successful poet.
First a surgeon, he was later ordained priest.

CRASHAW, Richard 1613?–49
Son of a noted Puritan divine, he later became a Roman Catholic.
He lived in Paris, Rome and Loreto.

CROSSMAN, Samuel 1624–83
Preacher, writer and hymn-writer. He was appointed Dean of Bristol Cathedral
a few weeks before his death.

CRUM, J.M.C. 1872–1958
Ordained and became Canon of Canterbury Cathedral.
He wrote on St Mark's Gospel.

CULBERTSON, E. Neil 20th century
American poet. He was a chaplain's assistant during the Vietnam War.

CYNEWULF 820?
Anglo-Saxon poet and scholar from Mercia or Northumberland.
His identity is known only from his own runic inscriptions on texts.

DAVENANT, Sir William 1606–68
Poet and playwright, Poet Laureate after Ben Jonson. He also opened a theatre.

DAVIE, Donald 20th century
Distinguished scholar, poet and literary critic, who has published his collected poems
and edited several anthologies.

DAVIES, W.H. 1871–1940
English poet who emigrated to the USA, returning to England, where he lived as a tramp
and pedlar to raise money for his verses to be collected.

DICKINSON, Barbara 20th century
Civil servant who edited poetry magazines and published two collections.

DICKINSON, Emily 1830–86
American poet, a recluse who wrote over a thousand poems—original in thought and style—most of
them discovered and published after her death.

DICKINSON, Patric 20th century
Academic, educator and poet who has won poetry awards. He was Poetry Editor for the BBC.

DINES, Jennifer 20th century
Member of a Roman Catholic religious order, she teaches Biblical Studies at Heythrop College,
University of London.

DOBSON, Rosemary 20th century
Australian poet, lives in Sydney. She has compiled anthologies and published
several collections of verse.

DODDRIDGE, Philip 1702–51
Nonconformist clergyman, a pastor and president of a theological college,
who wrote several well-known hymns.

DOLBEN, Digby Mackworth 1848–67
Educated at Eton, where he wrote his devotional poems. He became a Benedictine monk. He was
drowned in a swimming accident, aged 19.

DONNE, John 1572–1631
Metaphysical poet, who sailed with the Earl of Essex to Cadiz. He was later ordained,
and became Dean of St Paul's and the greatest preacher of his time.

DOWDEN, Edward 1843–1913

Irish writer, critic and poet. Became professor of English literature at Trinity College, Dublin, only four years after graduating there.

DOWDEN, Mrs Edward 19th century

The poem's author is probably Dowden's second wife, Elizabeth Dickinson (née West) who edited her husband's poems after his death.

DOWSON, Ernest 1867–1900

Poet and translator of French classics, friend of W.B. Yeats. He lived in France, and died there of tuberculosis and alcoholism.

DRUMMOND, William, of Hawthornden 1585–1649

Son of a courtier, who devoted his life to poetry and mechanical experiments. Friend of Ben Jonson. His death was hastened by grief for Charles I's execution.

DRYDEN, John 1631–1700

Poet, playwright and political satiririst. He became a Roman Catholic and lost his appointments as Poet Laureate and Historiographer Royal in the revolution of 1688.

DUGUID, Sandra 20th century

American teacher and poet with an MA in creative writing from Johns Hopkins University.

DUNBAR, William 1460?–1520?

May have graduated from St Andrews University and become a Franciscan novice. By 1504 he had taken priest's orders.

DURIEZ, Colin 20th century

Brought up in Wales, lived and studied in Istanbul. Now lives in Northern Ireland.

EARLE, John Charles 1749–1818

Roman Catholic, one of the officiating priests at the Spanish Ambassador's Chapel in London.

ELIOT T.S. 1888–1965

Verse playwright and leading poet of the modern movement. He was born in America but became a British citizen and joined the Church of England.

L'ENGLE, Madeleine 20th century

American poet and award-winning writer of children's books, converted from atheism. She was librarian and writer-in-residence at the Cathedral of St. John the Divine, New York.

FANTHORPE, U.A. 20th century

One-time teacher at Cheltenham Ladies College, who has had several collections of poems published.

FARJEON, Eleanor 1881–1965

Wrote fantasies and children's stories. There is a Farjeon Award for outstanding work in children's books.

FENWICK, R.P. 20th century

Served in the Second World War and began writing poetry as a POW. He joined a Roman Catholic religious order and became a priest in 1984.

FIELD, Michael

The pen name of Katharine Bradley, 1846–1914, and her niece Edith Cooper, 1862–1913 who lived together and wrote tragedies and volumes of verse. Both became Roman Catholics. They died of cancer within a year of each other.

FLETCHER, Giles 1586–1623

Brother of Phineas Fletcher and cousin of John Fletcher, the dramatist. Reader in Greek at Cambridge. He took a country living, but his parishioners did not appreciate him.

FLETCHER, Phineas 1582–1650

Held a fellowship at King's College, Cambridge. He was Rector of Hilgay in Norfolk from 1621 until his death.

GASCOIGNE, George 1542–97

Poet, dramatist and translator from Greek, Latin and Italian. Member of Parliament for Bedford, disinherited for his extravagance.

DE GASZTOLD, Carmen 20th century

Wrote her *Prayers from the Ark* in a French convent. They were translated into English by the novelist Rumer Godden.

GERSHON, Karen 20th century

Poet, novelist and translator, born in Germany and came to England in 1938. Her German parents died in Hitler's concentration camps.

GIFFORD, Humphrey 1580?

His work was described as 'a posy of gillyflowers, each differing from other in colour and odour, yet all sweet'.

GILMAN, Charlotte Perkins 1860–1935

American feminist writer. She lectured on ethics, economics and sociology.

GIOVANNI, Nikki 20th century

Afro-American poet, writer and recording artist. She produced a collection of poems for young children. She has won awards of many kinds.

GIRLING, Clare 20th century

Retired teacher now living in Anglesey.

GODFREY, Jan 20th century

Freelance writer, married to a clergyman, closely involved with the Fellowship of Christian Writers.

GODOLPHIN, Sidney 1610–43

Friend of Ben Jonson's circle. A Member of Parliament who joined the forces of Charles I and was killed in a skirmish.

GOLDSMITH, Oliver 1728–74

Irish playwright, novelist and poet. Best known for *She Stoops to Conquer*.

GONZALEZ, Anson 20th century

Poet, teacher, broadcaster and writer from Trinidad and Tobago, crucial influence in the development of Caribbean writing in the 70s and 80s.

GRAVES, Robert 1895–1985

Poet, novelist, essayist and critic. Served in the First World War. Best known for his novels *I, Claudius* and *Claudius the God*.

GRAY, Cecil 20th century

Poet, anthologist and lecturer from Trinidad and Tobago, who greatly influenced Caribbean students. He now lives in Canada.

GREENWELL, Dora 1821–82

Struggled with poverty and ill-health, but published six volumes of poetry.
She pleaded for greater work opportunities for educated women.

GREVILLE, Fulke, first Lord Brooke 1554–1628

Friend of Sir Philip Sidney, active in politics and a patron of young writers.
He was killed by one of his servants.

HABINGTON, William 1605–54

His father was imprisoned and his uncle executed for conspiring with
Babington to murder Queen Elizabeth I. He wrote metaphysical lyrics and a play.

HALDEN, Alistair 20th century

Educated at Glasgow University, he became an English teacher. He has won poetry prizes.

HALL, John 1627–56

Poet and pamphleteer from Durham. Wrote rapidly and had a marvellous memory.
Cromwell awarded him a pension for his pamphleteering.

HALSALL, Martyn 20th century

Teacher, then a journalist with *The Guardian*. He lives in Lancashire and is the paper's northern
industrial correspondent.

HANN, Isaac 1690–1778

The verses in this anthology hang framed in the ancient Loughwood Baptist Meeting House,
near Axminster, Devon, England, where Hann was once minister.

HARDY, Thomas 1840–1928

Novelist, poet and dramatist. Practised as an architect and church restorer for a time.
Not an orthodox believer.

HARVEY, Christopher 1597–1663

Poet, rector and headmaster, friend of Izaak Walton, who quoted some of his verses
in an edition of *The Compleat Angler*.

HARVEY, Frederick William 1888–1957

Served in the First World War and wrote when a prisoner of war.
His verse is now largely forgotten.

HATCH, Edwin 1835–89

Friend of some pre-Raphaelites, including William Morris. He became
Professor of Classics at Toronto University and held academic posts at
the University of Oxford.

HAVERGAL, Frances Ridley 1836–79

Knew Greek and Hebrew as well as several modern languages. Remembered for her hymns,
especially 'Take my life and let it be'.

HAWKER, Robert Stephen 1804–73

Published poems and hymns. An Anglican priest, he was received into the
Roman Catholic church the evening before he died.

HEANEY, Seamus 20th century

Irish poet and critic. He lectured at Queen's College, Belfast, before becoming
a full-time writer.

HEATH-STUBBS, John 20th century

Poet, critic, anthologist and translator. Described as a 'Johnsonian presence with a Miltonic disability'
(a reference to his blindness).

HEBER, Reginald 1783–1826
Hymn-writer and compiler, who became Bishop of Calcutta.
His best-known hymn is 'Holy, holy, holy, Lord God almighty'.

HECTOR, Rosemary 20th century
Irish poet, now living in England. She has won the Edinburgh City Poetry Prize.

HEMANS, Felicia Dorothea 1793–1835
Published her first volume of poetry at 14 and wrote prolifically for children and adults.
She was praised by Shelley and befriended by Scott and Wordsworth.

HENDERSON, Stewart 20th century
Writer and performance poet, born in Liverpool, who has introduced poetry
to audiences unfamiliar with it.

HERBERT, George 1593–1632
Classical scholar, musician and poet of the Metaphysical school. He was a member of Parliament with
good connections at court, but relinquished them to become a parish priest near Salisbury.

HERBERT, Mary, Countess of Pembroke 1561–1621
Sister of Sir Philip Sidney, and patron of poets. She revised Sidney's *Arcadia* after his death.

HERRICK, Robert 1591–1674
Parish priest, described as the most pagan of English poets in spite of his religious poetry.
He insisted that his life was not to be judged by his verse.

HEYWOOD, Thomas 1574–1641?
Dramatist, poet and actor, had a large part in the writing of 220 plays,
the best known of which is *A Woman Killed with Kindness*.

HILL, Geoffrey 20th century
Followed an academic career. His poetry is much concerned with death,
sex and religion and his poems have won prestigious prizes.

HINKSON, Katharine Tynan 1861–1931
Irish poet and novelist, close friend of Alice Meynell and a leading light in the Irish Celtic Revival.

HODGSON, Ralph 1872–1962
A journalist in London, he published three volumes of poems about nature and England.
After lecturing in Japan (1924–1938) he made his home in Ohio, USA.

HOGGARD, Trevor 20th century
Born in Nottinghamshire, he trained for the ministry.

HOPKINS, Gerard Manley 1844–89
Life-long friend of Robert Bridges; Jesuit novice then priest. His verse was experimental,
using what he called 'sprung rhythm'.

HOPKINS, Nancy 20th century
Poet, writer of articles and short stories, born in Ireland.
She came to London and lived in Germany for three years.

HORNE, Frank 20th century
Caribbean writer.

HOUGHTON, Frank 1894–1972
Was ordained and went as a missionary to China. He became Bishop of Eastern Szechwan,
then General Director of the China Inland Mission.

HOW, William Walsham 1823–97
Bishop of Wakefield. He wrote sermons, a Bible commentary and nearly sixty hymns, some still popular today.

HOWE, Julia Ward 1819–1910
American poet, married Samuel Howe, an anti-slavery campaigner. She wrote 'The Battle Hymn of the Republic' for the Northern States in the American Civil War.

HRABANUS MAURUS 776–856
Born in Mainz, became abbot of the monastery at Tours and later Archbishop of Mainz, where he dealt with heresy and was 'the greatest archbishop since Boniface'.

HUGHES, Ted 20th century
Yorkshire poet and children's writer, married the American writer Sylvia Plath. He studied archaeology and anthropology and worked as zookeeper, nightwatchman and gardener before teaching. Became Poet Laureate in 1984.

HULL, Eleanor 1860–1935
Wrote on Celtic folklore. She wrote 'Be thou my vision' in verse after it had been translated from the original Irish (8th century) by Mary Byrne.

HYLAND, Paul 20th century
Writer and poet, many of his poems have been broadcast on BBC radio. A new collection of his poetry has recently been published.

IDLE, Christopher 20th century
Formerly Rector of churches in inner London and in rural Suffolk; writer (including hymns) and editor.

IMAGE, Selwyn 1849–1930
Studied under John Ruskin at the Slade School and became Slade Professor of Fine Art. Ordained in the Anglican church, he published carols and poems.

JELLEMA, Roderick 20th century
American, grew up in Michigan. Teacher of English at the University of Maryland and co-director of the Washington National Poetry Centre.

JENNINGS, Elizabeth 20th century
Acclaimed poet. Her Roman Catholic faith and her poems are the most important things in her life. Once a library assistant and publisher's reader.

JOHNSON, Lionel 1867–1902
Educated at Winchester and Oxford, he became a Roman Catholic. A member of the Rhymers' Club. Destroyed by drink.

JONSON, Ben 1572?–1637
Dramatist and poet, who joined an acting company. He killed a fellow player in a duel and escaped execution by appealing to the clerical courts. Shakespeare acted in his play, *Every Man in his Humour.*

KAVANAGH, Patrick 20th century
Irish poet and novelist, he farmed before leaving Dublin to work as a writer and journalist.

KEBLE, John 1792–1866
Clergyman and poet, a leading light in the high-church Tractarian movement, along with Newman and Pusey. Wrote *The Christian Year* (poems).

KELLY, Gerard 20th century
Poet and performer at the Greenbelt Festival and in schools, churches and youth events. He has had a poetry collection published.

KEN, Thomas 1637–1711

Clergyman and hymnwriter. A royal chaplain, he refused to give up his house to Nell Gwynne, when Charles II visited Winchester. Deprived of the bishopric of Bath and Wells when he refused to take the oath of allegiance in 1688.

KENNELLY, Brendan 20th century

Irish poet, playwright, novelist and anthologist of Irish verse. University lecturer living in Dublin.

KING, Henry 1592–1669

Bishop of Chichester, and a royal chaplain, suffered loss during the Civil War. He was a friend of Ben Jonson and Izaak Walton and a close friend of John Donne.

KIPLING, Rudyard 1865–1936

Journalist, poet and writer also for children. Born in India, and lived there later. His 'Recessional' was written for Queen Victoria's diamond jubilee.

KIRKUP, James 20th century

Poet, anthologist and translator. He has been a professor of English in Spain and Japan and poet in residence in the USA.

KLUG, Ronald 20th century

American book editor, he has also taught English at the American School, Madagascar.

LAMB, Mary 1765–1847

Sister of Charles Lamb. In a fit of insanity she killed her mother with a table knife. She and Charles together wrote *Tales from Shakespeare* and poems and stories for children.

LANGLAND, William 1330?–1400?

The allegorical poem *Piers Plowman* has been attributed to him since the 15th century. He lived in a hovel in London for a while, married and had a daughter.

LANIER, Sidney 1842–81

American academic, author, poet and musician. He fought with the Confederates in the American Civil War, where he developed tuberculosis, which later caused his death.

LAWRENCE, D.H. 1885–1930

Novelist, poet amd essayist. Son of a miner, he became a teacher then full-time writer. He rejected orthodox Christianity but later recognized the importance of spiritual realities.

LEAX, John 20th century

American poet, teaches English at Houghton College. He has had a collection published.

LEE, Laurie 20th century

Poet, author and scriptwriter. He travelled widely and has written about many parts of the world. *Cider with Rosie* describes his rural childhood.

LEWIN, Ann 20th century

Formerly a teacher, now a writer, tutor and workshop leader.

LEWIS, Cecil Day 1904–72

Irish poet, critic and detective story writer, under the pseudonym of Nicholas Blake. Once associated with left-wing causes, he renounced communism in 1939. Professor of Poetry at the Universities of Oxford and Harvard. Became Poet Laureate.

LEWIS C.S 1898–1963

Irish-born professor of English and writer, converted to Christianity. His broadcasts and books made Christian apologetics popular. He wrote children's books about the imaginary land of Narnia and an adult science fiction trilogy.

LEWIS, Janet Born 1899

American writer best known as a novelist, she has also written children's books and opera librettos. She has taught at universities in the United States.

LLOYD, Cyril 20th century

Born in Wales, now living in England. He is a minister of religion.

LONGFELLOW, Henry Wadsworth 1807–82

American poet and academic. His poetry—which included 'Hiawatha' and 'The Wreck of the Hesperus'—was very popular in his lifetime.

LONGFELLOW, Samuel, 1819–92

American. Brother of Henry, ordained as a Unitarian minister. Edited hymnbooks and wrote hymns and a biography of his brother.

LUCAS, Tony 20th century

Vicar in south London. His poetry has appeared in various English and American anthologies.

LYDGATE, John 1370?–1450?

Benedictine monk who may have studied at Oxford and Cambridge. He travelled on the Continent and became a prior in Essex. In spite of a pension as court poet, he died in poverty.

LYTE, Henry Francis 1793–1847

Scottish hymnwriter, vicar in Devon, England, for twenty-five years. Best known for his hymn 'Abide with me'.

MACDONALD, George 1824–1905

Scottish poet and novelist, best known for his children's books. He was a Congregationalist pastor and later a university professor. Admired and revered by C.S. Lewis.

MANGAN, James Clarence 1803–49

Irish poet with a life of 'hapless love, poverty and intemperance'. He translated Irish and German poets.

MANNYNG, Robert, (also known as Robert of Brunne) 1325?

English poet and chronicler. In 1288 he entered the Gilbertine monastery near his home.

MANWARING, Randle 20th century

London-born poet, now lives in Sussex. Deputy Chairman of Church Society and Crusaders.

de la MARE, Walter 1873–1956

English poet and novelist, retired from work on a state pension in 1908 to write full-time. He wrote for children as well as adults.

MARVELL, Andrew 1621–78

Son of a Calvinist clergyman, he became Milton's assistant, and a member of Parliament. He tolerantly accepted the Restoration while still admiring Cromwell.

MASEFIELD, John 1878–1967

Poet, novelist and journalist. He retired from the Merchant Navy because of ill-health. Appointed Poet Laureate in 1930.

MASON, John 1645–94?

Priest and hymnwriter, had a vision of Jesus and preached that the Second Coming was near. His last words: 'I am full of the loving kindness of the Lord'.

MEETER, Merle 20th century

American poet, teaches English at Dordt College.

MEW, Charlotte 1861–1928

Poet and short story writer, admired by Thomas Hardy. Troubled by illness and family worries, she committed suicide after her sister's death.

MEYNELL, Alice 1847–1922

Poet, essayist, lecturer and journalist. She became a Roman Catholic, and married Wilfred Meynell, by whom she had eight children. They befriended Francis Thompson.

MILLER, Vassar 20th century

American poet who has written three volumes of poetry.

MILMAN, Henry Hart 1791–1868

Theologian, church historian, poet and hymnwriter. Professor of Poetry at Oxford and Dean of St Paul's. Described as 'the last of the great conversers'.

MILTON, John 1608–74

Great poet and writer of religious and political pamphlets. He became totally blind but probably wrote *Paradise Lost*, *Paradise Regained* and *Samson Agonistes* at the end of his life.

MITCHELL, Susan 1866–1926

Irish poet, who mixed in Irish literary circles, wrote for Irish journals and produced several volumes of religious verse.

MOLLINEUX, Mary 1648?–95

Imprisoned for attending Quaker meetings, she met and later married Henry Mollineux. She wrote *Fruits of Retirement or Miscellaneous Poems Moral and Divine*.

MORE, Sir Thomas 1478–1535

Statesman, scholar and writer. Tried to retire as Lord High Chancellor rather than consent to Henry VIII's divorce and breach with the Roman Catholic Church. Executed for failing to take the Oath of Supremacy. Canonized in 1935.

MORGAN, Angela Died 1957

An American poet, she gave readings across the United States.

MORRIS, Mervyn 20th century

Jamaican poet, academic and poetry prizewinner. He is Reader in West Indian Literature at the University of the West Indies.

MUIR, Edwin 1887–1959

Born in Orkney, moved to Glasgow when he was 14, he was self-educated. He came to Christian faith late in life and wrote no poetry until he was 35.

MURRAY, Les A. 20th century

Australian poet, leading literary figure, author of five collections of poetry. He worked as a translator but has been a full-time writer for some years.

MYERS, Frederick William Henry 1843–1901

Became an Inspector of Schools. He was president of the Society for Psychical Research. Best known for his poem 'St Paul'.

NASH, Ogden 20th century

American light versifier, who used puns, parody and alliteration to amuse and to shock. Contributed often to the *New Yorker* magazine.

NEALE, John Mason 1818–66

Hymnwriter and high churchman, who also wrote on church history.

NEILL, William 20th century
Former airman and teacher, now lives in Galloway. He writes in Gaelic, Scots and English and has published at least eight collections of poetry.

NELSON, Alice Dunbar 1875–1935
American writer and teacher. Her husband, Paul Dunbar, was the first Black poet widely accepted in America. Together they collected great Black literature to be performed on stage.

NEWMAN, John Henry 1801–90
Priest and theologian, who wrote for the Tractarian movement of the Church of England but later joined the Roman Catholic Church and became a cardinal.

NEWTON, John 1725–1807
Went to sea at 11 and later became a slave trader. Converted during a dangerous storm at sea. Ordained in 1764. He and William Cowper wrote the Olney Hymns. He helped Wilberforce in the anti slave-trade campaign.

NICHOLS, Grace 20th century
Novelist, poet and children's writer. Born in Guyana, she came to Britain in 1977. She won the Commonwealth Poetry Prize.

NICHOLS, Kevin 20th century
Poet, teacher and student chaplain who has written widely on literature and education. Now a parish priest in County Durham.

NICHOLSON, Norman 20th century
Poet, novelist and playwright. He lived near the English Lake District and wrote about its landscape.

OLDENBURG, E. William 20th century
American poet and professor of English who was killed in a car accident.

ORFORD, Margaret 20th century
Born in Harare, Zimbabwe, now lives in England. She has written historical novels and poetry.

PALGRAVE, Francis Turner 1825–97
Poet and critic, professor of poetry at Oxford. Best known as editor of the *Golden Treasury of Lyrical Poetry*.

PALMER, Herbert Edward 1880–1961
Poet and literary critic, taught English in England, France and Germany before becoming a full-time writer.

PATERSON, Evangeline 20th century
Poet, grew up in Dublin, Ireland, Deeply involved in revival of the arts among evangelical Christians. She has won major poetry prizes.

PATMAN, Keith 20th century
American, taught English, art and drama in North Carolina and is now working with his wife with Wycliffe Bible Translators.

PATMORE, Coventry 1823–96
Literary journalist, an assistant librarian at the British Museum. He was a friend of the Pre-Raphaelite brotherhood and became a Roman Catholic.

PATRICK patron saint of Ireland, 372–466
According to legend, carried off by pirates at the age of 15 and sold as a slave in Ireland.
He escaped, became a monk in France and later returned to Ireland
as a missionary.

PESTEL, Thomas 1584?–1659?
Chaplain to King Charles I and a rector until removed by the Westminster Assembly of 1646.
His hymns and sermons were published just before he died.

PITMAN, Marion 20th century
Poet, brought up in London and keeps a bookshop. She has won poetry competitions and
published a collection.

PITTER, Ruth Born 1897
Wrote verse from an early age, later encouraged by Hilaire Belloc. She won poetry prizes and
published collections of poetry.

PLUNKETT, Joseph Mary 1887–1916
Born in Dublin and edited the *Irish Review*. He suffered from ill-health and died in Dublin
during the Easter Rebellion.

POLLARD, Velma 20th century
Jamaican, lecturer at the University of the West Indies. She has edited schools anthologies
and published stories and poems.

POOLE, Peggy 20th century
Children's writer and poet, also a freelance journalist and broadcaster.
She has had several collections of her poetry published.

POPE, Alexander 1688–1744
A leading poet of his century, highly satirical, a convinced Roman Catholic. He suffered all his life from
ill-health. He was the first English poet to live by his writing.

POST, Marie J. 20th century
American poet, wife and mother from Grand Rapids.

PRIOR, Matthew 1664–1721
Poet and diplomat, who helped to bring about the Treaty of Utrecht (1713) for which he was
imprisoned after Queen Anne's death. Master of light, epigrammatic and satirical verse.

PRUDENTIUS 348–405?
Contemporary of Augustine, Jerome and Ambrose, greatest of the Christian Latin poets.
After a life in the law-courts he withdrew at 57 to seek the kingdom of God.

QUARLES, Francis 1592–1644
A staunch royalist. He married and had eighteen children and was equally prolific in his poetry.
His *Emblems* was the most popular book of the century.

RADBOD Died 917
Went to the court of Charles the Bald and studied at St Martin's at Tours. He was made
Bishop of Utrecht, where he was much loved.

RAINE, Kathleen 20th century
Poet who has lived and written in Northumberland, England, since her second marriage broke up.

RALEGH, Sir Walter 1552?–1618
Explorer, courtier, writer, one-time favourite with Queen Elizabeth. He spent twelve years
imprisoned in the Tower of London, where he wrote his *History of the World*.
Finally executed.

ROBERTSON, Jenny 20th century

Century social worker and writer of children's novels and poetry. She and her husband encourage support of Christians in Eastern Europe.

ROLLE, Richard, of Hampole 1290?–1349

About 1290–1349, mystic and poet, became a hermit at 19. He wrote lyrics, meditations and religious works in Latin and English and translated and expounded the Psalms.

ROONEY, Elizabeth 20th century

American poet and member of the Society of the Companions of the Holy Cross, an order of Episcopal laywomen. Her husband is an Episcopal priest.

ROSSETTI, Christina 1830–94

Prolific poet of considerable technical virtuosity, whose work ranged from poems of fantasy and verses for the young to ballads, love lyrics, sonnets and religious poetry; devout High Anglican.

ROWE, Elizabeth 1647–1737

Began writing verse at 12. She was courted by Matthew Prior, whom she rejected. She gave half her income to charity each year. Isaac Watts edited her *Devout Exercises of the Heart* after her death.

SANDYS, George 1578–1644

English colonist and traveller in Europe and the Middle East. He acted as treasurer of Virginia in America. He wrote poetic versions of the Psalms as well as translating Latin authors.

SASSOON, Siegfried 1886–1967

Poet of the First World War, who won the Military Cross. He made an official protest against the slaughter on the Western Front. He became a Roman Catholic.

SCANNELL, Vernon 20th century

Writer and poet, who has won awards. Once a professional boxer, then an educator and since 1962 a professional writer and broadcaster.

SCOTT, Dennis 20th century

Jamaican playwright, actor, dancer, teacher and poet. He has published several poetry collections including the prizewinning *Uncle Time*.

SCOTT, Sir Walter 1771–1832

Scottish novelist and poet who became a national figure. He wrote ballads and novels, many historical.

SEDULIUS, Scottus ?848–74

Scholar and poet. After his early life in Ireland he went to France and settled at Liege.

SEYMOUR, A.J. 20th century

Guyanan critic, anthologist and poet, one of the great men of Caribbean poetry. He published many collections of his poetry over 40 years.

SHAKESPEARE, William 1564–1616

Greatest English playwright and poet, also actor, joint-manager of a London acting company and part-owner of a theatre. His birthday is celebrated on 23 April, St George's Day.

SHAW, Luci 20th century

Poet grew up in England, Australia and Canada, studied in USA and married an American, with whom she ran a publishing firm. She lectures on poetry and creativity and has published five collections of poetry.

SHERBURNE, Sir Edward 1618–1702

Roman Catholic and royalist, deprived of his office as clerk of the ordnance during the Civil War. He wrote Latin tragedy and verse.

SHIRLEY, Sir James 1596–1666
Dramatist. He went into the Anglican Church, later becoming a Roman Catholic. He taught then became a playwright. He died in the Great Fire.

SIDNEY, Sir Philip 1554–86
Courtier, soldier, scholar and poet. He spent two years abroad at foreign courts and later served in Flushing. Died after a wound in battle.

SISSON, C.H. 20th century
Poet, served with British Army Intelligence in India then in Parliament (Under Secretary of State).

SITWELL, Edith 1887–1964
She and her brothers, Osbert and Sacheverell, were patrons of the arts. She became a Roman Catholic. Her later poetry is concerned with the suffering of the world.

SKELTON, Philip 1707–87
Son of an English settler in Ireland, fatherless at 11, grew up in extreme poverty as one of 10 children. When teacher and curate he gave away half his income and cared for others with generosity and compassion.

SMART, Christopher 1722–71
Had periods of madness throughout his life. He was confined in Bedlam, where he is said to have written 'Song to David'. He died heavily in debt. 'Rejoice in the Lamb' was not published until 1939.

SMITH, Joshua 18th century
American, compiled a book of *Divine Hymns or Spiritual Songs* in New Hampshire in 1784.

SOUTHWELL, Robert 1561–95
Poet and Jesuit martyr. Educated at Douai and Rome, he became chaplain to the Countess of Arundel. He was betrayed, thrown into the Tower of London, tortured thirteen times and hanged and quartered.

de SOUZA, Eunice 20th century
Born in India and educated at Bombay and Milwaukee Universities. Poet and literary columnist and Head of English at Bombay College.

SPEED, Samuel Died 1681
Stationer and bookseller who wrote verse. A contemporary of Samuel Speed, 1631–1681, a priest said to have fled the country for plotting against Cromwell and joined buccaneers in the West Indies.

SPENSER, Edmund 1552–99
Great poet, friend of Sir Philip Sidney and leader of a literary circle. His greatest work—unfinished—was *The Faerie Queene*, a tribute to Queen Elizabeth I.

STAINER, Pauline 20th century
Poet and beekeeper. Her first published collection was a Poetry Book Society recommendation.

STARKEY, Mike 20th century
Poet, newsreader and reporter on commercial radio. He has performed his poetry at Greenbelt Festival and on TV, and published a collection.

STEELE, Anne Died 1779?
Daughter of a and nonconformist preacher, she wrote a metrical version of the Psalms and many hymns.

STEPHENS, James 1882–1950
Irish poet and writer. Sent to an orphanage as a child, worked as a solicitor's clerk until successful enough to become a full-time writer.

STUDDERT-KENNEDY, G.A. 1883–1929
First World War chaplain, affectionately nicknamed Woodbine Willie, from his habit of giving cigarettes to the soldiers. Absent-minded, generous and much loved.

SUDERMAN, Elmer F. 20th century

American academic and poet of Mennonite upbringing, now a Methodist lay preacher.

SWETS, Robert D. 20th century

American poet and literary editor.

SYMONDS, John Addington 1840–93

Author and poet, who also translated from Latin and Italian. He wrote travel sketches and monographs on Shelley, Sidney and Jonson.

TABB, John Bannister 1845–1909

American who served in the Confederate Navy during the Civil War and met Sidney Lanier while a prisoner. Ordained, he became blind before he died.

TAMPLIN, Ronald 20th century

Academic and poet, who has translated Langland's poetry into idiomatic modern verse.

TAYLOR, Edward 1645–1729

English-born American colonist who became a Puritan pastor and poet.

TAYLOR, Jeremy 1613–67

Priest, theologian and writer, imprisoned three times during the English Civil War. Best known for *Holy Living and Holy Dying*.

TENNYSON, Alfred, Lord 1809–92

For many years poor, depressed and insecure before being hailed as the greatest poet of his day. Became Poet Laureate.

THOMAS, Nancy 20th century

American Quaker missionary—with her husband and their family—among the Aymara Indians of Bolivia.

THOMAS, R.S. 20th century

Welsh poet and priest. Awarded the Queen's Medal for poetry.

THOMPSON, Francis 1859–1907

Religious poet, who failed in his attempts to become a priest or a doctor. Rescued from opium addiction by Wilfred and Alice Meynell, who cared for him until he died of tuberculosis.

THRILLING, Isobel 20th century

Her poetry has been on radio and television and in anthologies. She began writing after eye operations which saved her sight.

TOLKIEN, J.R.R. 1892–1973

South African-born philologist and writer, best-known for his trilogy, *The Lord of the Rings*. He was one of the 'Inklings', the literary coterie to which C.S.Lewis belonged.

TOLLETT, Elizabeth 1694–1754

Grew up in the Tower of London, where her father had a house. Well-educated, she wrote poems in English and Latin and a verse drama.

TOPLADY, Augustus Montague 1740–78

Clergyman and hymnwriter, defended Calvinism and argued well. Best remembered for his hymn 'Rock of Ages'.

TRAHERNE, Thomas 1636?–74

Poet, author and clergyman, whose main writings were not discovered until 1896 and 1897 and published in the early 20th century.

TRENCH, Richard Chenevix 1807–86
Irish priest, philologist and poet, Professor of Theology at London University,
later Archbishop of Dublin.

TUCKWELL, Patience 20th century
Poet and educational therapist, who has worked in schools in the UK, Nigeria, Israel and America. She
is now disabled by multiple sclerosis.

TURNER, Steve 20th century
Poet, writer and performer. He has published several collections.

UNDERHILL, Evelyn 1875–1941
Poet and mystic, who lectured on the philosophy of religion.
She moved from agnosticism to Christianity.

UPDIKE, John 20th century
American novelist, poet and critic, once on the staff of the *New Yorker* magazine.
His main status is as a major novelist.

VANDER MEY, Randall 20th century
American graduate of Calvin college, he studied for a PhD in English at the University of Pennsylvania.

VATSA, Mamman Jiya 20th century
Nigerian poet and children's poet. A lietenant colonel in the army, he lives now in Nigeria where he
won a poetry award.

VAUGHAN, Henry 1622–95
Welsh poet, physician and Royalist supporter. He wrote only religious poetry after a spiritual
experience following serious illness.

VERY, Jones 1830–80
American mystic and poet, who lived a retired life in Salem. He became a Unitarian minister and was a
friend of Ralph Waldo Emerson.

WADDELL, Helen 1889–1965
English medievalist, born in Tokyo. She translated medieval Latin poetry into verse,
and also translated prose works.

WALING, Steven 20th century
Theology graduate who attends Quaker meetings. He launched and edits a magazine.

WALKER, Jeanne Murray 20th century
American Professor of Literature and Creative Writing at Haverford College.

WALLER, Edmund 1606–87
Poet and politician, cousin of John Hampden. A Member of Parliament, he plotted on behalf
of Charles I, was arrested and exiled for a time.

WALTON, John 1410?
An Augustinian canon of Osney Abbey. He translated the works of the Roman philosopher,
Boethius, popular in medieval Europe.

WALTON, Peter 20th century
Poet and academic and convinced Christian since student days.
Prize-winner in a BBC National Poetry Competition, his first published collection
won an award.

WANLEY, Nathaniel 1634–80
Poet and parish priest. His poems remained in manuscript until the 20th century.

WARREN, Eugene 20th century

American poet, grew up on a Kansas farm and teaches English at the University of Missouri.
Has published several collections of poetry.

WARREN, James E., Jr. 20th century

American academic and poet, member of the United Methodist Church.
He has published at least nine books of poems and many essays.

WASHBOURNE, Thomas 1606–87

Canon of Gloucester, published sermons and poems.

WATT, Jean M. 20th century

Of Scottish and Welsh parentage. One-time social worker, she has published poetry and prose
translations from French and German.

WATTS, Isaac 1674–1748

Hymnwriter, dissenting pastor and eminent preacher at an Independent Congregation.
He established the place of hymns in English worship.

WEDDERBRUN, James, John and Robert 1567?

Three sons of a Scottish merchant who all graduated at St Andrews University.
James upset the church authorities by the plays he wrote and fled to France.
John became a priest but was accused of heresy and fled to Wittenburg, joining Luther and other
reformers. He wrote and translated Psalms, hymns and ballads.
Robert became Vicar of Dundee and wrote some 'Gude and Godlie Ballates'.

WESLEY, Charles 1707–88

Scholar, clergyman and hymn-writer, younger brother of John Wesley. He joined his brother as an
itinerant missionary. He wrote over six thousand hymns, many of which are still favourites.

WESLEY, John 1703–91

Evangelist and founder of Methodism who travelled and preached in the open air. In over 50 years he
covered 25,0000 miles, mainly reaching working-class neighbourhoods.

WESTERDUIN, Grace 20th century

Irish born, graduate of Queen's University, Belfast.
She taught at Wilson College in Bombay,
married a Dutchman working with United Nations and now lives in Belgium.

WESTERFIELD, Nancy 20th century

American poet and English teacher.

WHEATLEY, Jeffery 20th century

Poet and business economist. He has written several books.

WHITING, William 1825–78

Poet and hymnwriter, known now only for 'Eternal Father Strong to Save'.

WHITTIER, John Greenleaf 1807–92

American Quaker writer, poet, journalist and abolitionist, highly acclaimed in his lifetime.

WILD, Robert 1609–79

Puritan clergyman and poet, son of a shoemaker. He was a satirist with a reputation for wit
and a friend of Richard Baxter.

WILDE, Oscar 1856–1900

Irish playwright, novelist, essayist, poet and wit. In later life he was prosecuted and
imprisoned for his homosexuality.

WILKINSON, Marguerite 1883–1928
Born in Canada and grew up in America, she was a lecturer and poetry reviewer, interested in Christian mysticism. She drowned in a swimming accident.

WILLIAMS, Dick 20th century
Born in Wales, clergyman, author and broadcaster.

WILLIAMS, Sarah 1841–68
Welsh writer, only child of a wealthy father. She gave all she earned from writing to the poor. Her poems were published posthumously.

WIRT, Sherwood E. 20th century
American who has written a number of books and was formerly editor of *Decision* magazine.

WOLCOT, John 1738–1839
Pseudonym Peter Pindar. He became physician-general of Jamaica. He became ordained but later devoted his time to writing satires in verse.

WOTTON, Sir Henry 1568–1639
Traveller, diplomatist, scholar and poet. Sent by James I as ambassador to Venice, he later became provost of Eton.

WRIGHT, Judith 20th century
Australian poet and keen conservationist. She has published at least ten volumes of poetry and won the Robert Frost award.

YOUNG, Andrew 1885–1971
Scottish poet, attached to the YMCA in France during World War I. Minister of an English Presbyterian church, he later became an Anglican vicar.

YOUNG, Edward 1683–1765
Poet and writer of satirical verses, he was made chaplain to the king. His *Night Thoughts* were very popular.

ZUNDEL, Veronica 20th century
Poet, Christian journalist and anthologist, born of Austrian parents, graduate of the University of Oxford.

INDEX OF FIRST LINES

ACKNOWLEDGMENTS

We would like to thank all those who have given us permission to include poems in this anthology. Every effort has been made to trace and contact copyright owners. If there are any inadvertent omissions in the acknowledgments we apologize to those concerned. Each figure refers to the page number of a poem.

Abelard, Peter: 302, from *Medieval Latin Lyrics*, tranlsated by Helen Waddell, Constable & Co. Ltd, 1933

Adam, David: 79, 352, from *The Edge of Glory*, 1985, used by permission of SPCK

Addink, Carol: 447

Agard, John: 353, by kind permission of John Agard c/o Caroline Sheldon Literary Agency, 'By All Means Bless', from *Lovelines from a Goat-Born Lady*, Serpent's Tail, 1949

Anderson, Cathy: 408

Ashby, Cliff: 20, 201, from *Plain Song*, Carcanet Press Limited, 1985

Ashworth, Anne: 103

Auden, W.H., 53, 510, from *Collected Poems*, Faber and Faber Ltd; 272, from *For the Time Being*, Faber and Faber Ltd

Avison, Margaret: 126, from *Winter Sun*, used by permission of McClelland & Stewart, Inc., The Canadian Publishers; 145, 203, from *The Dumbfounding*, used by permission of McClelland & Stewart, Inc., The Canadian Publishers

Babbage, Humphrey: 107, 122

Barendrecht, Cor W.: 82, 269

Bauckham, Richard: 411

Bayly, Joseph: 299, from *Psalms of My Life*, used by permission of Timothy B. Bayly

Baynes, Simon: 517

Bellerby, Frances: 159, from *Selected Poems*, Enitharmon Press, used with permission of David Higham Associates

Belloc, Hilaire: 382, from *Complete Verse*, Random House UK Ltd. Reprinted by permission of the Peters Fraser and Dunlop Group Limited on behalf of the Estate of Hilaire Belloc, © 1970 Estate of Hilaire Belloc

Bennett, John: 325, from *The Reformed Journal*, Wm. B. Eerdmans Publishing Co.

Berrigan, Daniel: 523, The World Publishing Company

Berry, Wendell: 208, 'The Slip', from *Collected Poems: 1957–1982* by Wendell Berry, © 1985 Wendell Berry. Reprinted by permission of North Point Press, a division of Farrar, Straus and Giroux, LLC

Berryman, John: 386, from *Henry's Fate and Other Poems 1967–1972*, Faber and Faber Ltd

Betjeman, John: 230, 401, 534, from *Collected Poems*, John Murray (Publishers) Ltd

Bidwell, Joan: 364

Bond, M.: 437

Borgman, Paul: 519

Braddock, Joseph: 522, from *Stronger Than a Flower*, Robert Hale Ltd

Braybrooke, Neville: 432

Brown, George Mackay: 180, 294, 359

Buning, Sietze: 345, 426

Byron, Catherine: 318

Caedmon: 57, from *Anglo-Saxon World*, Oxford University Press, 1984, used with permission of Rogers, Coleridge and White Ltd

Carlisle, Thomas John: 22, 348, 516

Carmichael, Amy: 124, Dohnavur Fellowship; 241, from *Rose from Brier*, used with permission of Christian Literature Crusade; 253, from *Gold Cord*, used with permission of Christian Literature Crusade

Carter, Sydney: 531, National Book League

Causley, Charles: 295, from *Collected Poems*, Macmillan, used with permission of David Higham Associates

Cave, Freda: 489

Chapman, Raymond: 243, 363

Chaucer, Geoffrey: 253, from *The Man Behind the Book*, translated by Henry Van Dyke, Charles Scribner's Sons; 537, from *The Canterbury Tales*, translated by Nevill Coghill, Penguin Classics, 1951, fourth revised edition, 1977, pp. 32–34, © 1951, 1958, 1960, 1975, 1977 Nevill Coghill. Reproduced by permission of Penguin Books Ltd

Clemo, Jack: 327, used with kind permission of Mrs R. Clemo; 176, 530, from *Selected Poems*, Bloodaxe Books, 1988, reprinted by permission of Bloodaxe Books Ltd

Crum, J.M.C.: 315, from the *Oxford Book of Carols*, © 1928. Reproduced by permission of Oxford University Press

Culbertson, E. Neil: 504

Cynewulf: 369, from *God of a Hundred Names*, translated by Sir Israel Gollancz, reproduced with kind permission of Victor Gollancz Ltd

Davie, Donald: 337, from *Brides of Reason*, Carcanet Press Limited, 1997

Dickinson, Barbara: 148

Dickinson, Patric: 526, from *The Bearing Beast*, Chatto & Windus Ltd, used with permission of Mrs Shiela Dickinson

Dines, Jennifer: 194

Dobson, Rosemary: 422, from *Collected Poems*, reproduced by permission of HarperCollins Publishers Australia

Downing, Diane: 139

Duguid, Sandra: 507

Duriez, Colin: 161

University Press, by permission of the University Press of New England

Morgan, Angela: 490

Morris, Mervyn: 452, from *Shadowboxing* by Mervyn Morris, New Beacon Books Ltd, 1979, reprinted by permission of New Beacon Books Ltd

Muir, Edwin: 258, 468, 512, from *Collected Poems*, Faber and Faber Ltd

Murray, Les: 129, 491

Myrie, Daisy: 342, Nelson Caribbean

Nash, Ogden: 142, from *Verses from 1929 On*, © 1942 Ogden Nash, renewed, reprinted by permission of Curtis Brown Ltd, New York

Neill, William: 339

Nichols, Grace: 143, from *The Fat Black Woman's Poems*, Virago Press, reprinted by permission of Virago Press; 143, Curtis Brown Ltd

Nichols, Kevin: 180

Nicholson, Norman: 515, from *Five Rivers*, Faber and Faber Ltd

Oldenburg, E.W.: 339, from *Sightseers into Pilgrims*, Harold Shaw Publishers Ltd

Orford, Margaret: 142

Palmer, Herbert: 357, reprinted with permission of Mrs Phoebe Hesketh

Paterson, Evangeline: 193, 344, 412, 432, 440, 465, 477, 479, 494, 499, 532

Patman, Keith: 278

Pitman, Marion: 311

Pitter, Ruth: 137, from *Collected Poems 1926–1960*, reproduced by permission of Mark W.S. Pitter; 370, from *End of Drought*, reproduced by permission of Mark W.S. Pitter

Pollard, Velma: 120, from *Crown Point*, Peepal Tree Press

Poole, Peggy: 356, 392

Post, Marie J.: 296, 340

Prudentius: 379, from *Medieval Latin Lyrics*, translated by Helen Waddell, reprinted with permission of Constable & Co. Ltd

Radbod: 424, from *Medieval Latin Lyrics*, translated by Helen Waddell, reprinted with permission of Constable & Co. Ltd

Raine, Kathleen: 109

Robertson, Jenny: 430

Rooney, Elizabeth: 291, 308, 311, 350, the poems of Elizabeth Rooney are © Elizabeth Rooney and reprinted here with her permission

Sansom, Clive: 283, from *The Witnesses and Other Poems* by Clive Sansom, Methuen, reprinted by permission of David Higham Associates Ltd

Sassoon, Siegfried: 45, 203, 415, G.T. Sassoon

Scannell, Vernon: 402, 407, 445, from *Love, Shouts and Whispers*, Red Fox, reprinted by permission of the Random House Group Ltd

Scott, Dennis: 398, 'Epitaph', from *Uncle Time* by Dennis Scott, © 1973. Reprinted by permission of the University of Pittsburgh Press

Scottus, Sedulius: 232, from *Medieval Latin Lyrics*, translated by Helen Waddell, reprinted with permission of Constable & Co. Ltd

Seymour, A.J.: 360, from *Kyk-Over-Al*, reprinted with permission of Ian McDonald

Shaw, Luci: 39, 171, 410, from *The Sighting*, © 1981 Luci Shaw, used by permission of Harold Shaw Publishers, Wheaton, IL, USA

Singh, Kamal: 102

Sisson, C.H.: 453, 539, from *Collected Poems*, Carcanet Press Limited, 1998

Sitwell, Edith: 395, from *Collected Poems*, Sinclair Stevenson, reprinted by permission of David Higham Associates

de Souza, Eunice: 382

Stainer, Pauline: 430, from *The Honeycomb*, Bloodaxe Books, 1989, reprinted with permission of Bloodaxe Books

Starkey, Mike: 389

Stephens, James: 14, reprinted with permission of the Society of Authors on behalf of the copyright owner, Mrs Iris Wise

Suderman, Elmer R.: 201, 334, 443

Swets, Robert D.: 448

Tamplin, Ronald: 398

Tatum, John: 192

Thomas, Nancy: 86, 338

Thomas, R.S.: 199, 231, 394, 413, from *Mass for Hard Times* by R.S. Thomas, reprinted by permission of Bloodaxe Books Ltd; 208, 340, from *Selected Poems 1946–1968* by R.S. Thomas, reprinted by permission of Bloodaxe Books Ltd; 333, 535, reprinted by permission of R.S. Thomas

Thrilling, Isobel: 194, 309, 423

Tolkien, J.R.R.: 181, 196, from *Lord of the Rings*, reproduced by permission of HarperCollins Publishers Ltd

Tripp, Diane Karay: 46

Tuckwell, Patience: 431, 438

Turner, Steve: 136, 150, 384, 441, 460, 472, from *Up to Date*, reproduced by permission of Hodder and Stoughton Limited

Updike, John: 317, from *Collected Poems 1953–1993*, Hamish Hamilton, 1993, pp. 20–21, © 1960, 1993 John Updike. Reproduced by permission of Penguin Books Ltd

Vander Mey, Randall: 315

Vasta, Mamman J.: 505

Walker, Jeanne Murray: 25, 528

Walton, Peter: 111

Ward, Rodney: 136

Warren, Eugene: 538

Warren, James E. Jr: 78, 485

Watt, Jean M.: 169

Weldon-Searle, Joyce: 169

Westerduin, Grace: 351, 451, 513

Westerfield, Nancy: 443, *Christianity Today*

Wheatley, Jeffery: 290

Williams, Dick: 416

Winnell, Robert: 407

Wirt, Sherwood E.: 523, from *Decision*, Billy Graham Evangelistic Association

Wright, Judith: 429

Zundel, Veronica: 24, 307